BELGIUM

SAMUEL HUMES

Belgium

Long United, Long Divided

Foreword by

Wilfred Martens,
former prime minister of Belgium

HURST & COMPANY, LONDON

First published in the United Kingdom in 2014 by
C. Hurst & Co. (Publishers) Ltd,
41 Great Russell Street, London, WC1B 3PL

Printed in India

Distributed in the United States, Canada and Latin America by
Oxford University Press, 198 Madison Avenue, New York ,NY 10016,
United States of America.

A Cataloguing-in-Publication data record for this book is available from the British Library.

ISBN: 978-1-84904-146-1 *paperback*

This book is printed using paper from registered sustainable and managed sources.

www.hurstpublishers.com

For my sons Hamilton and Hans,
and my grandchildren Willem, Hendrik, Kees, Etta and Elias
—that they may more fully appreciate the homeland of their
Low Country ancestors.

CONTENTS

LIST OF MAPS

LIST OF ILLUSTRATIONS

ACKNOWLEDGEMENTS

James MacGregor Burns, a Pulitzer Prize winner and my Williams College honours mentor, reminded me that 'Writing about past events is a collective enterprise.' Many scholars, from Henri Pirenne to Els Witte, contributed to this effort. My debt to the scholars ('the giants upon whose shoulders we may stand' as my Leiden University doctorate 'promoter', C. H. Polak, often reminded me) who have preceded me is indicated only in part by the *Notes* that state the sources of the quotations.

Many read critically part or all of the text. They include Wulf Bodenstein, Franz Burnett, James M. Burns, Sam Crane, Thomas Coomans, Frank Daelemans, James C. Davis, Lynne De Lay, the late Roger Gillette, Samuel Hamilton Humes, John Hyde, Dirk Imhoff, Wilfried Martens, Quentin Martin, Cleveland Moffet, Arnold Ricks, the late Whitney Stoddard, Anthony Teasdale, Guy Vanthemsche and Robert L. Volz. Needless to say, the sole responsibility for what I have written and for what I have omitted is mine.

The Institut Royal du Patrimoine Artistique, the Belgian Royal Library, and the Sawyer Library, Center for Environmental Studies, the Chapin Rare Books Library, and the Office of Information Technology of Williams College provided indispensable assistance.

Thomas Coomans provided photographs as well as invaluable continuing advice and encouragement. Wilfried Martens not only wrote the introduction but also provided significant insights. Sharron J. Macklin used basic source ESRI data layers to develop the specialised maps that complement the textual narrative by depicting the changing borders that accompanied the transitions of Belgian political history. Michael Dwyer, of C. Hurst & Co., recognised the timeliness and appeal of a history of this long united, long divided country at the heart of northern Europe. Assisting him in transforming the manuscript into this attractive volume were Jonathan de Peyer (who graciously incorporated my post-deadline amendments into the text) and Fatima Jamadar (who designed the cover). I owe a long overdue thanks to Frances Dehandschutter and Dorothee Gilette for encouraging me to write a history of Belgium, and to Anne Rainbow and Joanne Thornton who typed the first draft of the manuscript.

I am especially grateful to Zirka Z. Filipczak, Frank Daelemans and Quentin Martin who wrote chapters describing specific aspects of Belgium's political, artistic and literary heritage. While much of their content has been incorporated in the text, unfortunately the exigencies of publishing led to these chapters being deleted from the final manuscript.

Lynne De Lay, my wife of thirty-six years, was my principal encourager and supporter in this long effort to appreciate the complex history of my second homeland. Perhaps she was motivated in part because she finds me more tolerable when writing a book than when I have no goal demanding my attention.

Brussels, Belgium
Williamstown, Massachusetts, USA

FOREWORD

In the autumn of 1991, Robert Senelle, a renowned constitutional commentator for Belgian television, declared 'Belgium will definitely not last till the year 2000 if the government continues to carry on like this.' According to Senelle, our country's fate was hanging by a thread and it was possible that within a few years Belgium would split into two or three parts. The reasons for so much concern lay in the political situation. Since the 1991 summer break, the government had done nothing but squabble over community dossiers. The Flemish and Walloon ministers began to clash more often and more bitterly. The situation was so difficult that as prime minister, I saw no other solution than to hand in my resignation to the King.

Now, twenty years later, we barely remember this government crisis. The storm would be merely a footnote in Belgian history had it not formed part of the lengthy struggle between the Flemish and French speakers. This conflict focuses not only on the balance in language usage but also on the clashing interests of Flanders and Wallonia. For an outsider, it is often difficult to understand why Belgians, who share a prosperous country with so many common assets, devote so much energy to things that at first sight seem to divide them. In fact, you have to be Belgian—or come from another multicultural state—in order to understand fully the friction the Walloon-Flanders conflict arouses. There are so many irrational aspects at stake. If neither the former nor the latter applies to you, this book should help shed some light on the subject. In this book, Samuel Humes gives us a brilliant insight into the age-long history of Belgium and tells how the linguistic and cultural divide determines the outlook of our country to this day.

Belgium: Long United, Long Divided has the merit of describing Belgian history without any complexes. Or should I say: without prejudice or bias. As he is an outsider, it is difficult to accuse Humes—an American academic who became more and more interested in the Belgian case in his long residence here—of one-sidedness. He differs in this from his Belgian historian and political scientist colleagues who, in the past at least, have tended to incorporate an ideologically coloured message in their historiography. *Histoire de la Belgique* by Henri Pirenne, for example, showed that the inhabitants of the Southern Low Countries formed a harmonious nation from the Middle Ages, while Jules Destrée and Paul Belien showed exactly the opposite in their respective historiographies.

The objectivity with which this work is steeped makes it particularly worthwhile reading for Belgians. From an outsider's perspective, Belgians can get to know their country better and discover that its main characteristic is perhaps a lack of chauvinism. 'Belgians are a modest people,' argues Humes, who cannot hide his love for this little country, which stands at the meeting point between Germanic and Romanic Europe. If Belgium did not exist, it would have been invented. Not because Belgium is a model of political stability or socio-economic foresight, but because this country has a mission in the world of tomorrow. After all, it proves that it is possible, as a multi-ethnic state, to reconcile fundamental differences and have different language communities living and working together in a coordinated whole. Differences and disagreements are not necessarily handicaps but can also add value, as long as they pair with a minimum amount of shared identity and unity.

Readers of this book learn that in the course of its history, Belgium has already succeeded relatively well in this task. Before the Burgundians united the southern Low Countries, divisiveness often prevailed over unity, but rulers always re-established hegemony. Burgundian, then Spanish and then Austrian Habsburgs, followed by Dutch rule, governed lands that while linguistically divided developed not only a centralised administration but also a stronger sense of community and a shared southern Low Country cultural heritage, which Humes' narrative highlights as an important aspect of its history. As long as they showed enough respect for the individuality of its citizens and avoided trampling on local rights and regional autonomy, they governed with little unrest. Examples of this are the unsuccessful experiments of the

Austrian Emperor Joseph II, the Dutch King Willem I, and eventually the independent unitary Belgian state.

The fact that the Belgian state initially attempted to stimulate a national consciousness of unity by eliminating all forms of difference is well known and requires no further explanation here. It is more important that the aberrations—including the systematic subordination of Flemish language and culture—belong permanently in the past since Belgium became a federation. The way in which this federation came about—via complex compromise solutions and institutional high technology—has nevertheless been criticised by many a political scientist and historian. One of the criticisms is that the federalisation process has not made Belgium stronger but a lot weaker, and that since then, the oppositions have never been so great. Does this explain the panicky reaction of Robert Senelle on the eve of the last large-scale state reform?

As a one-time constitution reformer, I am grateful to Samuel Humes because he evaluates the constitutional reform in a positive way. Naturally, the Belgian federal construction is particularly complex, as he establishes in his analysis, but at the same time it is also particularly ingenious, and even more importantly, it meets its objective. Because thanks to federalism, in Belgium two language communities still live in harmony. With the exception of Switzerland, no other European country has followed this course.

Today, the Belgians see this as self-evident. Humes, as a political scientist, is also familiar with the history of other multicultural countries and understands that it could have happened very differently in Belgium; less peacefully as in Yugoslavia where people fought out their differences with weapons, or with a so-called *Velvet Divorce* as was the case in Czechoslovakia. Perhaps it is for this reason that in his closing chapter, he sets aside his neutral role as historian and speaks out for maintaining Belgian unity. In his opinion, separation is not worth the political price the Belgians would have to pay in return for the loss of influence on the international scene. Moreover, a divided Belgium would be giving the world a particularly bad sign if the country were to split up. Because, in Humes's words, 'what can the world expect from the many other divided countries if Belgium—with its long shared collective identity and tradition of leaders committed to resolving conflicts and finding compromises—cannot remain united?' As a former prime minister, I can only agree with this conclusion. I consider it the wisdom of a politically experienced academic who over the years has found that real wealth lies in multiculturalism and diversity.

Wilfried Martens
Former prime minister of Belgium

Wilfried Martens was prime minister of Belgium from 3 April 1979 to 21 September 1988 (with the exception of a few months in 1981), during which time he led eight cabinets. He led the efforts that enacted two of the four critical constitutional reforms transforming Belgium from a unitary state into a federation.

PREFACE

A LAND LONG UNITED BY GOVERNMENT, LONG DIVIDED BY LANGUAGE

Increasingly strident separatism is splitting Dutch-speaking Flanders from French-speaking Wallonia. How and why is Belgium, a country so long divided yet long united, having its unity so threatened? Growing tension between Flanders and Wallonia has driven Belgium to enact constitutional revisions that converted its unitary state into a federation. Yet many voice the concern that continuing separatist pressures will break up Belgium.

Examination of this separatist threat to the unity of the land leads to the consideration of other questions. How and why did this long linguistically divided country over several centuries develop a sense of national unity sufficient to win independence in 1830, over the reluctance of most of the major European powers? How and why, despite a large Flemish-speaking community, did a minute Francophone, propertied power elite dominate Belgian politics for so long? How and why did a Flemish movement develop and in the final decades of the twentieth century force a split of the parties and then the transformation of the Belgian unitary state into a federation? And how and why, despite successive constitutional changes that granted more and more power to newly constituted federated parts, do separatist forces continue to demand increased devolution or secession? How long can this multilingual country remain united? This book responds to these questions by tracing the transitions that forged its history and its present crisis.

The cleavage between Dutch-speaking Flanders and French-speaking Wallonia highlights the paradox of how a long linguistically divided, yet long governmentally united country finally succumbed to language-driven sectional pressures, transforming its unitary state into a federation. Understanding this enigma requires appreciating how more than 2,000 years of transitions have transformed Belgica into Belgium. From Julius Caesar's 57 BCE conquest of Belgica to Belgium's present political predicament, the land has metamorphosed from a collection of tribes on the frontier of the Roman Empire to a bifurcated country at the governmental heart of the European Union. This transmutation includes a number of significant transitions:

- The Roman conquest of northern Gaul in the first century BCE, which unified the country's governance and named it Belgica.
- The Frankish invasion in the fifth century CE, which established the Germanic-Romanic linguistic and cultural fault-line.
- The southern Low Country counts' assertion of military prowess and autonomy in the tenth century, which broke down the Frankish empires into numerous principalities.
- The reunification of the southern Low Country principalities in the fifteenth century, which then became part of the Duchy of Burgundy, and then come under Austrian and Spanish rule.
- The Low Countries' revolt that won the Dutch their effective independence by the end of the sixteenth century, but left the southern provinces under Spanish rule.
- Absorption by the French Empire and then merger into the newly-created united Kingdom of the Netherlands at the beginning of the nineteenth century.
- Belgium's independence in the early nineteenth century.
- The concomitant rise of labour, the advent of Flemish consciousness, the increase in schooling and literacy and the gradual introduction of universal suffrage, which drove the rise of Flemish-Walloon friction and sectionalism and led to four constitutional revisions in the late twentieth century. These split the converted Belgian polity and converted its unitary state into a complex federation, increasing Flemish-Walloon friction and frustrating the ability to form coalitions and cope with political and policy issues.
- Included in these transitions, almost ceaseless invasions from Belgica's early history to the more recent French and German ones; seismic events such as the Renaissance, the Reformation and the Enlightenment; and many changing premises underlying governance,

from the 'divine right of kings' to the 'nation-state' to 'representative government'.

As a frontier of the Roman Empire, as the medieval and later commercial and artistic crossroads of northern Europe, and as the perennial cockpit of battles that forged the course of European history, the area has been the seat of interaction between the contending forces of Germanic and Romanic Europe. Battles that have critically affected European history include Bouvines in 1214, Sluys in 1340, Crécy in 1346 (then part of the Low Countries), Waterloo in 1815, Ypres/Ieper in 1914–18 and 'the Bulge' in 1944–45. The forces that transformed Belgium were a microcosm of those that drove European history.

No book in English covers the two millennia of Belgium's history beginning with Caesar's conquest, through the unification of the southern Low Country principalities in the fifteenth century, past independence in the nineteenth century, and extends to the twentieth century sectional schism that has split the Belgian polity. The title of a recent book asks: *How Can One Not Be Interested in Belgian History?* The usual neglect of the subject is not just unfortunate, it is lamentable given the proliferation of histories of the country's neighbours. European historians have tended to focus their attention on Britain, France and Germany. They leave themselves open to the myopia of appreciating only the roles of the biggest and strongest countries. The experiences of Europe's smaller countries have affected and reflected the course of its history in remarkable ways. This is especially true of Belgium, which has seen invasions of aggressive European powers and the continent's ideological divisions played out. My goal has been to write the book that I would have liked to read when I first visited Belgium in 1948, and later when I moved to Belgium in 1984. This narrative describes the traditions and transitions that have transformed the southern Low Countries: from myriad Belgic tribes to part of three successive empires (Roman, Merovingian and Carolingian), to a collection of principalities, to a prestigious Burgundian duchy, to part of three more empires (Spanish, then Austrian, then French), a part of the united Netherlands, and then finally to an independent nation-state. Since the unification of Belgium under the Burgundians in the fifteenth century, its rulers have steadily taken steps to centralise its governance. Not until recent years has the long-existing language divide threatened the unity of this land.

The lack of a book tracing the two millennia of Belgium's recorded history led me, as an 'outsider', to write the book that I searched for when I first came to Belgium. This short narrative, aimed at the general reader, focuses on the leaders and events, as seen in their international context, which over centuries developed a nation-state and then over the last few decades led to the present cleavage between Dutch-speaking Flanders and French-speaking Wallonia. As a student in the Low Countries in the 1950s and a professor in Brussels from the 1980s, many aspects of Belgium's long history have especially intrigued me. For example, in the fifteenth and early sixteenth centuries Burgundy, of which present-day Belgium was a major part, was one of the most prosperous, powerful and culturally influential states in Europe. The war that won the Netherlands its independence actually began in what is now Belgium, was initiated not by Hollanders but by Brabanters and was mainly fought in what is now Belgium. Moreover, French-speaking Walloons, not Hollanders, first settled Manhattan Island. More recently, the growing gulf between the late twentieth century's sister parties led them to change their strategies, their rhetoric and even their names. The complexity of its federation indicates the severity of the challenge the country has faced and the ingenuity of its leaders.

Belgians are a modest people who have much to be immodest about. Divided by language and culture, they neglect to nurture their common history, heritage, and heroes—let alone brag about them. Countless foreign interventions and invasions have determined Belgium's borders, its drive for independence and its present schism. A long history of contending with external threats accounts in part for Belgium's leadership in the forming and sustaining of the European Community/Union (EU) and the North Atlantic Treaty Organization (NATO)—and providing both institutions with their homes; this demonstrates how immodest Belgians deserve to be. Their lack of chauvinism, combined with their increased tendency to identify primarily with Flanders or Wallonia or Brussels, has led to too many knowing too little about this land.

Belgium's present political crisis raises several additional questions regarding its past: why and how did a language-divided country develop over many centuries into a united nation? Why and how did the fact that governance of this multilingual southern Low Country was conducted solely in French for so long raise so little Flemish concern, even for many decades after independence? Why and how did Flemish sectionalism gather momentum sufficient to split the parties and the Belgium polity in the twentieth century? And why and how did Belgium over the past few decades resist the onslaught of a linguistically driven sectional schism and remain united? The schism prompts many to question its future.

Belgium is not the only country whose governance has been centralised and is now confronted with threats to its unity. As I noted in the opening lines of a previous book, *National Power and Local Governance*, 'A number of fundamental societal changes have concentrated power in national governments ... and thus demeaned local governance. In most developed countries the process of change extended over centuries ... In less developed countries the process has been more recent, more rapid and more traumatic.' The experience of Belgium may provide some perspective to the sectional challenges faced by other countries.

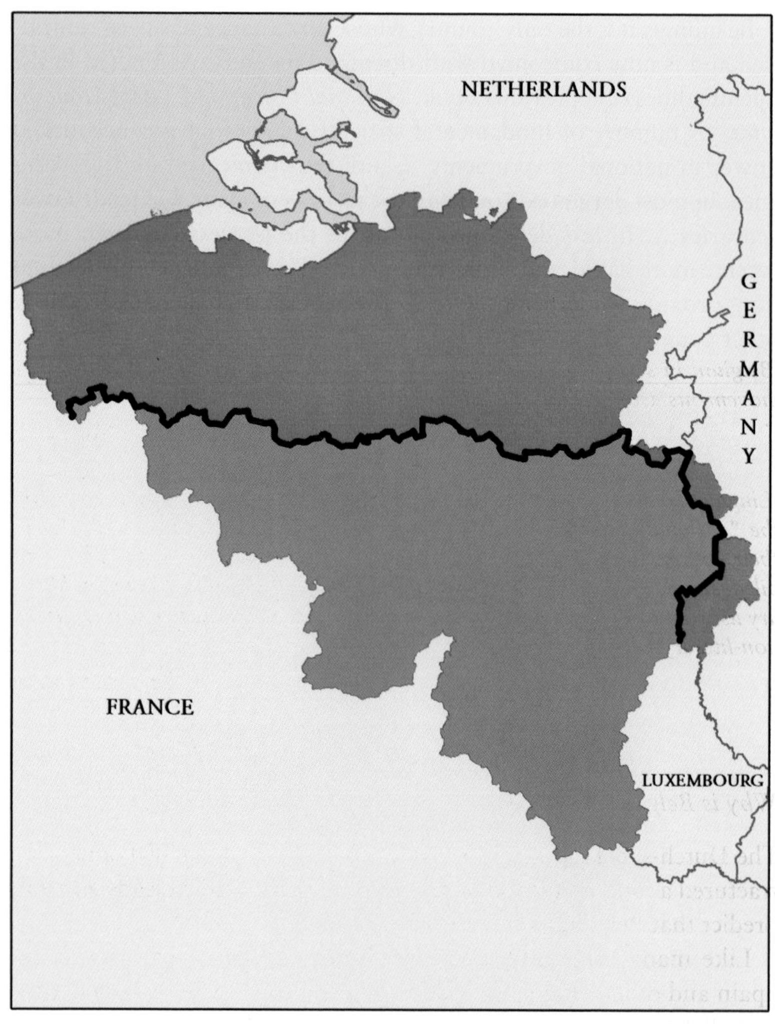

Map 1. The Belgian language frontier stems from the fifth century Frankish invasions and colonisation. Since then, Germanic tongues have dominated in the north and the east of the southern Low Countries, and Romanic ones have prevailed in the south. This map shows the language frontier superimposed on present-day Belgium.

From Belgica to Belgium

'Belgium in short combined all the ingredients of nationalist and separatist movements across Europe...'[1]

Tony Judt

'Linguistic nationalism was the creation of people who wrote and read. And the "national languages" in which they discovered the essential character of their nations were, more often than not, artefacts, since they had to be compiled, standardized, homogenized and modernized for contemporary and literary use, out of the jigsaw puzzle of local or regional dialects which constituted non-literary languages as spoken.'[2]

Eric Hobsbawm

Why is Belgium dividing?

The Dutch-speaking Flemish and the French-speaking Walloons have fractured a long-united Belgium. Continuing separatism leads many to predict that Belgium will not survive.

Like many other countries, developed ones such as Britain and Spain and others that gained their independence in the twentieth century, Belgium is anxiously coping with separatist threats to its unity. Despite a series of recent constitutional revisions that transformed this unitary state into a federation, language-driven tensions continue to escalate. Following its 2007 general election, three different prime ministers stumbled through a series of stop-gap, short-term, temporising, essentially caretaker coalitions. The 2010 general election reflected increasing tensions, a forewarning of decreasing prospects for stable coalitions.

Why now is Belgium threatening to split? While the southern Low Countries have been divided linguistically for more than 1,500 years, the country has possessed a common government for almost 600 years, albeit one that was subject to foreign rule from the late fifteenth to the early nineteenth century. Belgium began developing a sense of national identity when Caesar conquered and named the country Belgica more than 2,000 years ago. Unified governance since the fifteenth century, along with growing resentment of foreign rule and accompanying rising national aspirations, helped foster the 1830 Belgian-wide revolution that won independence and developed a modern nation-state.

In the course of tracking the evolution of Belgian governance, this book describes why and how the dominance of the French-speaking propertied elite eroded after having monopolised the land's governance for centuries. The extension of the suffrage, combined with the rise of literacy and schooling, enabled labour and Flemish movements to gather sufficient momentum to fracture the Belgian polity, splitting its parties and frustrating its politics. The presence of the EU and the NATO has, in a tangential way, enabled the Belgian separatists to discount the merit of a national government that is no longer needed to defend the country militarily and economically.

The traditions and transitions that over 2,000 years have developed in Belgium a sense of shared identity, common government and a centralised nation-state—and then over a few recent decades paved the way for the Flemish-Walloon schism that now threatens Belgium—respond to the question: why does a government, unified for more than 600 years, no longer seem capable of holding together a linguistically divided country?

Separatism: a global issue

Language-driven pressures threaten the unity of many countries. Where individual communities have distinct languages, and ethnic, and related cultural differences, they develop an acute sense of local identity and belonging. The rise of modern democracy, which has mitigated the process of rule by and for a dominant class by extending voting rights to a mass electorate, has increased the political assertiveness of communities with distinctive languages, histories and heritages. Discrimination and oppression, and memories thereof, generate sectional movements. So do globalisation and the rise of supranational organisations providing the military and economic security that was long a major *raison d'être* of national governments. Sectionalism has split many countries and threatens many more. The phenomenon prevails not only in many countries that achieved their independence after World War II, but also in many longer established ones. Countries that have fragmented include the Soviet Union, Yugoslavia and Czechoslovakia, as well as many in the developing world. Others such as the United Kingdom, Spain and Italy have granted a significant degree of autonomy to distinctive parts of their countries. China, India, Indonesia and Nigeria provide a few examples of large 'third world' countries in which sectional demands continue to challenge the national government. No country, though, that has remained united has constitutionally devolved more power across the whole country than Belgium has. While the complexity of this devolution baffles and confuses many, the creativity required to develop a system responding to so many cross pressures, and at least alleviating the sectional pressures, deserves respect.

Belgium is a particularly interesting example of a land in which language-driven sectional pressures have forced the division of its people, its parties and its government. Having been independent for almost two centuries and having had a sense of common identity, at least among the elite, that traces its roots back to the first millennium, Belgium is a long-established country. In 1993, Belgium revised its constitution for the fourth time in twenty-three years, thus completing its transformation from a unitary state into a complex federation. Since then it has adopted a fifth revision. Other countries facing sectional pressures demanding more autonomy or even independence may find Belgium's experience worth noting.

Long united, long divided Belgium

Caesar first united Belgium more than twenty centuries ago. The Franks divided it linguistically more than fifteen centuries ago. Belgium's ruling caste relied upon a Romanic tongue for its governance through almost all of its history. From the fifteenth century to the nineteenth century, despite the linguistic frontier that divided the land, a series of foreign rulers progressively unified the country and centralised its governance. The presence of a sense of national community enabled Belgian leaders to secure independence in the early nineteenth century, after which a Francophone, propertied elite dominated its governance until the latter part of the twentieth century. Not until then did language-driven sectionalism develop sufficient momentum to divide the Belgian polity, splitting Dutch-speaking Flanders from French-speaking Wallonia. This narrative focuses on the question: how, despite the language frontier, did Belgium unify and develop as a nation, but then erupt in the twentieth century to convert its unitary state into a federation with two sets of constituent parts? The initiatives taken in recent decades by Belgian political leaders to contain the sectional pressures by devolving significant power to constituent parts have been resolute and innovative, and deserve attention.

Low Country rulers from Caesar, Clovis and Charlemagne to Baldwin the Iron Arm, Philip the Good and Charles V, and to those of modern Belgium, have faced the challenge of governing a divided country. Caesar first united Belgica. Clovis took advantage of the weakening of the Roman Empire to expand from his Low Country base to create the Merovingian Empire, which his descendants divided amongst themselves. Charlemagne reunited the Low Counties within his Carolingian Empire; but when fratricidal wars again broke the empire apart, counts fragmented the Low Countries into principalities. Burgundian dukes and then Habsburg rulers later reunited the Low Countries.

In considering how the language-driven cultural frontier, which had remained politically benign for so many centuries, finally erupted in the twentieth century to split Belgium, this book addresses several questions. How did the Germanic-Romanic linguistic frontier begin? How, despite the language divide, did the Burgundian and Habsburg rulers unite Low Country governance and promote a sense of community among the court, church and commercial leaders? How, despite the linguistic divide and continued foreign rule from the war that won the Dutch their independence to the revolt that won the Belgians theirs, did the southern Low Countries continue developing a collective identity? How, despite so many Flemish-speakers, did the French-speaking elite of independent Belgium ignore Flemish interests in their governance of Belgium for so long? And why and how did the Flemish-Walloon schism finally erupt?

As long as the minute, essentially unilingual, ruling elite monopolised the land's governance, the fact that the population was linguistically divided did not impact its governance. However, just as currents erode the base of a riverbank causing it in time to collapse, so as the march of democracy extended the right to vote, it undermined the long-dominant Francophone propertied and professional power elite, leading the language crisis to erupt and divide the country. Flemish-speakers demanded that their interests no longer be ignored, and not satisfied with progress many have demanded autonomy or secession. The continued severity of the Flemish-Walloon split leads many to question whether a linguistically divided Belgium will remain united.

Belgium's past illustrates the vision and vigour of leaders forging a land's unification. Its present political schism demonstrates the challenge of keeping a divided country united. Belgium is only one of many countries that struggle with sectional pressures for more autonomy or secession. These movements are generally basically language-driven, but ethnic, socio-economic and cultural differences, along with contrasting versions of their histories, reinforce the schism. While the sectional movements that resort to extremism gain more attention, there are many more that fervently press their cause.

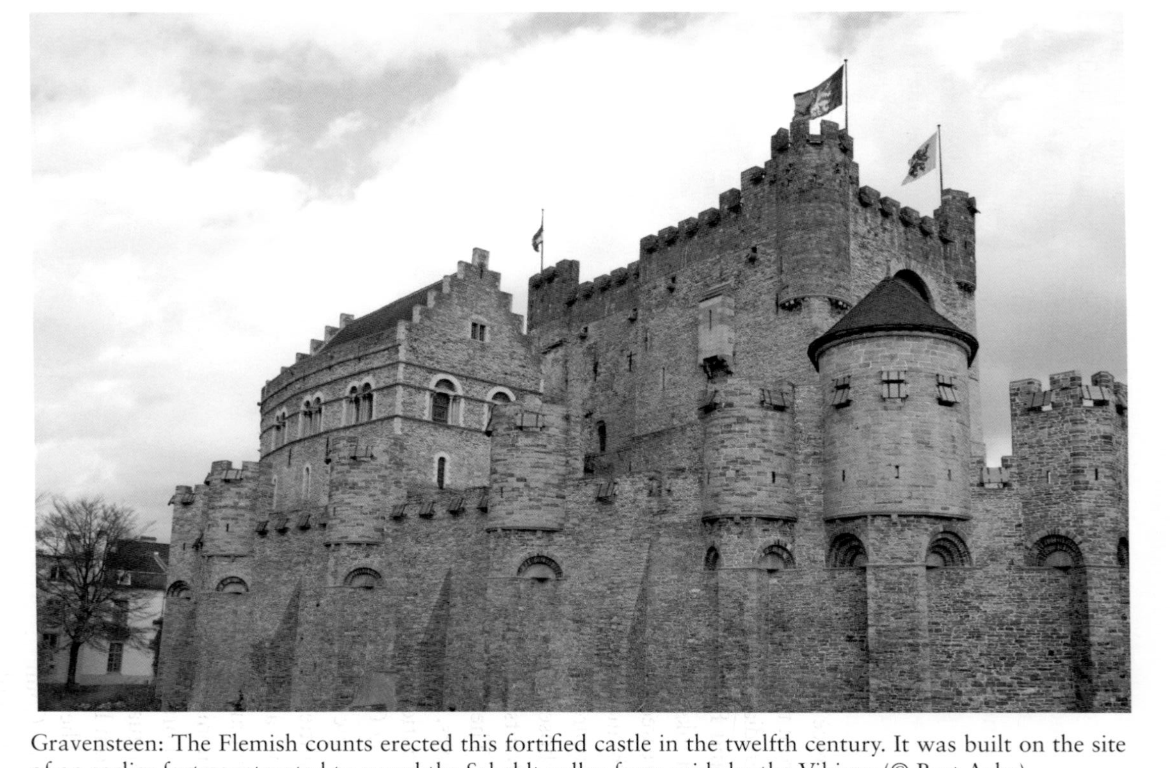

Gravensteen: The Flemish counts erected this fortified castle in the twelfth century. It was built on the site of an earlier fort constructed to guard the Scheldt valley from raids by the Vikings (© Bart Acke).

Belgica

Three beginnings mark the 1,500 years of Belgian history, which extend from the Roman conquest of the Belgic tribes to the advent of the Burgundian dukes. The Romans, by conquering northern Gaul, calling the land Belgica and colonising it, first gave it a collective identity. The Franks, when they invaded and occupied the land in the fifth century, created the Romanic-Germanic language frontier. The growth of Flemish and Lotharingian towns following the break-up of the Carolingian empire marked the emergence of prosperous Low Country towns, whose sense of community was strengthened by ties among the merchants, the nobles and the clerical hierarchy, as well as binding all three.

The colonisation of Belgica divided the land and its people in three ways. One, the Rhine River, which initially served as the northern frontier of the Roman Empire and divided the northern and southern Low Countries. Two, the vertical border that once separated the two Belgic Roman frontier provinces and later divided the eastern principalities owing titular allegiance to the French king from the western ones at least nominally subject to the German emperor. Three, the split that arose in the fifth century when the Frankish conquest and uneven colonisation divided the land linguistically between a Germanic patois in north Belgica and a Romanic dialect in the south—thus creating the language frontier that continues to separate French-speaking Wallonia from Dutch-speaking Flanders.

These physical frontiers profoundly shaped the early history of the Low Countries. The vertical split along the Scheldt did not fade politically until the fifteenth century when the Burgundian dukes extended their rule to include principalities in the valley of the Meuse as well as the Scheldt. The divide along the lower stretch of the Rhine surfaced in the sixteenth century war that won the Dutch their independence and critically separated the northern and southern Low Countries. The language-driven cultural split, politically benign for centuries, emerged in the twentieth century to divide the major Belgian parties, forge sectional parties and break the country into a complex federation.

Ideological as well as physical divides also affected the evolution of southern Low Country polity. The Church developed sufficient strength to dominate Low Country political and social life for most of its history. Conflict between the clerical hierarchy and civil authorities led to the eleventh and twelfth centuries 'investiture' controversy (over whether the sacred or secular leaders would select new bishops and abbots), the Reformation and the civil war that led to Dutch independence in the sixteenth and seventeenth centuries, and the nineteenth and twentieth century 'school wars' which until the rise of the language schism were the principal issue igniting Belgian politics. Paralleling these splits was the shift in power as the merchant and artisan classes grew to challenge the power of the nobility.

How did the Germanic-Romanic language frontier begin? The Romans sowed seeds of the divide when they colonised the more fertile south of the land rather than the north. When the Franks invaded Belgica their Germanic dialects prevailed in the less colonised north, but over time Romanised customs and speech predominated in what became Wallonia. The major feudal principalities that arose in Belgica extended across this language frontier. With minor changes, the language frontier that had its origin in the fifth century continues to divide Belgium today.

Map 2. 'A Map of Belgium'—Catrou and Rosille (1737) shows the location of the major Celtic tribes, the dense forests that stretched across the land and the major rivers that provided military and commercial access from the south.

1

THE ROMANS CONQUER, NAME AND COLONISE BELGICA

57BCE–406CE

'Gaul consists of three regions, inhabited respectively by the Belgae, the Aquitani, and a people who call themselves Celts, but are known to us as Galli … Variations in custom, language, and law distinguish these three people of whom the sturdiest are the Belgae.'[1]

Julius Caesar

'Caesar uses the term Belgae or Belgians fairly vaguely … The area was much wider than modern Belgium, and included not only parts of Holland, but much of northern France.'[2]

Adrian Goldsworthy

Caesar conquers and calls Northern Gaul 'Belgica'

The conquest of northern Gaul by Gaius Julius Caesar marks the entry into written history of the land that he named Belgica. His lucid account of his campaigns in *The Gallic Wars*, which opens with the sentences quoted above, contributed to his lasting literary as well as military reputation (and introduced generations of students to the study of Latin). The Roman conquest and colonisation introduced a sense of extended community to Belgica.

Archaeological evidence indicates that centuries before the Roman conquest, the people Caesar called the Belgae were part of a migration from the east. Caesar's conquest, undertaken without the sanction of the Roman Senate, strengthened his military and political prestige and power within the Roman Empire. By uniting under one rule the tribes inhabiting the lands drained by the Scheldt and the Meuse, he was the first of a long line of foreigners whose rule over the land profoundly affected the course of Belgian history.

The Rhine delta, which includes its tributaries the Scheldt and the Meuse and their numerous tributaries such as the Lys, Dyle, Lesse and Semois, provide the core of the Low Countries, which once included not only Belgium, the Netherlands and Luxembourg but also part of modern north-western France and the slice of western Germany along the lower Rhine. Through most of its recorded history, Belgica and the Netherlands were interchangeable names for all of the Low Countries. The name Belgica stems from the name Caesar called its people, the Belgae. The name the Low Lands (*de Nederlanden* in Dutch, *les Pays-Bas* in French and the Low Countries in English) reflects the region's predominant physical feature: the delta. Since the Dutch appropriated the name Netherlands for their northern Low Country nation, when the Belgians won their independence in 1830 they adopted the name Belgium.

The Scheldt and Meuse (Maas) rivers trisect the land now comprising Belgium. In the Roman era its northern coast and the land along the Rhine and Meuse estuaries were sandy and interspersed with marshes. In contrast, forests covered the more fertile southern part. These physical conditions encouraged the Romans to develop the southern part of Belgica more intensively than the northern part. The more intensive development of the southern part of the land (what is now called Wallonia) led to its more Romanised inhabitants having a significant impact on the language and culture of the Franks when they invaded Belgica in the waning decades of the Roman Empire.

Caesar's conquest

In 57 BCE Caesar invaded northern Gaul, extending the boundary of the Roman Empire to the Rhine. His troops moved into land inhabited by independent tribes, which he collectively called the Belgae, by marching north along the Scheldt and Sambre (a Meuse tributary) rivers, which provided a gateway through the hilly, forested Ardennes. Several tribes surrendered without a fight, but not the Nervi, whom

Caesar called 'the remotest and reputedly most warlike of the Belgic tribes.'[3] When the Nervi ambushed his troops, Caesar rallied his forces and in the battle of the Sambre defeated the attackers, whose heroism nevertheless earned his tribute to their bravery. When, after surrendering, the Nervi attempted to escape, Caesar defeated them again and exacted severe revenge by selling all its men, women and children into slavery. This act not only signalled to the other tribes the penalty for revolt but also enhanced his personal fortune. Soon more northern Gallic tribes surrendered; Caesar conquered the others.

When two years later the Eburones, led by a local chief named Ambiorix, lured a Roman force into a trap and massacred them, Caesar ravaged this tribe. To warn off distant tribes he undertook short forays across the Rhine and the Channel in 54–53 BCE before resuming his subjugation of northern Gaul. Thereafter the Romans dominated the area to the extent that no Belgic tribe dared side with a later unsuccessful revolt further south in Gaul. In 49 BCE Caesar left Gaul for Italy, crossed the Rubicon, defeated Pompey in a civil war and established himself as Roman dictator.

In 22 BCE, Emperor Augustus divided the *Provincia Belgica* into three parts. The area between the Scheldt and the sea became the province of *Belgica Secunda*, with Rheims as the seat. Between the Scheldt and the lower Rhine was the province of *Germania Secunda*, with Cologne as the seat. To its south was *Belgica Prima*, administered from Trier. The provinces were divided into districts, called *civitates*, which generally following the tribal areas.

Roman colonisation: villas, crossroads and provinces

In the next century, the Roman Empire extended its frontier north of the Rhine into the present-day Netherlands. The *Pax Romana* brought peace and promoted prosperity. The Romans brought economic growth by improving transport links: dredging rivers, building a canal linking the tributaries of the Meuse and the Rhine, and constructing a network of roads. A major road ran from Cologne to Maastricht, to Tongeren, to Kortrijk and then to Boulogne on the coast. At Tongeren, this east-west road formed a crossroads with a north-south one that extended to Arlon. At Kortrijk another road went south to Tournai and on to Rheims. At the crossing of these roads and rivers, the Romans established the seats for the administration of the surrounding *civitates*.

These towns attracted the markets for the surrounding countryside. The largest of these early settlements were Tongeren and Tournai.

The economy developed. Agriculture and fisheries produced pip-free apples, geese (for their livers), and oysters. A textile industry in Flanders and the Artois produced tunics and cloaks for export, and a metal industry in Hainaut supplied weapons for the Roman legions.

Most inhabitants lived in the more fertile southern part of Belgica, in 'villas' that were self-contained economic and social units with tenants, servants and slaves. Many of the artisans, labourers and soldiers were Romans, including retired legionaries, sent to live in the area to help assimilate the conquered peoples and encourage them to identify with Rome and its way of life. Kupchan notes that 'The goal was to cultivate allegiance toward rather than resentment of Roman rule; assimilation was a cheaper and more effective way to extend control than coercion.'[4] The Gallo-Roman settlements and villas led in time to the Franks adopting Roman customs, clothing styles, language and other aspects of culture.

The Roman Empire recruited Franks and others to help defend their frontiers. Many of these recruits reached high ranks in the service of Rome. The continuing influx of soldiers and settlers from beyond the Rhine contributed to the Germanisation of the Low Countries.

Constantine's conversion to Christianity in 312 had little impact on the Low Countries. The Church established two bishoprics: the one headquartered in Rheims initially covered the area between the Scheldt and the sea; the other in Trier covered the area east of the Scheldt extending through the valley of the Meuse.

Roman rule over Belgica lasted until the fifth century when the Franks overran the land and the Romans could no longer defend their frontiers. The concentration of Roman colonisation in southern Belgica led to an uneven impact of the Frankish invasion upon the language and culture of its people. While in northern Belgica Frankish practices and patois prevailed, over time in the south, Romanised customs and patois came to predominate. The Germanic-Romanic frontier that was created has remained fundamentally unaltered to the present day.

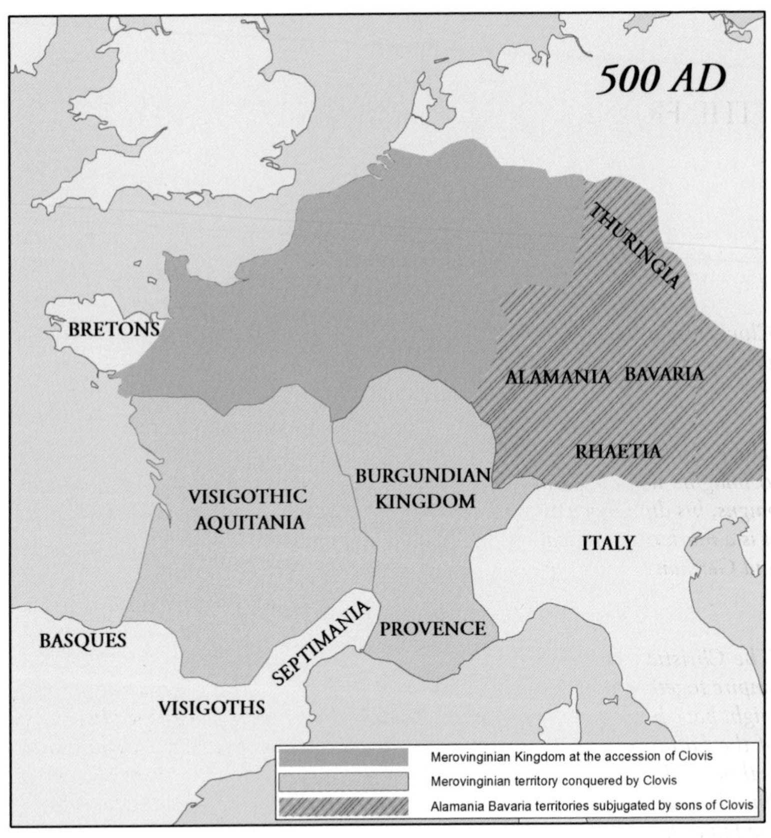

Map 3. Merovingian expansion: Clovis extended his Tournai-based realm to cover most of present-day France; his sons extended Merovingian rule to include most of Germany.

2

THE FRANKS CREATE A LINGUISTIC FRONTIER

406–861

'Clovis was a bold warrior who, with a tiny army … was able to subdue the whole of Gaul …'[1]

Adrien de Meeus

'There can be no doubt of [Charlemagne's] claim to greatness. It is impossible to imagine what European history would have been like without his campaigns, his diplomacy and his imagination—he shaped it for a thousand years. It is a mark of historical importance that he is a national hero of both France and Germany; a unique achievement.'[2]

Friedrich Heer

'The Christian faith offered an essential common culture to bind this huge empire together, however varied the liturgical practice and religious experience might have been. The organization of ecclesiastical institutions, the observance of the faith in ritual, the promotion of Christian morality, the definition of orthodox doctrine, and the dissemination of essential texts were all part of this. The new churches and monasteries established in the landscape, both in the Frankish heartlands and the newly conquered regions, were essential markers of Charlemagne's power.'[3]

Rosamond McKitterick

Low Country born-and-bred, Clovis and Charlemagne develop empires

Decisive events in the early evolution of the Low Countries included the decline of the Roman Empire, the rise and fall of the Merovingian

Empire and the successor Carolingian Empire, the advent of autonomous feudal principalities and the emergence of a Catholic clerical hierarchy that politically as well as spiritually dominated medieval life.

Two Frankish rulers, Clovis (his Latin name, in Frankish Chlodowech) and Charlemagne (Carolus Magnus), dominated the history of Western Europe from the fall of the Roman Empire until the breakdown of the Carolingian Empire that facilitated the rise of feudalism. Both rulers were born and raised in Low Country valleys: one in the Scheldt, the other in the Meuse. Both expanded and ruled extensive domains.

In the waning days of the Roman Empire, Clovis expanded his Tournai-based Merovingian kingdom to the Pyrenees. His sons extended the realm into much of Germany. The disparate impact on northern and southern Belgica of Frankish subjugation and colonisation created a language frontier cutting horizontally across the southern Low Countries. In the more barren and hence more sparsely populated lands along the coast and the lower estuaries of the Rhine, the Meuse and the Scheldt, Frankish customs and Germanic tongues continued to dominate, but in the more fertile south where more Romanised villas and villages had developed, the Franks gradually integrated with the inhabitants and adopted Roman ways and Romanic speech. The Germanic-Romanic confrontation created a language frontier that has changed little since then.

Clovis' feuding descendants split the Merovingian Empire, dividing the Low Countries roughly along the Scheldt border, which once separated two Roman Belgic provinces.

Charlemagne's forefathers displaced the Merovingian rulers. He extended the borders of the empire he inherited to include most of Western Europe. The Viking raids exploited the division of the empire and facilitated the rise of counts, who secured the succession of their progeny as rulers of the autonomous principalities. Not until the fifteenth century did the Burgundian dukes reunite the land.

Christian mission efforts successfully evangelised the Low Countries. By the time of Charlemagne, the church hierarchy played a major role in secular administration as well as sacred affairs. This development affected the political dynamics of the southern Low Countries and led to political clashes particularly evident in the eleventh and twelfth century investiture controversies, the sixteenth and seventeenth century Reformation and Eighty Years War, and the nineteenth and twentieth century school wars.

The Merovingians: the Franks overrun Belgica

By the late fourth century, in successive waves of immigration two Frankish tribes had settled along the lower Rhine. The Riparian Franks (dwellers by the riverbank—*ripa*) settled in the land between the Meuse and the Rhine. The Salian Franks (dwellers by the sea—*sal*) settled along the lower Rhine estuaries and the sea. By treaty, Salian Franks served as Roman allies guarding the frontier and providing contingents serving in the Roman army. Many Salian Franks rose high in the ranks of imperial service.

Pressed by a Hun invasion from the east, in the winter of 406–407 a major Frankish migration crossed the frozen Rhine into Belgica. After Germanic tribes sacked Rome in 410, the empire recalled frontier troops to Italy, leaving Belgica virtually undefended. Taking advantage of the Roman's plight, Salian Franks under Clodio renounced Roman rule, seized Tournai and Cambrai and moved southwest destroying towns as far south as Arras and Boulogne-sur-mer. The Romans finally defeated Clodio in 431. While they allowed him to keep most of his conquests, he was forced to acknowledge his subsidiary status. Clodio's son Merovech (from whom the Merovingian dynasty derived its name) and grandson Childeric continued as client rulers.

The impact of Frankish colonisation differed in the north and the south of Belgica. In the less populated north, where there had been fewer Roman settlements and Franks had long resided, they dominated the land culturally and linguistically as well as politically, but in the more arable south, where the Romans had built more villas and villages, the Franks interacted and intermarried with the more numerous Gallo-Romans (the Latinised Gauls) and adopted their Roman customs and used Latin as the official language. Artistic works found in Childeric's grave in 1653 attest to the Roman-style splendour of his court. The Franks called their Gallic subjects the *Wal*—their pronunciation of the Roman word *Gaul* and the origin of the word Walloon.

Clovis, who at fourteen years of age succeeded his father Childeric, took advantage of the continuing disintegration of the Western Roman Empire to shake off his subject status and expand his small coastal kingdom to one that covered almost all Gaul. Having secured a firm Frankish base, Clovis extended his rule to the Loire by defeating Roman forces outside Soissons. He then defeated a Burgundian king near Dijon, and later a Visigoth king at Vouillé, extending his kingdom to the Pyrenees. He married Clotilda, a Burgundian Catholic princess, and had their children, but not himself, baptised. Edward Gibbon describes the events that led to Clovis' own conversion: 'In distress of the battle of Tolbiac, Clovis loudly invoked the God of Clotilda and the Christians; and victory disposed him to hear, with respectful gratitude, the eloquent Remigius, bishop of Rheims, who forcibly displayed the temporal and spiritual advantages of conversion. The king declared himself satisfied of the truth of the Catholic faith; and the political reasons which might have suspended his public profession were removed by the devout or loyal acclamations of the Franks, who showed themselves alike prepared to follow their heroic leader to the field of battle or to the baptismal font.'[4] Clovis and 3,000 of his followers were baptised at Rheims. His Catholic baptism helped consolidate the Gallo-Roman population of the conquered territory into his Frankish kingdom by gaining the support of the Catholic bishops, who in the Athanasian-Arian schism then splitting the Christian world, promoted the three-in-one Trinity against the Arian denial of Christ's full divinity.

With the enlargement of his empire, Clovis moved his capital from Tournai to Paris. This Frankish warrior, by embracing the doctrine and mantle of the Roman church and the veneer of Roman ways, enhanced his royal power and prestige in a manner that led to a fusion of religious and secular politics which continued for centuries.

The Merovingian Empire breaks down

Clovis' sons expanded the kingdom beyond the boundaries of present-day France to include much of Western Europe, but the Frankish tradition of dividing the inheritance among the surviving sons, combined with the viciousness of fraternal strife, broke up the Merovingian kingdom. Centuries of fierce internecine conflict followed Clovis's death in 511. An early observer described Merovingian rule as 'a regime of despotism tempered by assassination.'[5]

While rival Merovingian kings generally divided the land, a few energetic and ruthless rulers, notably Clotaire I from 558, Clotaire II from 613 and Dagobert I from 629, reunited them. But their successors continued to partition the empire among their sons. By the early eighth century, the Merovingian Empire was divided between Austrasia (the mainly Germanic '*auster*' or east land) and Neustria (the mainly Gallo-Romanic land to the west). While through most of Europe the boundary separating Neustria and Austrasia followed the Romanic-Germanic language frontier, within the Low Countries the border ran along the Scheldt, thus cutting across the language frontier—so that in the Low Countries both the eastern and western Merovingian kingdoms included Germanic and Romanic speakers.

Significant efforts to Christianise the Low Countries began in the early seventh century, about the time St Augustine began his work in Kent. Amand (later a Saint) founded the St Bavo monastery, around which the city of Ghent later grew. Emboldened by early successes Amand tried to make baptism compulsory; in reaction the townspeople forced him to leave town in 648. Later as bishop of Tongeren he continued his missionary work and founded many monasteries and abbeys.

By the time of Charlemagne, there were twenty-five or more large abbeys in what is now Wallonia and at least three in the northern part of the land. Since stone is more plentiful in the hilly south than in the north, abbeys in Wallonia were more likely to be made of stone and thus more likely to have left traces. Bishoprics at Cologne, Tongeren, Cambrai, Tournai and Arras served the Low Country population. Their boundaries ran in north-south directions; thus each included those speaking Germanic and Romanic dialects. The Christian missions produced an environment in which a man's fidelity to his church rivalled his loyalty to his secular lord.

The Carolingians displace the Merovingians

In time, the feuding descendants of Clovis became *rois fainéants* (do-nothing or lazy kings) who relied upon the top officer of their court, the so-called 'mayor of the palace' to govern their kingdoms. In 688 Pepin II of Herstal, an Austrasian mayor of the palace who through a maternal Merovingian line was descended from Clovis, defeated the forces of Neustria in 687 and imposed his rule upon both realms. His illegitimate son, Charles Martel (the name Martel 'the hammer' was added after he turned back Muslim forces at Poitiers, forcing them from France) effectively ended the *rois fainéants* charade. When in 751 Charles Martel's son, Pepin III ('the Short'), with the support of the Pope whose endorsement was facilitated by promised military support against the Lombards, declared himself king, the Pepin-founded dynasty, later called Carolingian after Charles Martel, legitimised its take-over from the Merovingian line.

Charlemagne and his brother Carloman jointly succeeded their father, Pepin III, in 768, but when Carloman died in 771, Charlemagne exiled his nephews and ruled alone. Charlemagne's military exploits, organisational acumen and cultural vision demonstrated his energetic leadership. He expanded his domains throughout Europe, fighting more than fifty campaigns in forty-six years: in the Papal States, Lombardy, Bavaria, Saxony, and along the Slavic and Spanish frontiers. His conquests extended his realm to include most of Western Europe. Pope Leo III crowned him Holy Roman Emperor in 800.

To govern this expanded territory with its extraordinary diversity, inadequate revenue and slow and unreliable travel dependent upon rivers and dilapidated Roman roads, Charlemagne systematised and extended across the empire governmental institutions developed by the Merovingian rulers and further developed by his grandfather, Charles Martel. At the height of its expansion, the empire consisted of more than 200 parts, each of which came under an emperor's deputy, called a count, who was charged with keeping order, presiding at the local court, levying taxes and carrying out royal commands. In his biography of Charlemagne, Barbero notes that 'In itself the system was not new, because Frankish kings had already made use of a network of local representatives ... whose origins went right back to the administration of late Roman Gaul....'[6]

Initially counts served at the emperor's pleasure and he appointed their successors. Over time, though, most counts held their posts for life and their eldest sons succeeded them. In this transition from serving at the pleasure of the emperor to a virtual patrimony, Marc Bloch observes: 'Nothing is more instructive, in this respect, than the arrangement made by Charles the Bald in 877, in the famous *placitum* of Quierzy. On the eve of his departure for Italy he was concerned for the government of the kingdom in his absence ... the proclamation ... gave official recognition ... to what was already a customary privilege.'[7] Maintaining central control over local heads has long been a challenge for rulers of extensive realms, especially when communications are poor. The transition demonstrated the growing unfettered power of the post-Carolingian counts. Given little help from the empire in defending their lands and their people, they felt little obligation to their overlord and augmented their autonomy.

In governing, Charlemagne relied heavily upon clergy, who provided a major source of talent for the imperial administration as well as the

Church. The work of both the secular and clerical hierarchies closely interlocked and complemented one another. In his central administration, Charlemagne relied upon clerics to fill critical posts. At the local level, he used archbishops and bishops not only to oversee the work of the counts but also to carry out many secular functions. Both the clerical and secular hierarchies were subject to his orders for he employed both as complementary organisations for governing his empire.

The empire developed schools for educating sons of the aristocracy and young clerics who were destined to be leaders in secular as well as church administration. Alcuin, an English scholar who was Charlemagne's most trusted intellectual and spiritual adviser, helped inspire a Carolingian Renaissance, which included building and rehabilitating monasteries and churches, copying manuscripts, developing libraries and preparing a revised text of the Bible. With regard to the significance of these achievements, Roger Collins in his biography of Charlemagne writes, 'It could well be argued that Charles' military conquests ... were of far less significance for the future development of European civilisation than the parallel program of intellectual and spiritual reform and revival.'[8]

During the Carolingian era the rise of Islam interfered with European trade with west Asia and North Africa, thus reorienting European commerce from the Mediterranean to north Europe—an event that helped develop Low Country trade and prosperity. Flemish cloth and Walloon metal products sold throughout Europe. An increasing amount of commerce flowed through southern Low Country ports.

The glory of Charlemagne was magnified by his former courtier and lay abbot Einhard, who in his hagiography, *Life of Charlemagne*, masked the problems bequeathed to his successors. It is ironic that the counts, whose role Carolingian rulers had strengthened to increase the effectiveness of imperial administration, later helped undermine the empire their forerunners had supported.

The Carolingian Empire splits

The fervent zealotry of Louis the Pious, Charles' only surviving legitimate son and successor, drove him to cleanse the court, church hierarchy and abbeys of disreputable persons and practices. However, Louis' preoccupation with this effort, his lack of attention and skill in military matters, and the treachery of his sons undermined his effectiveness as

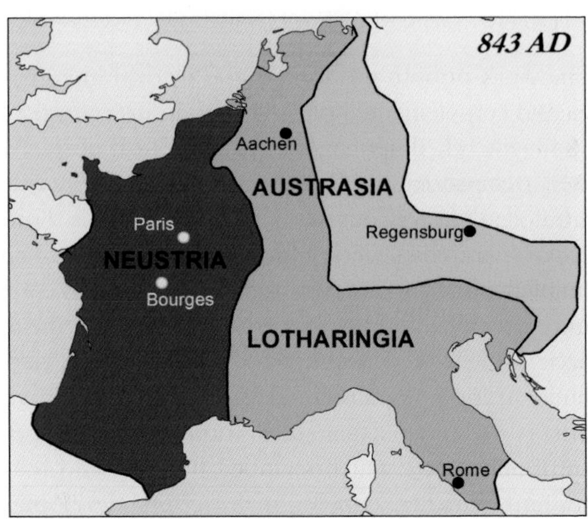

Map 4. Dividing the Carolingian Empire: by the Treaty of Verdun (843) the grandsons of Charlemagne split his empire into three kingdoms—with the ruler of the middle kingdom Lotharingia also titled as emperor. Neustria, later West Francia, included Flanders and much of present-day France. Austrasia, later East Francia, lay to the east and included much of present-day Germany. Lotharingia stretched from Friesland to Italy, including that part of the Low Countries east and north of the Scheldt (see upper map). Under the Treaty of Mersen (870), following the death of Lothair II, the second Lotharingian king and two of his three sons, the rulers of Neustria and Austrasia, divided most of Lotharingia between them, leaving only a south European fraction for the heirs of Lothair II (see lower map).

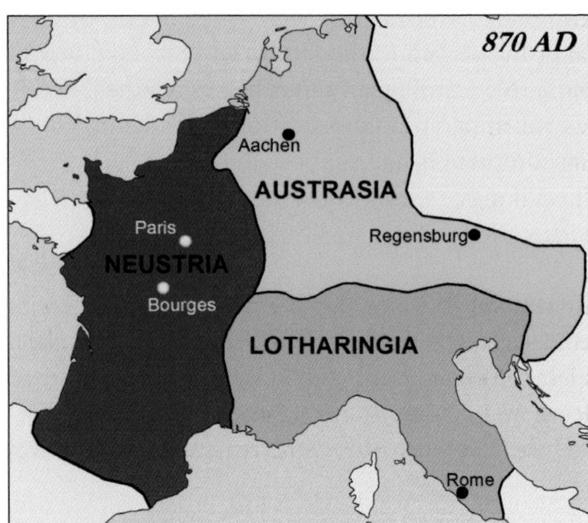

a ruler—and thus the prospects for preserving the empire's unity. His sons unsuccessfully revolted against him in 829–30. Following Louis' death in 840, his three sons divided the empire in the 843 Treaty of Verdun. Maurois points out: 'The partition of Verdun has created two of the States of modern Europe: France and Germany. And it opened the road to the long continued violence between the two countries by creating between them that Lotharingian corridor which both countries would contest ...'[9] and continue to contest for more than 1,100 years. The struggle for Belgium and Lorraine in two wars in the early twentieth century was the latest phase in a struggle that began in the ninth century.

In this partition, Louis the German got the mainly Germanic Austrasia kingdom, the part of the empire east of the Rhine. Charles the Bald took the Neustrasia kingdom that generally approximated medieval France and included Flanders. The third son Lothair, in addition to the empty title of emperor, got the middle kingdom, Lotharingia, that extended from the North Sea to the Mediterranean and included Low Countries east of the Scheldt. Following the death of Lothair, one of his sons got Italy, another received the land between the Alps and the Rhone, called Burgundy, and the third received the northern third of the middle kingdom. In 870, following the death of two of Lothair's sons, their uncles Charles the Bald and Louis the German, by the Treaty of Mersen, split the northern part of the middle kingdom between East and West Francia. The Scheldt border that had divided two Roman Belgic provinces became the frontier separating the Eastern and Western Frankish kingdoms. The break-up of the Empire facilitated the Viking raids upon the Low Countries.

Motivated by adventure, plunder and conquest, the Vikings, also known as the Norsemen or Northmen, ventured widely: eastward to Russia, westward to Greenland and North America, and southward to the Mediterranean. The raids on the Low Countries were especially severe. The Vikings attacked the most vulnerable and valuable parts using the network of navigable rivers that gave access to the continent, including the Rhine, Scheldt and Meuse and their tributaries. With the Low Countries split between East and West Francia, neither dynasty considered their border areas critical. The defence of the Low Countries was left to the counts. By 850, Vikings had settled on the banks of the Meuse and established a fortified base in Louvain. From these camps, they stepped up their raids, reaching as far as Cambrai and

Arras in the western Low Countries and Tongeren and Liège in the east, devastating the land. Viking raids on the Low Countries did not stop until Low Country forces defeated the Norsemen at Louvain in 891. By then the land was stricken, with little trade or cultivation.

Further down the Atlantic coast, the French king granted land for the sake of peace. Peter Sawyer notes that in 911 'The West Frankish king granted Rouen and surrounding territory on the lower Seine to a Viking leader named Rollo in the hope that he would deny other Viking raiders passage of the Seine.'[10] Within a few generations, these Vikings who had settled in what had become known as Normandy (the land of the Norsemen) had intermarried, adopted the Christian faith, acquired Romanised customs and developed a Norman French dialect. It was this Norman French that William the Bastard, Rollo's great-great-great grandson, and his Norman and southern Low Country invaders took with them when they invaded and conquered England in 1066. Modern English is a result of this multi-century integration of the tongues of two language groups, Germanic Old English and Romanic Norman French.

As the first nine centuries of recorded Low Country history neared its close, the land fragmented. The Frankish practice of rulers dividing their realms among their sons—rather than vesting all in the eldest, the ablest or the most favoured son—led to fratricidal warfare. This weakening, which the Viking raids highlighted, facilitated the rise of the counts, who ruled virtually autonomously and secured the succession of their chosen heirs. The resulting feudal dynasties split the Low Countries into many principalities, with Flanders at least nominally owing its allegiance to France and the others to the Holy Roman Empire. This split cut perpendicularly across the Romano-Germanic language frontier so that each of the larger principalities included both those speaking local Germanic dialects and those using Romanic patois.

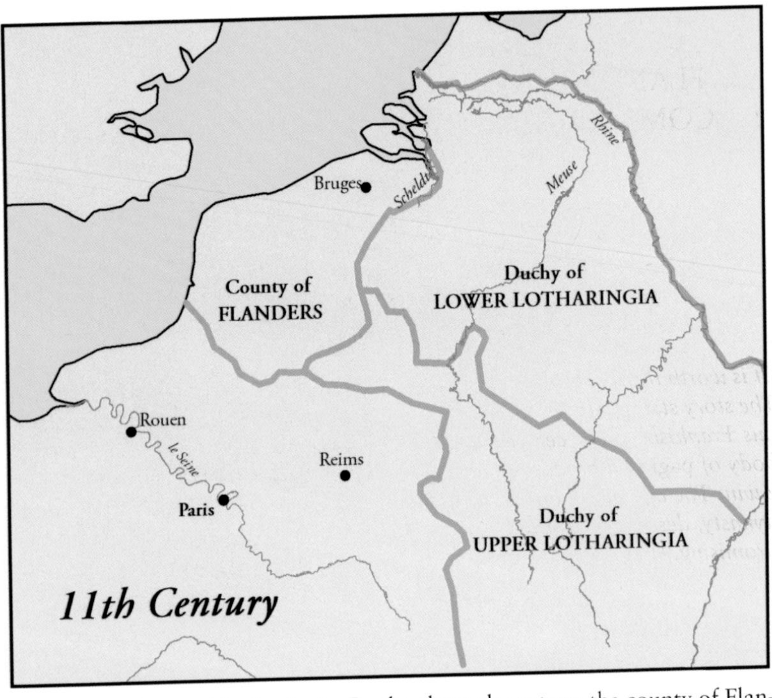

Map 5. Flanders and Lotharingia: By the eleventh century, the county of Flanders, a nominal fief of West Francia (France), ruled the coastal area west of the Scheldt. East of the Scheldt was the East Francia (German) duchy of Lotharingia. After the emperor divided Upper and Lower Lotharingia, the latter later fragmented into several principalities.

3

FLANDERS AND LOTHARINGIA DEVELOP COMMERCE, CITIES AND CIVIC CONFLICT

861–1384

'It is worth the trouble to follow the ups and downs of the county of Flanders. The story starts with the pagus Flandrensis, *a rather marginal and inconspicuous Frankish region centred on Bruges, which gave its name to a compact body of* pagi *in a broad strip along the North Sea between the rivers Aa and Zwin. The common bond that held this area together was above all its ruling dynasty, descended from the Frankish aristocracy. The start was not all that promising.'*[1]

Raoul C. Van Caenegem

The Rise of Commerce and Cities: from Baldwin the Iron Arm and Regnier the Long-Necked to Margaret of Flanders

By the early tenth century the empire of Charlemagne had badly fragmented. In the west, Flanders, Brittany, Aquitaine and Normandy (given to Rollo, the Viking), were effectively independent. In the east the death in 911 of the German King Louis the Child ended the Carolingian dynasty. By the time Henry the Fowler and Otto the Great, founders of the Saxon dynasty, restored order, many of the principalities, including Lotharingia, had asserted autonomy.

The Carolingian empire breakdown fuelled the rise of headstrong, aggressive counts who dominated the Low Countries during the feudal age. Counts asserted their power and gained autonomy. The Church solidified its authority throughout the land. Propelled by the clearing of forests and the reclaiming of land from marshes and the sea, commerce prospered and towns grew. Trade nurtured a merchant and artisan class that promoted communal organisations, which in time challenged the nobles.

The feudal era began with counts, notably Baldwin the Iron Arm, defending their principalities against the Vikings and asserting their autonomy against their overlords, such as Baldwin against the French king and Regnier the Long Necked against the German emperor. The lords fought, as did John II of Brabant against those opposed to his annexation of Limburg. Nobles allied with their suzerain powers in fighting the Crusades. Burghers, notably Jacob van Artevelde and his son Philip, resisted and revolted against their feudal lords. France, Germany and England frequently intervened and invaded. The Low Countries were directly involved in the intrigues and warfare of the Hundred Years War. Feudal fragmentation led each principality to develop distinctive traditions, institutions and grievances; but Low Country-wide ties among the nobility, the clerics and the merchants increased a sense of an extended community.

Romance, legend and mythology have glorified and romanticised the chivalry, magnificent pageantry, impressive tournaments, gallant knights and fair ladies of the medieval age. The imagery has obscured the reality of the protracted brutality that pervaded feudal life. As King John II of France noted during the Hundred Years War, 'many deadly battles have been fought; people slaughtered; churches robbed; souls destroyed; young women and virgins deflowered; respectable wives and widows dishonoured; towns, manors and buildings burned; and robberies, cruelties and ambushes committed ...'[2]

From 1000, Flanders developed its agriculture and commerce, which depended largely upon its trade with England.

The rise of counts, clerical hierarchy, commerce and communal organisation

The rise of counts and dukes, bishops and abbots, and merchants and artisans energised the southern Low Countries and spurred the growth of its cities. The first counts of Flanders, Baldwin the Iron Arm and his successors, exploiting the weakness of the early French kings, extended

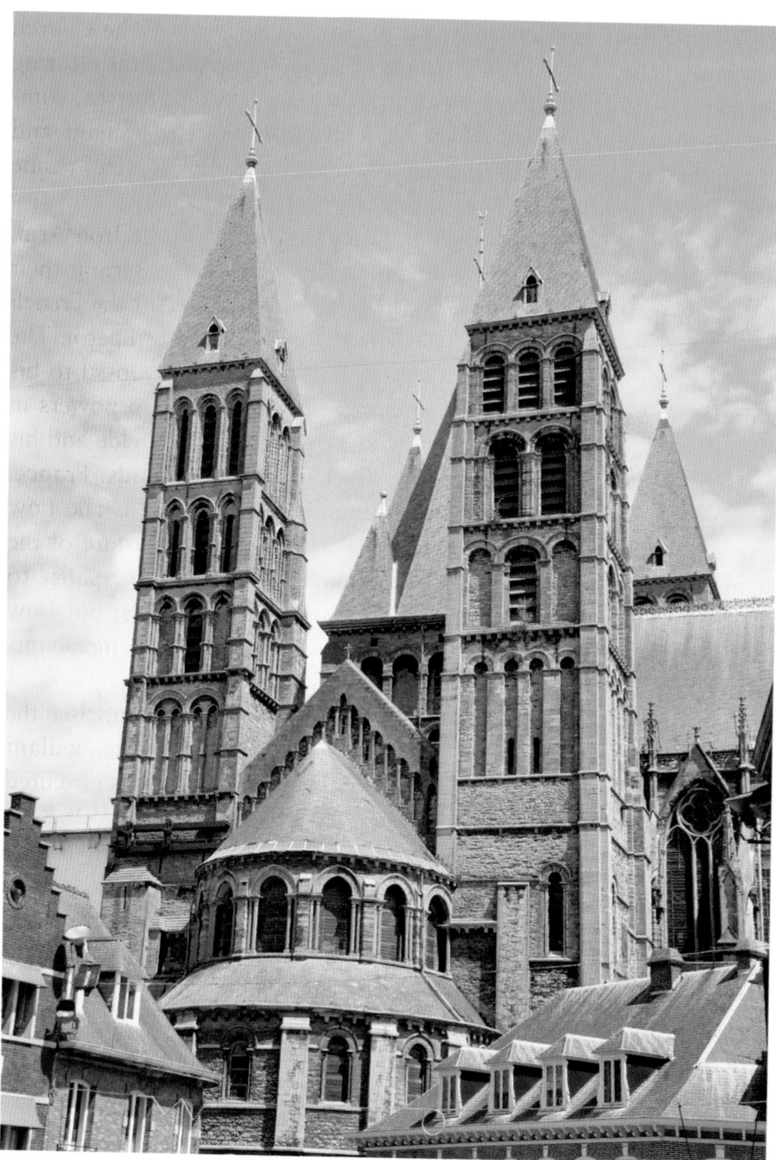

Tournai Cathedral was built in three stages over more than 150 years. A comparison of the style and scale of the Romanesque nave (early twelfth century), the transept with five towers (late twelfth century) and the huge Gothic choir (late thirteenth century) illustrates not only the changing architectural influences but also increasing prosperity that marked those centuries (© Sealine, istockphoto.com).

their campaigns southward as far as Normandy, only to have their autonomy later threatened by stronger French monarchs. A Lotharingian count, Regnier the Long-Necked, won a battle against the forces of the German king and established the autonomy of the rebel duchy. While the Low Countries fragmented, the Church through its hierarchy, the merchants through their commercial connections and the feudal courts through marriages and other alliances fostered a sense of extended community, if only among the elite.

The dynasties of Flanders, Brabant, Hainaut and Namur gained legitimacy by their descent from Charlemagne, through two of his great-granddaughters. One married Baldwin the Iron Arm, who founded the Flemish dynasty. Another great-granddaughter was the mother of Regnier the Long Necked, whose descendants included not only the counts of Louvain (whose descendants became the dukes of Brabant) but also of Hainaut and Namur. Frequent dynastic intermarriages reflected and affected alliances that sometimes led to one ruler heading two or more principalities (see genealogical chart in Appendix 2). The lords exerted their dominance not only through their control of the principalities but also by their younger sons and other relatives pervading the upper ranks of the Church. The merchants and the artisans gained participation in the governing process only after continued struggles.

'The most powerful force in Western Europe at this time was the Church which asserted itself in open and subtle ways ...'[3] says Robert Payne in his history of the Crusades. The work of the church was interwoven with the work of the government. The church ran the schools that provided the diplomats and advisers upon whom the rulers depended. Its influence pervaded all aspects of medieval life. A number of religious reformers led the revival of the once moribund Church. Among these were Bruno, who combined the offices of Archbishop of Cologne, Arch-Chancellor of the empire and Duke of Lotharingia, Notger (Prince-Bishop of Liège) and St Bernard (founder of the Cistercian 'white monks'). These efforts revitalised the church, encouraged church building, and escalated the role of the Church in secular governance and daily life.

Low Country nobles played leading roles in the Crusades. The First Crusade (1095–99) attracted, along with other European nobles, the counts of Flanders, Hainaut and Bouillon. The latter mortgaged his county to the Liège prince-bishopric when he departed on the crusade that led to his crowning as the first king of Jerusalem in 1099. Low Country leaders in the Second Crusade (1147–49) included Thierry of Alsace, Count of Flanders, who brought back the Holy Blood reliquary carried in the annual procession at Bruges. In the Third Crusade (1189–92), Philip of Alsace, Count of Flanders, participated with the kings of Germany, France and England. The Fourth Crusade (1202–04) led to the capture of Constantinople and the crowning of Baldwin IX, Count of Flanders, as Emperor of Constantinople. Generations of returning Low Country Crusaders awakened western European materialistic, commercial, intellectual and artistic interests.

Striking medieval castles, churches, market halls, belfries and city halls continue to highlight Belgian townscapes and demonstrate the invigorated civic life that drove the architectural flowering of Belgian towns in the medieval era. Early settlements grew on sites critical for travel and trade: the crossing of two main roads by a river as at Tournai, the confluence of two rivers as at Liège and Ghent, and the most inland navigable point of a river as at Brussels. At these crossroads

Hastiere, built around 1035, is a Mosan Romanesque former Benedictine abbey church in the Meuse valley, a major commercial and cultural traffic corridor (© Jean-Pol Grandmont, from Wikimedia Commons).

Bruges Cloth Hall with Belfry is a medieval merchants' hall topped by its belfry. Initially the cloth hall housed the town administration as well (© Ulrich Knaupe).

lords built castles, clerics erected abbeys and churches and merchants developed markets, then market halls. Pride motivated the building of edifices that matched or surpassed those of other cities. Prosperity and pride provided the wealth that funded their construction.

Changing challenges drove successive transitions in Belgium's architectural heritage. Each shift introduced a new emphasis in the purpose for which edifices were built. In the ninth and tenth centuries, when the Carolingian Empire broke down and the Viking threat grew, bold counts built fortified castles along the Scheldt in Antwerp and Ghent. In the Ardennes local lords built forts, such as Bouillon, Dinant,

The Ghent Belfry, unlike the Bruges one, stands apart from the Lakenhalle, or covered market (© Bart Acke).

Namur, Spontin and Laarne, on natural rock escarpments along a river, generally overlooking a settlement. The religious zeal of the eleventh to thirteenth centuries, as well as fuelling the Crusades, promoted monasteries such as those at Hastiere, Nivelles and Villers. The rise of commerce and civic pride promoted the construction of the market halls and bell-towers, such as those at Ghent, Bruges and Ieper. Belfries, market halls and city halls followed in the fourteenth and fifteenth centuries, driven by increased mercantile prosperity and civic pride. The building of castles, churches and markets stimulated the growth of cities as centres for security, worship and trade, as well as the development of civic life. While Romanic influences initially predominated in the Scheldt basin, the Gothic style prevailed in the valley of the Meuse. In the middle was Brabant, which mixed and blended these influences.

International contacts and accompanying new ideas and tastes stimulated artistry and trade. The growing economy spurred the growth of cities. Le Goff points out: 'the tangle of Flemish rivers, extended from the twelfth century on by a whole network of artificial canals ... produced a thirteenth century commercial evolution comparable to the eighteenth century industrial revolution.'[4] The aristocratic character of rural institutions in the Frankish period and the aristocratic character which was soon to mark urban administration are explicable by the rapid concentration of capital, whether consisting of land or of moveable property, in the hands of a few privileged persons.[5] The *Gros Brief*, which the count of Flanders initiated in 1187 following the example of the English Doomsday Book in recording the landholdings, fostered the development of commerce as well as improving the tax base. The rise of merchant guilds and later craft guilds spearheaded the rise of an urban-based merchant class that challenged the rule of the nobility. The first guilds were merchant associations, whose ranks excluded shopkeeper-artisans as well as the hand-workers. Little by little, a middle class evolved. 'The guild not only laid the foundations of the urban constitution, but also, among the crowd of immigrants who had come in from the country, it was the starting point for the formation of different social classes.'[5]

By the beginning of the twelfth century, Flemish towns possessed municipal councils. By mid-century, they supported primary schools for burgher children. Until the Renaissance, though, secondary education remained the monopoly of clerical schools, from which came the 'clerks' who, starting at the end of the twelfth century, were charged with the correspondence and accounts of the city. Towns, says Richard Vaughan 'evolved spontaneously from the eleventh and twelfth centuries onwards in all parts of Europe, but they were most numerous and most powerful in the Low Countries, along the Rhine and in Northern Italy'[6] where they became strong enough to gain virtual autonomy. During this period artisans, copying the tapestry and metallurgy trades that abbeys and monasteries had long nurtured, established themselves as secular enterprises. The keen desire of sovereigns, nobles and merchants for ostentatious displays of costly furnishings provided artisans with patronage assuring their prosperity. By the thirteenth century, merchant guilds dominated Flemish politics as well as commerce. Bruges, along with Lübeck, Hamburg, Bergen and London, was a major member of the Hanseatic League, which controlled the trade of northern Europe from the late thirteenth to the late fifteenth century. The members exchanged the furs, fish, and other products from northeast Europe for the cloth and manufactures of Flanders and its hinterland.

Exclusion of the artisans from civic power led to the rise of craft guilds, such as the metalworkers, leatherworkers, butchers, bakers and weavers, who defended their political and economic interests and controlled the standards of their products. Low wages and festering social conditions fomented serious uprisings in Douai, Ieper, Bruges, Tournai and Liege, signalling the unrest that led to the growing power of guilds and their integration into the governance of medieval Belgian cities.

The rise, expansion and decline of Flanders

An early history, the *Chronique de Flandre*, describes the broad strip of land along the North Sea between the rivers Aa and Zwin as 'an infertile strip of land, of little value and full of swamps.'[7] Yet by the twelfth century the county had grown into one of the most populous and prosperous parts of Europe. Its importance led the English to call all the Low Countries 'Flanders'. Similarly, many Dutch as well as others have long called the entire kingdom of the Netherlands 'Holland', even though the county of Holland, now the two provinces of North and South Holland, is only part of that country. Likewise many Europeans and Americans call all residents of the United Kingdom English—to the annoyance of the Welsh, Scots and northern Irish. In the same way many non-Americans call all Americans, not just New Englanders, 'Yankees' despite the heated objections of Americans from south of the Mason-Dixon line, where the ravages of the 'damn Yankees' during the American Civil War are not forgotten; they have long been telling the 'damn Yankees' to go home.

Conflict with the nominal overlord, the French king, forged Flemish medieval history. Initially the Flemish counts exploited the weakness of the French kings, but later French monarchs frequently invaded and intervened in the affairs of their nominal fief. The seesawing of political and military advantage, which arose from ambiguous and often hostile feudal relations, encouraged frequent external interventions and internal insurrections, which kept the southern boundary of medieval

Flanders in constant flux. Throughout the feudal era Flemish rule extended south-west of the Flemish-Walloon language frontier, and thus the county included not only those speaking a Germanic tongue but also many speaking a Romanic one. The latter were in the area referred to as *Walloon Flanders*, which now includes part of Hainaut and north-western France.

The first Count of Flanders was Baldwin the Iron Arm. His family, David Nicholas writes, 'had furnished three counts of *pagi* between the Scheldt and the Leie ... Baldwin was thus already a count ... when he established the basis of his family's fortune by eloping around Christmas 861 with Judith, the eldest child of King Charles the Bald. Judith was already the childless widow of two West Saxon kings when she returned to the continent at age sixteen in 860. Alfred the Great was her stepson; and Alfred's daughter ... would later marry Judith's son, Count Baldwin II'[8]. When Baldwin eloped with Judith, her angry father, deprived of arranging a third prestigious marriage, confiscated his property. However, the bishop of Rheims, backed up by the Pope, in addition to Baldwin's threats to ally with the Vikings, persuaded King Charles to accept Baldwin as his son-in-law, grant him the county of Flanders and charge him with defending the Scheldt estuary against the Vikings.

The raids of the Vikings upon the Low Countries did not cease until Baldwin's son, Baldwin II, with the help of German forces, defeated the Norsemen at Louvain in 891. Exploiting the weakness of France, the count and his descendants expanded Flanders to the south and west, consolidating their rule over a conglomerate of territories and exercising power more in their own name than as agents of their nominal suzerain, the French king. Baldwin IV and Baldwin V seized land east of the Scheldt River, subsequently called 'imperial' Flanders because it was within the Holy Roman Empire. The Flemish counts now owed homage to two overlords, a common feudal arrangement.

Baldwin V married his daughter Matilda to William, Duke of Normandy, the bastard who had won the duchy only after years of fierce conflict. The match secured William a major alliance, which not only strengthened his rule in Normandy but also assured William significant assistance in his 1066 invasion of England. Many Flemings settled in England and William granted titles and estates to a number of Flemish leaders.

When Baldwin VII died childless, Charles the Good, son of a Danish king whose wife was the daughter of a Flemish count, succeeded his cousin. Galbert of Bruges cites Charles' support of the poor, his military prowess, and the invitations he rejected to become King of Jerusalem and Holy Roman Emperor as indications of Flemish prosperity, power and prestige in the early twelfth century. His threat to depose his chief financial officer, a member of a powerful patrician clan, increased the friction between Charles the Good and the leading Burgher families that led to his assassination.

From the mid-twelfth century, when a strengthened French monarchy took steps to unify France, the king attempted to assert his suzerainty over Flanders, then its autonomous—and most prosperous—fief. French intervention in Flanders was especially evident in disputed successions. When the Flemish Count, Philip of Alsace died without an heir, only at the insistence of the archbishop of Rheims did the French King consent to the county passing to Philip of Alsace's sister Margaret and her husband Baldwin, who ruled Hainaut and Namur in his own right. The French again intervened when Baldwin and Margaret's son Baldwin IX, after becoming Emperor of Constantinople in 1204 and then being taken prisoner, died in captivity leaving two young daughters. The French King made the orphaned girls his wards, married the older daughter and heir Joan to Ferrand of Portugal and the younger Margaret to Bouchard of Avesnes. But Ferrand did not prove to be the loyal subject the French king sought.

The new Flemish count soon joined with the count of Holland, the duke of Brabant and other Low Country lords in rebelling against Philip II of France, known to history as Philip Augustus. King John of England sided with the rebels, for he had lost continental possessions to the French king; so did Otto IV, the Holy Roman Emperor. Supporting Philip were Pope Innocent III and the recently displaced German emperor. In the ensuing 1214 battle of Bouvines (near Tournai), the combined French-led forces decisively defeated the Low Country-English alliance in this conflict of Europe-wide interests. In the battle the French captured and imprisoned Ferrand in Paris and forced French counsellors upon Joan, thereby ensuring French control of Flanders. Upon Joan's death her younger sister Margaret became countess, the French forced her husband Bouchard of Avesnes into exile and she then married William of Dampierre. After Margaret's death, the French King again intervened in Flanders to arbitrate the conflicting claims of the heirs from each marriage, awarding Flanders to William's son Guy of Dampierre and Hainaut to Bouchard's son John of Avesnes who later inherited Holland and Zeeland from his mother.

When Bruges commoners took steps to limit the patrician dominance of town governance, the aristocrats asked the French King to send troops. Upon the troops' arrival, they ran up their *fleur-de-lys* banners on the ramparts and embroidered similar *fleur-de-lys* on their clothing and banners, thus becoming known as the *leeuwaerds (*men of the lily). The commoners mobilised and adopted as their emblem the heraldic claws of the Lion of Flanders, and thus became known as the *clauwaerds* (men of the claw). To counter the French, Guy of Dampierre took advantage of the ongoing war between France and England to revolt against France and asked the English for assistance. When the French invaded and the Bruges commoners revolted, the French governor made concessions that suspended the revolt. But at dawn the next day, 18 May 1302, the governor's forces 'were ambushed in the "the Matins of Bruges" when, at what seems to have been a prearranged signal (the cry "Shield and Friend"), the Claws, strengthened by numerous exiles who had been let back into the city during the night, massacred the French and their sympathisers.'[9]

The French then invaded Flanders with a large force of cavalry that included many Low Country nobles and aristocrats. Flemish commoners, led by Jan Breydel and Pieter de Cominck, head of the weavers, met this challenge outside Kortrijk on a marshy field they had prepared with ditches and spikes. Their 1302 rout of the French cavalry, in what has become known in history as the Battle of the Golden Spurs because the battlefield booty included costly spurs, continues to be regarded as an epic event in the Flemish struggle for independence. But its impact was short-lived, for the French navy defeated the Flemish at Zierikzee in 1304 and not long thereafter French forces prevailed against Bruges forces when Ghent, Ieper and Kortrijk troops prematurely left the field.

From 1337 to 1453, Flanders, with Brabant and Hainaut, took part in the intrigues and the prolonged series of campaigns and battles comprising what history has called the Hundred Years War. The confrontation began when Edward III of England coveted the French throne. Not only were the Low Countries involved, but also at various times the Holy Roman Empire, Burgundy, Scotland, Aragon, Castile and Portugal participated. In this war the Flemish count, Louis of Nevers, remained loyal to Philip VI of France, his nominal liege lord, and arrested English merchants in Flanders. In 1336 Edward reacted by forbidding the export of raw wool, of which England enjoyed a near monopoly, to Flanders. The embargo was devastating. With trade prohibited, the merchants could no longer trade and the weavers and other artisans no longer had work.

The situation led to a Flemish revolt in 1337 against the ineffective, unpopular and pro-French Count, Louis of Nevers. Leading the revolt was Jacob van Artevelde, a wealthy Ghent merchant who used his demagogic flair to assert dictatorial powers as *de facto* ruler of first Ghent and then all Flanders. Louis fled to France. Artevelde negotiated with Edward III of England to lift the wool blockade and subsidise the Flemish, Brabant and Hainaut forces to fight the French. With this support the English king proclaimed himself king of France in 1340 at Ghent. Shortly afterwards, in an effort to prevent the English from disembarking troops to invade the southern Low Countries, the French fleet attacked and destroyed the English fleet in the sea battle of Sluys (near Bruges). But the English king's continental campaign became so protracted and costs so prodigious that he could no longer pay his troops and subsidise the Low Country forces. His war efforts lapsed.

Disappointed with the course of the war and increasingly resentful of the arrogant dictatorial Artevelde, protesting crowds led by the weavers stormed his mansion and killed him. In the absence of the Count, who remained in France, powerful burghers of Ghent, Bruges and Ieper took control of the governments of Flanders. Renewed Anglo-French hostilities led to the battle of Crécy in 1346, in which Edward III, with his longbow archers defeated a much larger French force. In the battle, the exiled Louis of Nevers was killed, along with 1,500 lords and knights serving the French king. The Count's more politically skilful son, Louis of Maele, escaped his Flemish Burgher captors, fled to Brabant and married the daughter of its Duke. With the support of his new Brabant father-in-law, he invaded and secured Flanders, but when the weavers revolted, Louis capitulated.

At this point the guilds of the butchers and fishermen, who had long opposed the alliance of the weavers and merchants, helped Louis recapture Bruges and besiege Ghent. Despite overwhelming odds, Jacob van Artevelde's son Philip defeated Louis of Maele, who fled to Paris where he asked the French for help. Philip the Bold, the French king's younger son who had married Louis de Maele's daughter and heiress, intervened to help Louis regain his land and restore peace. These events so affected Flemish cities that Ghent's population dropped from about 50,000 in 1357 to about 25,000 in 1385 and Ieper's from about 20,000 in 1311 to less than 11,000 in 1412. The decline of Flanders facilitated the rise of Brabant.

The Duchy of Brabant succeeds the Duchy of Lotharingia

While the early Flemish counts were taking advantage of the vulnerable West Francia kings by expanding southwest, the aggrandising counts within Lotharingia exploited the German-French rivalry to assert their autonomy and undermine East Francia rule. Whereas Flanders remained united under its count, Lotharingia fragmented into many principalities, including Brabant, Hainaut, Limburg, Luxembourg, Namur, the large ecclesiastical one of Liège, and the smaller ecclesiastical ones of Cambrai, Douai, Mechelen and Stavelot-Malmedy. Each developed distinctive traditions that adversely affected the emergence of a united Belgium.

The role of Regnier the Long-Necked, whose father had eloped with or abducted the German Emperor's daughter, parallels that of Baldwin the Iron Arm in Flanders. When the German emperor appointed his bastard son Zwentibold as the Lotharingian duke, Regnier, with the French King's help, defeated and killed the son—and then ruled Lotharingia. While the counts within Lotharingia established the right of succession for their heirs earlier, the early emperors frequently changed dukes, whose major role was military coordination of the counties. Upon Regnier's death, the then German Emperor appointed Regnier's son as duke. When Regnier's son was defeated and drowned in a revolt against the empire, the Emperor appointed his own brother, Bruno, already the archbishop of Cologne, as duke. In 959, the Emperor divided Upper Lotharingia (Lorraine) from Lower Lotharingia (eastern Belgium). A later emperor appointed a brother of the French king as duke of Lower Lotharingia, rewarding him for allying with Germany against France. Later Godfrey of Bouillon was duke—until he left for the first Crusade and became the first King of Jerusalem. In 1106 the Count of Leuven, Godfrey the Bearded, when appointed as Duke of Lotharingia changed his title to Duke of Brabant.

In 1283 John I, Duke of Brabant, enlarged his realm by gaining possession of neighbouring Limburg, which gave him control of the Bruges-Cologne trade route. When the archbishop of Cologne and the Dukes of Luxembourg and Gelderland attempted to forbid this annexation, John defeated them at the battle of Worringen (1288). His grandson, John III, gained the support of the communal leaders and nobles by issuing the Charter of Cortenburg, an early assurance of communal rights that limited the imposition of taxes. His daughter

Joanna secured her inheritance by making a 'Joyous Entry' with her husband Wenceslaus I, Duke of Luxembourg, enhancing their acceptance by confirming the Cortenburg Charter and granting the communes more rights including no taxation without popular consent, a precedent for their successors. In contrast to the strained relations in Flanders, the closer working relations between the Brabant duke and the town burghers led to more harmony with the 'estates', the council of the duchy composed of clergy, nobles and town representatives. When the ducal heirs were children or female, the efforts to appease the elite increased. New rulers generally began their reigns with a 'Joyous Entry' into the seat of the principality. The less fractious Brabant environment later helped shift commercial and political power from Flanders to Brabant and from the sixteenth century Brabant became the leading Low Country principality.

Hainaut, Namur, Luxembourg and Liège split from Lotharingia

Beside Brabant, four Belgian principalities emerged from the duchy of Lotharingia: Hainaut, Namur, Luxembourg and Liège. Like medieval Flanders and Brabant, the extensive medieval Liège and Luxembourg principalities included significant numbers of those speaking a Germanic dialect as well as those speaking a French one. Today, with altered borders, these four principalities along with the recently created Brabant-Wallonia province comprise Wallonia. While each of these French-speaking provinces has a distinctive history, all shared traditions that differed critically from Flanders and Brabant, differences that led them to play a less enthusiastic role in the war that led to Dutch independence. Long ingrained differences in outlook dating back to the Romans persist in the partisan cleavages today.

The first Count of Hainaut was Regnier the Long-Necked, whose eldest son later succeeded his father as Duke of Lotharingia, whilst his younger son inherited Hainaut. Regnier's grandson was deposed, but his great-grandson, son-in-law of Hugh Capet who took the French throne in 987, regained the county. After Baldwin, Count of Flanders, married the Hainaut heiress, Flemish counts ruled Hainaut from 1051 until 1071 and from 1191 to 1278. When Margaret of Flanders (see above) died, different heirs inherited the two counties. The Hainaut one later inherited Holland and a descendant later ceded Hainaut to Philip the Good.

The county of Namur emerged as a small principality, squeezed between Hainaut and Liège, under Berenger of Namur, a son-in-law of Regnier the Long-Necked. Berenger's sixth generation descendant Henry the Blind inherited Luxembourg from his mother as well as Namur from his father. In 1188 his nephew Baldwin VIII of Flanders and V of Hainaut seized the county. In 1263 the Namur ruler, who was then also Emperor of Constantinople, sold Namur to Guy de Dampierre. A descendant of Guy's younger son sold his inheritance to Philip the Good in 1421; upon John's death Namur passed to Burgundian rule.

Luxembourg aligned itself more closely with the empire than the other Low Country principalities, from which it was geographically separated by the extensive Liège prince-bishopric. The German Emperor Charles IV made the county a duchy in 1354, shortly after relinquishing it to his younger half-brother, who married Joanna, Duchess of Brabant. The close involvement of the House of Luxembourg in empire affairs led four of its members to secure the German imperial crown. Henry VII (1308–1313), Charles IV (1346–1378), Wenceslaus (1378–1408) and Sigismund (1410–1437) interrupted the long chain of Habsburg emperors that began with Rudolph I in 1273 and ended with Francis II in 1806 when the empire was dissolved. In 1415 Wenceslaus pawned Luxembourg to his niece, Charles IV's granddaughter Elizabeth of Goerlitz, who was married to Anthony, Duke of Burgundy and brother of John the Fearless, from 1409 to 1415. Elizabeth ceded the duchy to her nephew Philip the Good in 1443. In 1815 eastern Luxembourg became an independent grand duchy under its Grand Duke, William I, who was also the new King of the united Netherlands. The western half continued as a Belgian province.

The Prince-Bishopric of Liège has a separate history from the other Low Country principalities. While neighbouring dynasties could not arrange marital alliances with its celibate clerical rulers, they did succeed in placing family members as prince-bishops. In 972, a few years after the bishops of Liège became lords temporal as well as spiritual, the German Emperor selected his nephew Notger as prince-bishop. He had not only ecclesiastical power over an area extending from Utrecht to Champagne, but also temporal power over an area comprising twenty-three towns, twelve Germanic-speaking and eleven Romanic-speaking, stretching along the Meuse from above Maastricht to below Dinant. Notger enlarged St Lambert's Cathedral, built other churches, developed fortifications and beautified the city. The temporal rule of the prince-bishopric increased with the annexation of the lordship of Bouillon, after Godfrey of Bouillon had mortgaged it in 1095 to fund his venture in the Crusade.

As in the other Low Country principalities, Liège endured a continuing power struggle. A vivid example occurred in 1312 after the guilds won demands to be represented on the town council. The nobles and patricians so resented the encroachment that on an August night, they entered the city through St Martin's Gate and marched to the market place. The artisans ambushed the armed men, forced them to seek refuge in St Martin's Church and set it on fire, killing those trapped within. After this massacre, known to history as the Mal St Martin, the surviving patricians agreed to an assembly with craft guild representation as its main institution. The massacres and sackings of the city by successive Burgundian dukes (described in Chapter four), inflicted not only an immediate impact but also a long-term one upon relations of the duchy with the other Low Country principalities.

The divergence of traditions, contrasting community identities and bitter inter-principality memories nurtured distinctive parochial loyalties long past the feudal age. Intermarriages among Low Country dynasties, a strong clerical hierarchy and a well-connected mercantile class, however, cultivated an extended Low Country community. These ties facilitated the efforts of the Burgundian dukes and Habsburg monarchs to unite most of the Low Countries under their rule. Urban growth fostered the development of the middle class for the role which it was to play in the Renaissance, the Reformation, the Counter-Reformation and later the winning of Belgian independence.

Oudenaarde Stadhuis was built between 1526 and 1537. While the Burgundian dukes were centralising their power, the pride of the Burghers spurred their development of civic organisations and their construction of municipal structures symbolising their assertiveness against the dukes (© Torsade de Pointes, http://en.structurae.de/photos/index.cfm?JS=111746).

Burgundy

The growth of commerce, emergence of centralised bureaucracies, the Renaissance and the Reformation transformed fifteenth and sixteenth century Europe, especially the southern Low Countries. From Philip the Bold until Philip II of Spain, Burgundian dukes and their Habsburg successors unified the Low Countries, centralised their governance, promoted their artistic creativity and cultivated a sense of extended community. Religious dissension, the anti-heretical prosecuting vigour of Philip II and the stubborn zeal of moderate Catholics as well as Protestants combined to split the northern from the southern Low Countries.

Four Burgundian dukes advanced the state-building process by uniting the several Low Country principalities under their rule and developing central institutions to oversee their governance. Later, Charles V added more principalities north of the Rhine, created the Burgundian Circle and further centralised Low Country governance. During a little more than two hundred years, Low Country rulers converted an agglomeration of feudal fiefs into a unified polity with a central bureaucracy, revenue sources and military prowess, and fostered a growing sense of commonality that laid the foundation for Belgian nationhood.

Increasing prosperity facilitated an artistic surge. The patronage of the Burgundian and Habsburg rulers, other nobles, and prosperous merchants supported creativity in the fields of painting, music, printing and cartography that sparked the southern Low Country-based Burgundian Golden Age.

Increased centralisation combined with the impact of the Reformation generated conflict in the Low Countries. Since new ideas germinate more quickly in urban than rural areas, the Reformation initially had more impact in southern Low Country cities such as Antwerp, Brussels, Bruges, Ghent and Oudenaarde. In the more rural northern Low Countries only a few cities, notably Amsterdam, had Protestant congregations. Charles V took relatively few steps to control the growing Reformation heresy. His son Philip II, far more concerned with the increasing threat to his Catholic faith and his autocratic rule in the Low Countries, sent the Duke of Alva to impose his views. By unleashing a reign of terror, he escalated the civic strife into civil war. The revolt that began south of the Rhine ended with the northern provinces gaining their independence under Protestant leadership and the southern ones continuing to be ruled by Catholic Spain. The war that won the Dutch Republic its independence split what the Burgundians and Habsburgs had put together.

How did the language frontier affect Burgundian and early Habsburg efforts to govern the Low Countries? Its leaders from Philip the Bold to Charles V extended their lands and centralised their governance with minimal resistance from those who did not speak proper French, which included not only the peasants in the north who spoke a Flemish dialect but also those who spoke one of the Walloon varieties of French in the south. Religion combined with arbitrary and harsh rule, not language, precipitated the war that lost Philip II the northern Low Countries.

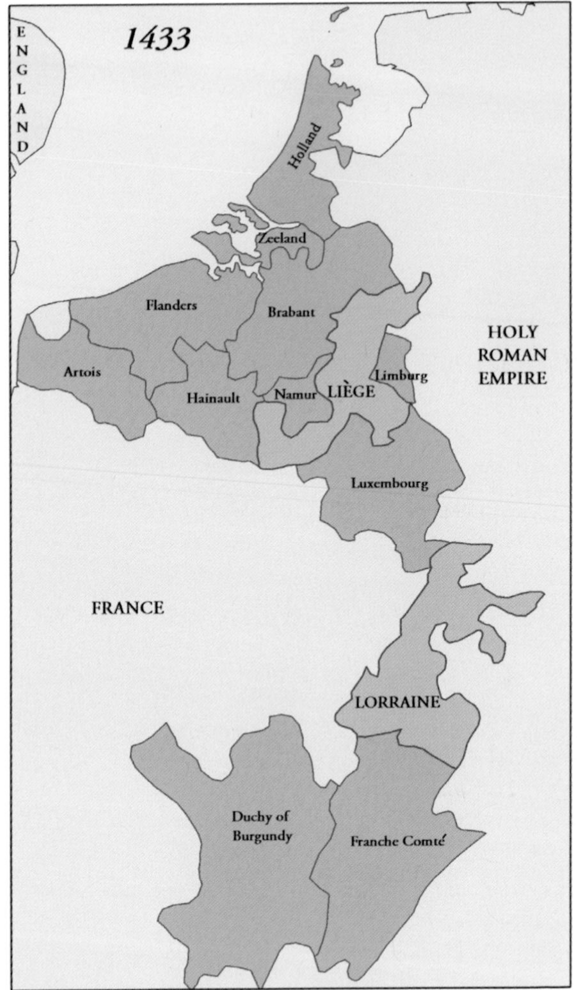

Map 6. Burgundian possessions: Philip the Good extended his rule of the Low Countries by adding several Low Country principalities to those inherited from his father, John the Fearless. Philip's Burgundian possessions initially included Burgundy of which Philip the Bold, Philip the Good's grandfather, was Duke before his marriage to the Flemish heiress, Margaret, who united Flanders with 'the other Burgundy' in the duchy of Burgundy. As this map demonstrates, the Burgundian duchy was not contiguous: the Prince-Bishopric of Liège and the duchy of Lorraine separated 'the other Burgundy' (Franche-Comté and Burgundy) from the Low Country principalities governed by the Burgundian dynasty. This simplified map does not show the by then only nominally independent ecclesiastical entities: Mechelen, Cambrai and Tournai.

4

BURGUNDIAN DUKES UNITE THE SOUTHERN LOW COUNTRIES

1384–1477

'The history of Burgundy itself, and above all the behaviour and ambitions of the last Valois duke, Charles the Bold, exemplifies very well the portentous and nearly ubiquitous increase in the authority of central governments that took place in the 15th century... The acquisition of more power by princes, the emergence of larger polities, the growing arbitrariness of government; these changes, which took place at the expense of the nobles...were often connected with the rise to power of a single remarkable, and usually purposeful rule.'[1]

Richard Vaughan

'In all branches of intellectual activity, Belgium enters decidedly, from the beginning of the 15th century, into the Renaissance period.'[2]

Emile Cammaerts

Philip the Bold to Charles the Bold

'It would be hard to mention any geographical name which, by its application at different times to different districts, has caused, and continues to cause, more confusion than this name Burgundy ...' says Bryce, who notes 'ten senses in which the name is most frequently to be met ...'[3]. Not only the Burgundy duchy described here but also several other kingdoms and polities, and a present day French region, have existed at different times and places from the North Sea to the

Mediterranean. The Low Country-centred Burgundian dynasty began with Margaret of Maele and ended with Mary of Burgundy. In each case, the lack of a male heir led the Low Country ruler to arrange for his heiress to marry the son of a foreign ruler—thus subjugating the principality to foreign rule. In 1384, on the death of Margaret's father, the County of Flanders and the Duchy of Burgundy united under Margaret and her husband, Philip the Bold, the Duke of Burgundy, the French king's son. In 1477 Mary, the only legitimate child of Charles the Bold and the great-great granddaughter of Margaret, married Maximilian, the Habsburg heir and future Holy Roman Emperor, making the Burgundian Low Countries a Habsburg possession.

The intervening years were decisive in unifying Belgium. When Margaret and Philip the Bold succeeded Louis of Maele, the French court expected Flanders to follow French interests. Once again, as when French kings married the successive Flemish heiresses to Ferrand of Portugal and Guy de Dampierre, the arranged marriage did not provide the French crown with its long sought hegemony over Flanders. The Burgundian dukes pursued their own dynastic interests—by marital alliances and military force—building a realm that politically, but not geographically, joined most of Low Countries with the Duchy of Burgundy (Bourgogne) and the Franche-Comté. Low Country governance continued to be affected by the vicissitudes of the Hundred Years War, which was fought in part in Flemish lands and lasted until 1453 when Charles VII of France, with the help of Philip the Good who had switched sides, drove the English forces from all but Calais.

Four successive Burgundian dukes, supported by the prosperity and power generated by the wool industry and international trade, scheming marriages, skilful diplomacy and military prowess, united the southern Low Countries. They developed the centralised institutions of governance that drove the state-building process. With their patronage, they also nurtured a Burgundian Golden Age. Given the ravages of the Hundred Years War and the Black Death, which killed a third of the population of northwest Europe in the fourteenth and fifteenth centuries, these are remarkable accomplishments.

Margaret of Maele, Countess of Flanders, marries Philip the Bold, Duke of Burgundy

Engaged in fighting each other as they were in the Hundred Years War, both the English and the French Kings sought a dynastic linkage with

Margaret of Maele, the only legitimate heir of Louis of Maele, Count of Flanders. When the English King negotiated a marriage for Margaret to his fourth surviving son, the French convinced the Pope to refuse permission for this proposed marriage of cousins. The French King then arranged for Margaret to marry his younger son Philip the Bold, to whom the duchy of Burgundy had been granted in 1363. To achieve this politically advantageous marriage the French King agreed to return the Artois to Flanders. Margaret had inherited Franche-Comté, adjacent to the duchy of Burgundy, from her mother, and thus her marriage to Philip added this principality as well as the county of Flanders to the Burgundian realm.

The French King expected that this marriage would resolve the long vexing Flemish suzerainty issue by gaining peacefully the county for which his predecessors had for centuries been finagling and fighting. Instead of the French King strengthening his suzerainty over Flanders, though, the expanded Burgundian duchy soon rivalled and warred with France. The Burgundian rulers soon became mortal enemies of their cousins, a senior Orleans branch of the French dynasty. During the minority and the later insanity of Charles VI, Philip engaged in a power struggle with his nephew, Louis Duke of Orleans. During these years, Seward describes the struggle saying: 'When the king was crazy France was ruled by [the duke of] Burgundy, who annually diverted one-eighth to one-sixth of the revenues to his own treasury. When Charles was sane the king's brother, Louis Duke of Orleans, held power, no less a bloodsucker than his uncle Philip.'[4] While active in the French court, Philip worked closely with Margaret in governing Flanders, creating common institutions for administering the affairs of the two-part realm, and taking steps that in time significantly increased the size, power, prestige and wealth of the duchy.

England joined with many Flemish towns in opposing the extent to which Philip's French interests determined his Burgundian ones. When Ghent raised the English flag and accepted a governor appointed by the English king, France invaded Flanders, then negotiated a peace and granted a general amnesty—but also took precautionary steps, including building new castles, strengthening its border fortifications and cutting off trade with England. Since the Flemish towns depended upon the wool trade for their prosperity and thus wanted to continue their unrestricted trade with England, they revolted, as they had earlier, first under Jacob van Artevelde and later under his son Philip. Philip the Bold suppressed these insurrections, in 1387 and 1391 in Bruges and 1392 in Ghent, in a manner showing that while not vindictive, he did not temporise.

With no threats from or expansion opportunities in France, Philip the Bold looked east and north. When the neighbouring duchy of Gelderland threatened the duchy of Brabant he offered to help the duchess—but only if she named Margaret, her niece and his wife, as heiress to the duchy. To the north, Philip succeeded in pushing his dynastic interests with a double marriage: his daughter to the son and heir to William, the Count of Hainaut, Holland and Zeeland, and his son John the Fearless to William's sister. These steps laid the foundation for the later expansion of the Burgundian possessions north of the Rhine. In Philip and Margaret's court, the official language remained French. Philip never learned Flemish; Margaret, though born and raised in Flanders, never became fluent.

John the Fearless extends his hegemony

When John the Fearless succeeded his parents in 1404, the leading Flemish towns confronted him with demands, which included residing in Flanders, remaining neutral in the continuing war between England and France, using Flemish in dealings with the county, and not maintaining foreign non-Flemish troops on Flemish soil. Unlike his father, John was generally conciliatory, but he did not remove foreign troops. In 1406, there were uprisings in Flanders. To win over Ghent and shame Bruges, he moved the Flemish Council there in 1407. The Bruges disturbances ended only when Ghent withdrew its support.

Continuing the dynastic aggrandisement begun by their father, John worked with his brother Anthony who had inherited Brabant from his mother (who, as already noted, had received it from her aunt, the Duchess of Brabant) and ruled Luxemburg through marriage with its duchess, Elizabeth of Görlitz. The brothers arranged the marriage of Anthony's son with the heiress of Holland, Zeeland, Friesland and Hainaut, thus facilitating the later unification of the Low Countries.

John also gained control of the Liège prince-bishopric. When in 1408 the Liégeois revolted against their Prince-Bishop, who was John's brother-in-law for whom John's father had secured the appointment, John marched on Liège, defeated its militia, occupied the area and exacted vengeance by throwing into the river and drowning the priests appointed by the replacement Prince-Bishop. Henceforth John was the *de facto* ruler of the prince-bishopric.

The intermittent madness of the French King Charles VI intensified the feud between the Burgundian and Orleans branches of the French royal family. Barker points out that John, who 'in an age not noted for the delicacy of its morals, [was the] most unscrupulous of all the princes of France ...'[5] After murdering his cousin, the King's brother and duke of Orleans, he entered Paris unopposed and by the end of 1409 was *de facto* king of France. When the Orleans faction regained strength, their feud with the Burgundians again escalated. England took this opportunity to invade, thus beginning another round of the Hundred Years War. John did not support the French (mainly Orleans) forces that fought the English and lost the invasion's decisive encounter, the 1415 Battle of Agincourt. In retaliation for the murder of Louis of Orleans, the Orleans faction murdered John on the bridge at Montereau when he arrived for a peace conference in 1419. The assassination drove John's son Philip into open alliance with the English.

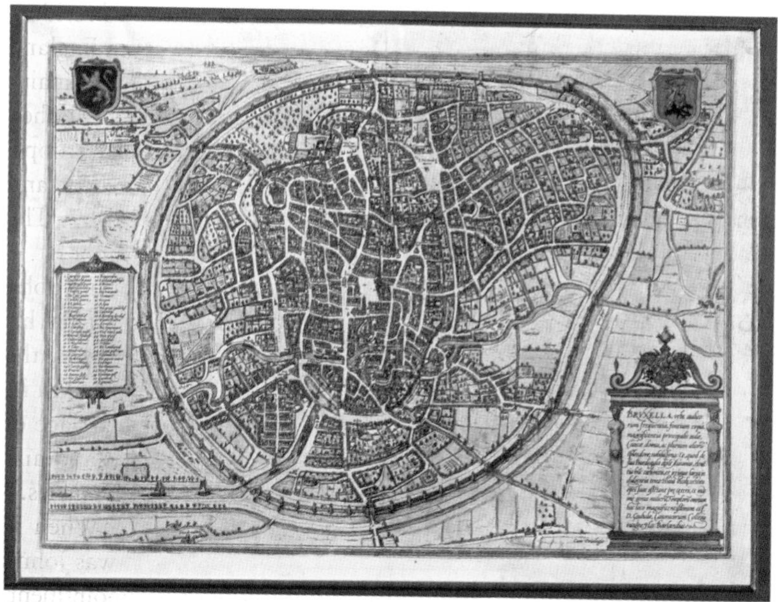

Map 7. 'Bruxella'—George Braun & Frans Hogenberg (1574). It depicts Brussels surrounded by a moat and city wall; an 'inner ring' motorway now stands in their place.

Philip the Good: 'The Founder of Belgium'

Philip was called 'the Good' for his uniting of the southern Low Countries and the majesty of his court, not for his character or personal morals. Desmond Seward describes him as 'Splendid in appearance, he was arrogant and violent tempered ... and extremely touchy. Still more disconcerting, this pillar of chivalry was a notorious liar; little reliance could be placed on his word, for he was whimsical and changeable ... a notorious lecher with thirty mistresses.'[6] Robert Neillands adds that he 'ruled Burgundy not like a vassal of France but like the great prince he was ... He maintained two capitals, at Dijon and Brussels, founded his own Order of Chivalry, the *Toison d'Or* (the Golden Fleece), fought several campaigns against his overlord and against rebellious subjects in the Low Countries, and meddled ceaselessly in the affairs of France and England.'[7] The splendour of his court, enhanced by the pomp of the Order of the Golden Fleece and the works of Northern Europe's great painters, sculptors and musicians, outshone that of any other. The pomp, ritual and ceremony of his duchy provided spectacles, as Roman circuses once did, and diverted attention from the reality of increasing centralisation. 'It was indeed above all late medieval Burgundy,' John Hale notes, 'that had created the image of a princely court ... as being the place where great men came together to add lustre to their reputations, and lesser ones to cadge a job or a free meal in memory of which they could dine out for the rest of their lives.'[8]

The continuing dynamics of the Hundred Years War affected Philip's foreign policy. The necessities of the wool trade, the Flemish habit of seeking English support to stop French intervention and Philip's rivalry with the house of Orleans spurred by his desire to avenge his father's murder, led him to welcome an English alliance. It was as an English ally that Philip's troops captured Joan of Arc and turned her over to the English. After 1430 when the French began recovering the north of France, however, the Burgundian-English alliance cooled. It only regained its strength when Philip arranged the third marriage of his son Charles the Bold with Margaret of York, sister of the English King in an event celebrated with elaborate pomp and ceremony.

Philip the Good considered the Low Countries—not France or the 'other' Burgundy to the south—to be his home, a fact that facilitated his successful reign. While engaged in the Hundred Years War, he continued efforts to unite the Low Countries, expedited by earlier marriage alliances, timely deaths and bold diplomatic and military aggrandisement. He inherited Brabant when his uncle, Anthony of Burgundy, was killed at Agincourt in 1415, leaving no heir. He bought Namur in 1429. He forced his cousin Jacqueline to cede her rights to Holland, Zeeland and Hainaut in 1433. Elizabeth of Görlitz, the childless widow of Anthony of Burgundy and ruler of Luxemburg, ceded her duchy in 1443. Philip further extended his rule over the Low Countries by forcing protectorate status upon the ecclesiastical entities of Tournai, Cambrai and Utrecht, making himself the *de facto* ruler of these principalities.

As his father had done in 1408, Philip strengthened his hold on the prince-bishopric of Liège. He invited its Prince-Bishop to dinner and then gave him the choice of death or resignation. When the cleric resigned, Philip installed his own eighteen-year-old nephew as prince-bishop. When the clergy, nobility and commoners, with the support of the French King, drove out the nephew, Philip sent an army that defeated the Liège forces and installed himself as regent. When in 1465 Dinant rebelled against Burgundian rule, Philip with his son Charles sacked and burned Dinant, destroyed its cathedral, confined a number of leading citizens in a building and burned them alive, drowned 800 persons by tying them in pairs and throwing them into the river and razed the city. When in 1467 Liège forces attacked his army, the duke allowed his troops to plunder, kill and burn the episcopal city. His vindictive brutality expedited his goal of unifying the Low Countries, but it also left bitter memories, which for centuries affected the relations of the Liégois with the rest of the Low Countries.

Having brought Low Country principalities from the Zuider Zee to the Somme under his personal rule, Philip the Good developed central governing institutions, staffed them with professional civil servants trained at the University of Louvain and thus reduced the role of the leading nobles in Low Country administration. Blockmans points out that 'Philip was well-acquainted with the centralized construction of the French state and he regarded it as a model for his own lands. To conform his dominions to French statecraft, the duke employed three methods which built on each other. First, he built a number of overarching structures which had authority over all his possessions ... in the Low Countries. Second, he standardized the administration of the various principalities. Last, he attempted to break local resistance to his rule by offering attractive incentives to regional elites—and by crushing them by armed force if they refused. As a result of these measures, the period from 1435 to 1476 witnessed the rise of a powerful monarchical state in Burgundian principalities.'[9] A special judicial body, eventually called the Grand Council, grew out of the duke of Burgundy's council and gradually assumed the powers of a central high court whose decisions took precedence over all local and regional interests. Historians generally consider this development as the birth of what has become the Belgian state. In 1464 Philip summoned representatives of the estates of the leading principalities to Bruges for meetings that came to be called the Estates-General; this met regularly from 1477 to 1576. While Philip continued to appoint nobles to the Grand Council and other high posts, he limited these appointments to those with a Low Countrywide rather than a parochial perspective. Philip's institution of the Order of the Golden Fleece was a stroke of genius, for it encouraged a Burgundian-wide loyalty and perspective among the magnates serving as councillors and provincial *stadhouders* (governors) and provided a means of rewarding them.

Philip's renown stemmed from not only his unification of Low Country principalities. His efforts to enhance the splendour of his court led him, and consequently many nobles and wealthy merchants, to support the work of painters and tapestry makers, metallurgists, writers and printers, musicians and cartographers who cultivated a spirit of creativity that drew aspiring talent from all over Europe. This period, recognised as the Burgundian Golden Age, featured the painting of Jan van Eyck, Pieter Brueghel the Elder and his sons among others. Mercator and Abraham Ortelius established the lead in mapmaking in the new era of global exploration. The artistic environment attracted students from throughout the continent. The careers of Pieter Paul Rubens, Anthony van Dyck, who spent most of his career in London, Genoa and Paris, and Jacob Jordaens in the seventeenth century marked the brilliant sunset of the southern Low Country-based Burgundian Golden Age. Art historian Zirka Filipczak points out that ironically, except for Jan van Eyck and a few early Low Country painters, most of the painters contributing to the glories of this period were from Brabant, not Flanders; but the earlier established foreign tendency to call all the Low Countries Flanders led the international artistic community to continue to call the southern Low Country artists Flemish. Only after Belgium won its independence in 1830 did the international artistic community refer to the work of southern Low Country artists as 'Belgian'.

The Grand Duke of the West, as Philip the Good was called, according to his own words could 'have been king if he had only willed it'—that is if he had been willing to pay homage to the German Emperor. Philip's unification of the southern Low Countries led the seventeenth century humanist Justus Lipsius to credit him as the *conditor Belgii* (the founder of Belgium).

Charles the Bold (or the Rash)

Philip the Good, by expanding his realm to the east and north, had succeeded in removing the political frontiers of the Scheldt and lower Rhine that had long divided the Low Countries. His son Charles the Bold continued the effort to expand his realm by annexing the land between the original duchy given to Philip the Bold by his French King father and the southern Low Countries that had been secured by marriage to its heiress. If successful, Charles would have reconstituted the northern part of the ninth century Lotharingian 'middle kingdom'. Charles was bold in his plans to expand, but he was reckless in his pursuit; thus the name 'the Rash' *(le Téméraire)* that French historians later ascribed to him. The use of contrasting words such as 'bold' and 'rash' to describe a leader illustrates not only whether his critical ventures succeeded or failed but also whether it is his admirers or detractors who apply them.

In 1467, Charles followed up the sacking of Dinant (noted earlier) by moving the seat of the prince-bishopric from Liège and removing its revered Perron, its prized civic monument, to Brussels. Many Liégeois were executed. Counting on French support Liège mustered men to counter Charles. When the French King Louis XI accepted Charles' invitation to meet to reconcile differences, Charles took him captive and forced him to witness the burning and the pillaging of Liège and the massacre of its citizens. Charles then appointed himself as 'protector' (that is the secular ruler) of the Liège prince-bishopric.

Charles the Bold further developed three unifying institutions: a court of appeals, a treasury and a governing council that further centralised the Burgundian state. These steps paralleled the nation-building efforts then underway in England and France. Even more than his father, he gave priority to his role as duke of a united Burgundy—not a leading French prince.

The Low Country towns resented Charles' autocratic rule and the taxes demanded to support his expansionist military efforts. Unlike his father's practice of reacting prudently and allowing the towns to practice limited autonomy, Charles used mercenary forces frequently and capriciously. When the Ghent Burghers protested against taxes, Charles temporised by promising concessions; but a year later, he suspended the town council and made his councillors responsible for the town affairs.

Charles' ambitions to close the territorial gap between the Low Countries and the 'other' Burgundy led to his fate as the last Burgundian duke. Charles might have been more successful if, like his father, he had determined his objectives more strategically and implemented them less impetuously. His initial actions were successful, gaining control of Alsace, and then, in pursuit of his efforts to extend his rule further southward, he conquered Lorraine and installed his own governor, and entered into alliances with the Republic of Venice, the principality of Savoy and the Duke of Milan. The Swiss, alarmed by Charles' occupation of Lorraine and provoked by the massacre of one of its garrisons, helped the Lorraine Duke to recover his duchy. When Charles retreated, these forces pursued him.

Despite his allies' desertion and his generals' pleading, in 1477 Charles impulsively flung himself into battle near Nancy where he was defeated and killed. His frozen, naked body was not discovered until days later. The historian Francis Hackett reports that the French king 'Louis XI praised his God, Burgundy was at his feet. He saw Dijon [and with it the other Burgundy] revert to France, for lack of male succession.'[9]

Overcoming the border that had divided the Low Countries' eastern and western halves under the Roman, many Merovingian, and most Carolingian rulers, the Burgundian dukes united most of the southern Low Countries. The Burgundian expansion paralleled the consolidation process beginning throughout Europe that led to the emergence of the modern system of government. Whereas in 1500 there were approximately 500 autonomous political units in Europe, by 1800 there were only a few dozen—and that was before the nineteenth century unification of Germany and Italy. The centuries of consolidation ended, however, in the twentieth century with the post-Word War I breakup of the Austro-Hungarian and Ottoman empires and the late twentieth century disintegration of the Soviet Union and Yugoslavia, breakups that exemplify the politics of long submerged peoples with a distinctive sense of community identity.

Burgundian rule over Flanders under a French dynasty, H.A. L. Fisher points out, 'was the only time in its history [that it] was the heart and centre of an ambitious and conquering state.'[10] Speculating on the 'ifs' of history is seldom productive, but one cannot help but wonder how the course of European history might have proceeded if Charles the Bold had acted more prudently and succeeded in (re-) establishing a middle kingdom that had ended with Lothair II.

The hurried marriage of his daughter Mary to the Habsburg heir subjected the southern Low Countries to foreign rule for the next three centuries.

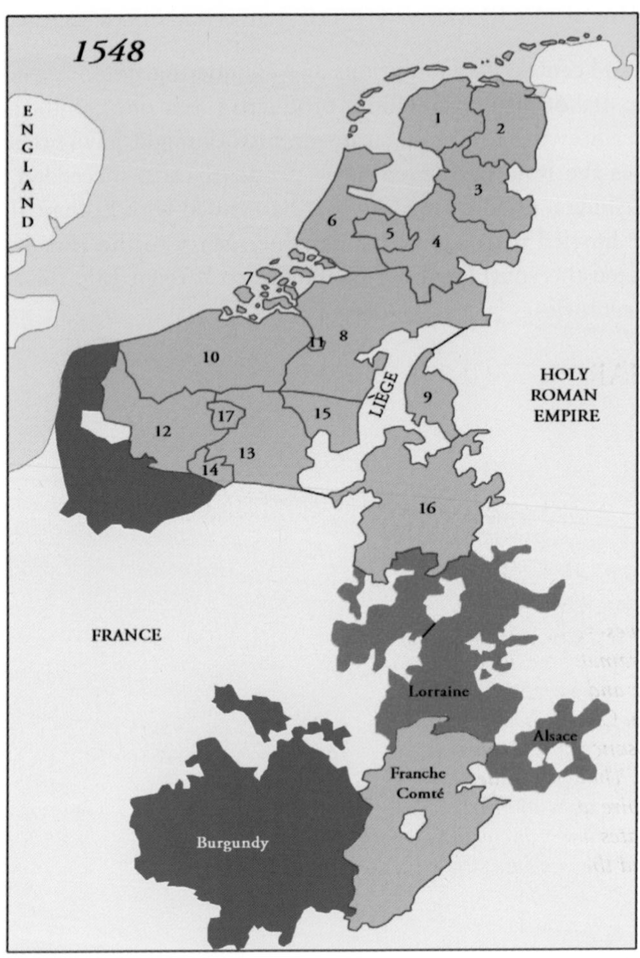

Map 8. Charles V's Low Country possessions in 1548: Charles the Bold had conquered Lorraine and Alsace in campaigns launched before 1476. But he lost battles of 1476–77 that culminated in his defeat and death in Nancy in 1477. After his death, France invaded and occupied the 'other Burgundy' (Burgundy and Franche-Comté) and part of Walloon Flanders including Picardy. Franche-Comté was later recovered in 1493.

Between 1524 and 1543 Charles V added five northern Low Country principalities to his Low Country possessions: Friesland in 1524, Groningen in 1526, Overijssel in 1538, Gelderland in 1543 and Utrecht in 1536. To unify Low Country governance and succession rights, he created the Burgundian Circle (shown in purple) out of the seventeen Low Country principalities: Friesland (1), Groningen (2), Overijssel (3), Gelderland (4), Utrecht (5), Holland (6), Zeeland (7), Brabant (8), Limburg (9), Flanders (10), Mechelen (11), Artois 12), Hainaut (13), Cambrai (14), Namur (15), Luxembourg (16), and Tournai (17).

5

CHARLES V UNITES ALL THE LOW COUNTRIES

1477–1555

'Few lives—and few eras—in the history of the world have been more filled with dramatic events or more important to the future development of both Europe and America than that of Charles V. His reign defies historical comparison. Charles lived from 1500 to 1558, an age that coincided with the later Renaissance, the Protestant Reformation, and the beginnings of Catholic reform. Though he ruled an Empire that stretched from Austria to Peru, it was an Empire with no heartland and few contiguous borders. Most of its component states and principalities were his by hereditary right, the product of good luck and the dynastic strategies of his grandfathers.'[1]

William Maltby

'The fall of Constantinople in 1453 and the identification at about the same time in Italy of a medium aevum separating the ancient from the contemporary world were in themselves sufficient to account for the subsequent adoption of the Renaissance as a turning-point in the history of western society. Bacon claimed further that printing, gunpowder and the magnet "have changed the whole face and state of things throughout the world". The political historians of the nineteenth century...saw in the fifteenth and early sixteenth century the emergence of phenomena regarded as characteristically "modern", nation-states, bureaucracy, secular values in public policy, and a balance of power.'[2]

Denys Hay

Maximilian to Charles V

Charles V, whose grandmother, Mary of Burgundy, married the Habsburg heir, Maximilian of Austria, inherited the largest disparate conglomeration of lands and people under one ruler that the world had seen. Through his mother Johanna, whose parents were Ferdinand and Isabella, he gained Castile, Aragon, Naples, Sicily and Spanish America. From his paternal grandfather, Maximilian, he inherited German principalities and from his paternal grandmother, Mary, the Duchy of Burgundy. As head of the House of Habsburg, he won the election to succeed his grandfather as emperor. Charles, born in Ghent and reared in the Low Countries where he was regarded as a native son, extended his personal domains to include almost all the Low Countries, created the Burgundian Circle that united these possessions and strengthened its central governance. When the Reformation threatened the religious integrity of his royal domains, he authorised steps to quell this heresy.

How was it possible that the Low Countries split so shortly after his abdication? What forces had emerged that precipitated the split of the Low Countries under his son? Critical factors were the laxity of the Catholic Church, the protests of Martin Luther and fervour of John Calvin that drove the rise of Protestantism and the advent of printing that expedited the spread of Protestant heresy. The puritanical and intolerant nature of Calvinism and its rapid expansion in the Low Countries provoked Charles to ban the possession of heretical literature, leading to the execution of a few Anabaptists. Charles' resignation left his son, Philip II, the problem of coping with the increasingly vibrant and resolute Calvinist heresy.

Mary of Burgundy marries Maximilian of Habsburg

Recognising the endangered position of his heir Mary of Burgundy, Charles the Bold conducted marriage negotiations with several European dynasties. He had arranged for her marriage to the Austrian heir Maximilian, but when the duke was killed on the Nancy battlefield, the wedding had not yet taken place. When news of the Nancy disaster and Charles' death reached Ghent, long-held resentment led the craft guilds to take the opportunity to rebel at the prospect of being ruled by a foreign prince, Maximilian. The States-General reformed itself into a constitutional assembly and forced Mary to cancel her father's centralising reforms by signing the Great Privilege of 1477, which restored some powers to the principalities—including the right of free assembly and participating in declarations of war.

Upon the death of Charles, under the pretext of defending Mary of Burgundy's rights, the French king invaded not only the Burgundian Low Countries but also 'the other Burgundy' to the south. At the same time the French king tried to marry Mary to his son the dauphin, rather than the Austrian heir. Incipient revolts in Low Country towns as well as the French invasion forced Mary to hurry wedding plans and marry Maximilian of Austria by proxy in August 1477. Maximilian arranged credit to fund a mercenary army that countered the threats to Artois, Hainaut and Flanders; but he was not able to prevent the loss of 'the other Burgundy' and Picardy, then in the southwest Low Countries, now in northwest France.

When Mary died in 1482, their son Philip the Handsome was only four years old. Maximilian assumed the regency, but the Flemings, still regarding him as a foreigner, revolted. While Antwerp, the major Low Country port, sided with him, the Flemish towns rebelled and sought support from the French King. Infuriated, Maximilian seized Ghent and executed thirty-three of the faction leaders. In Bruges, though, the rebels captured him and forced his acceptance of a new constitution, but when imperial forces arrived and freed him, he renounced the new constitution and forcefully subdued most of Flanders. When Ghent secured the help of French troops, Maximilian besieged the city and again forced its surrender, after which the whole of the Low Countries submitted. A year later upon his father's death, Maximilian won the election to succeed him as Holy Roman Emperor and left the Low Countries, appointing a regent to serve until his son came of age.

Philip the Handsome

When Philip the Handsome came of age at sixteen, the Low Countries greeted him with an enthusiasm that sharply contrasted with the continuing antipathy to Maximilian. Philip, who had never left the Low Countries and had been educated by Low Country tutors, was regarded as a native prince. When Philip made his 'Joyous Entry', the concessions earlier extracted from Mary and Maximilian lapsed. Philip re-established the advisory body at Mechelen as the Great Council. These steps led to the States-General having no difficulty in granting taxes. Philip's estrangement from his father, his exclusion of almost all foreigners from the Council and his readiness to heed the counsel of his advisers—to such an extent that he acquired the nickname of *Croit-conseil* (to trust or take advice)—facilitated his rapprochement with his subjects.

In his foreign affairs, Philip avoided foreign entanglements and war, despite his father's efforts to manipulate him into his Austrian adventures. While Henry VII of England had been so angry with Maximilian that he forbade trade with the Low Countries, in 1496 Philip negotiated the *Intercursus Magnus* (Large Intervention) that re-established trade relations. In 1498 he even recognised the loss of the 'other Burgundy', which his father had failed to recover—a move that helped Low Country relations with France at the expense of Habsburg dynastic interests.

When Philip's wife, Johanna 'the Mad', inherited the Spanish throne from her mother Isabella in 1504, Philip took the title of King of Castile despite the protests of his father-in-law, Ferdinand. With his attention now focused on Spanish governance, his Low Country interests suffered. With a view to conciliating England, Philip concluded a new treaty that was so unsatisfactory from a Low Country point of view that it was called *Intercursus Malus* (Bad Intervention).

Charles V annexes northern Low Country principalities and creates the Burgundian Circle

Philip the Handsome died in 1506 leaving his six-year-old son Charles V as heir. As they had when the four-year-old Philip inherited the throne, the towns again opposed Maximilian's effort to secure the regency. The French King's support of the efforts to keep the Emperor from becoming regent led the States-General to negotiate with Maximilian to appoint his illegitimate daughter, Margaret of Austria, as regent. Despite suspicions of Low Country lords headed by William de Croy, Lord of Chièvres, the continuing intrigues of the French crown, restlessness in Ghent, disturbances in Liège and trouble initiated from Gelderland, Margaret succeeded in bringing a period of peace. Pushed by the political machinations of Chièvres to discredit Margaret and the prodding of the States-General, Maximilian declared his fifteen-year-old son Charles of age. The 1516 accession of Charles was a triumph for the Low Country leaders, especially Charles' tutor Chièvres, who saw the young king, like his father John, as one born and bred in the Low Countries.

After the death of Ferdinand in 1516 and the continuing mental instability of his mother Johanna, Charles took the title King of Spain and left for Spain with Chièvres and other Low Country advisers. On the death of Maximilian in 1519, Charles bribed his way to election as the Holy Roman Emperor. His election was greeted with jubilation in the Low Countries, where there was little recognition that their interests in time might be overlooked among the empire's competing collage of pressures.

When Charles left the Low Countries for Spain, he brought back his aunt Margaret of Austria as governor. As earlier, she generally kept the Low Countries out of international entanglements. When war broke out between Spain and an Anglo-French alliance, she maintained trade with England. She kept the Low Countries from participating in Charles' efforts to restore his cousin Christian II to the Danish throne—a move that would have upset Low Country trade with the Danish and other Hanseatic League cities. She also negotiated the Treaty of Cambrai (1529) by which France confirmed its earlier abandonment of its suzerainty over Flanders and Artois, and Charles reiterated his renunciation of claims to 'the other Burgundy', lost following the defeat at Nancy and the death of Charles the Bold.

Upon the 1530 death of Margaret of Austria, Charles appointed his sister Mary of Hungary as governor. Although she was only twenty-five years of age when appointed, her intelligence and diplomatic skills enabled her to gain the respect of her brother in dealing with even graver problems than her aunt had faced. Early in her regency, Mary contended with town resistance arising from the growing costs of Charles' military adventures, including his military actions and acquisitions in the northern Low Countries. Riots erupted in Brussels in 1532. An especially severe revolt of Ghent in 1539 led Charles to send an army from Spain to put down the insurrection and suppress the town's privileges.

Initially Charles did use his power to advance his Low Country interests. After defeating and capturing the French king, Charles forced France to reaffirm its renunciation of its suzerainty over Artois and Flanders. He added northern Low Country principalities to his personal possessions, annexing Friesland in 1524, inducing the bishop of Utrecht to cede him the secular power over Overijssel and Utrecht, adding Gröningen and Drenthe in 1536 and after a quick victory forcing the Duke of Cleves to renounce his rights over Gelderland and Zutphen in 1543. His overlordship of the prince-bishopric of Liège, which Charles the Bold had established, continued.

While the great nobles continued to exercise significant powers as members of central councils and provincial governors (*stadhouders*), Charles strengthened central governance of his Low Country possessions, efforts that had been interrupted by Charles the Bold's ventures and Maximilian's neglect, expanding the role of the general assembly (the States-General) and the three central governing councils (for finance, justice and administration). He extended their purview to the newly annexed principalities north of the Rhine and further developed a civil service. These efforts accompanied Charles' move of the Low Country seat of government from Mechelen to Brussels in 1531.

In 1548 Charles further unified his Low Country possessions by creating the 'Burgundian Circle', converting the mix of duchies, counties, and other principalities into seventeen provinces and consolidating their succession rights. By calling the once more autonomous counties and duchies by the term 'provinces', Charles evoked memories of the Roman Empire. The consolidation nurtured a sense of collective community in the Low Countries, which was variously called the *Seventeen Provinces*, *Nederland* or *Netherlanden* in Dutch, *Pays-Bas* in French, and *Belgique* from Latin.

Thus, in this age of emerging nation-states, Low Country governance was projecting a more cohesive sense of common identity—one nurtured by the imposition of increased governmental unification. The strengthening of Low Country-wide institutions, similar to the ones France and England were developing, was particularly resented in the northern provinces that Charles had so recently annexed. Antipathy to the increasing exertion of power by a ruler to whom the Low Countries were by now a peripheral concern was a major source of tension, which later confronted Charles' son Philip II.

Another major source of tension was the rise of the Reformation that followed Luther's protest in 1517. As early as 1517, 1519, 1520 and 1521 Charles, through his regent and aunt Margaret of Austria, issued edicts ('placards') banning heretical works. His administration reacted to reform preaching by razing the Augustinian monasteries in Antwerp and burning two monks at the stake. But the early efforts to suppress the heresy were unevenly and only spasmodically enforced.

From 1550, when Calvinism began to spread rapidly, Blockmans notes 'the Inquisition redoubled its efforts to combat heresy...between 1521 and 1550, an average of thirteen persons was tried annually ... By the 1550's the average was sixty per year, and between 1561 and

1565 it was 264.'[3] Most victims were artisans and tradesmen from Antwerp and other large towns where they readily heard the new ideas rapidly gaining adherents and did not have sufficient political influence to avoid prosecution. Notable among those executed was William Tyndale, translator of the first English printed Bible, whom the Inquisition imprisoned, garrotted and burned in the courtyard of the Vilvoorde castle in 1536.

In 1555, overwhelmed with the burdens of a widespread empire and the growing threat of Protestantism, a tired, sick and discouraged Charles V turned over his rule of the Low Countries to his son Philip. Unable to speak French (or Flemish), Philip asked an official to read his speech of acceptance for him, an act that further undermined his new subjects' reception of their new Spanish-raised ruler. Standing at Charles' side at the abdication was William of Orange, a promising young noble who had grown up at the court where he had long been a favourite of the retiring ruler. Over the next decades, the new ruler and the protégé of the old one were locked in a bitter struggle that divided the Low Countries, separating the northern provinces from the southern ones.

Charles tried to avoid confrontations. His subjects may not have loved him, but because he was born and educated in the Low Countries, they at least accepted him as their ruler; 'But when the emperor pronounced his abdication in the palace of Brussel,' Koenigsberger notes, 'the Habsburg political system in the Netherlands was already near to dissolution.'[4] The cost of wars had escalated taxes and the economy had deteriorated. A few months later in 1557, the government declared financial bankruptcy. The Low Countries States-General became all but unmanageable. A few years later, the religious and social troubles came to a head, leading to eighty years of religious and civil war that not only undermined the empire but also broke apart the Low Countries. Philip, who had been born and raised in Spain, inherited the growing problems of Reformation along with the resentment against foreign rule. But the rigour of his convictions, his temperament and his Spanish upbringing magnified the challenges he faced when he succeeded his father.

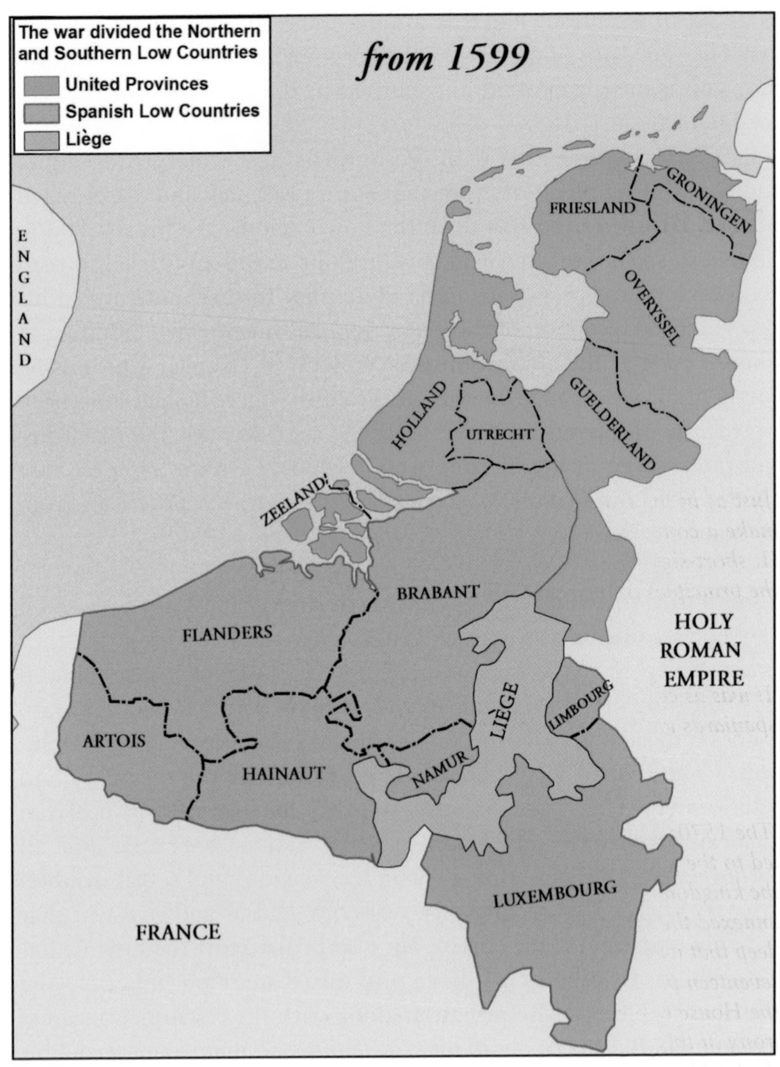

Map 9. War divides the northern seven United Provinces from the Spanish Low Countries

6

THE BEGGARS' REVOLT AGAINST SPAIN DIVIDES THE LOW COUNTRIES

1555–1599

'Just as in the case of Philip the Good and Charles the Bold, so it is usual to make a contrast between Charles V, wise, moderate, and popular, and Philip II, short-sighted, unbending, and detested, and to extend this contrast ... to the principles of their systems of government.'[1]

Pieter Geyl

'It was as certain that the Netherlanders would be fierce reformers as that the Spaniards would be uncompromising persecutors.'[2]

John Lothrop Motley

'The 1570s and 1580s saw the partition of the Low Countries that eventually led to the permanent establishment of a Roman Catholic southern state, now the kingdom of Belgium, and a Protestant north, which in its modern form has annexed the old name of the Netherlands. The ideological division became so deep that when in 1815 the victors of Waterloo tried to impose reunion on the seventeen provinces of the old Low Countries under a Protestant monarch of the House of Orange, the marriage proved impossible to sustain. There is an irony in this: in the early stages of the Dutch revolt in the 1560s and 1570s, the backbone of Protestant militancy had been the south, and in particular the great commercial city of Antwerp.'[3]

Diarmaid MacCulloch

The civil war called the 'Dutch Revolt'

The war that won the Protestant-led Dutch Republic its independence and its separation from the Spanish Low Countries did not begin as a 'Dutch revolt'; nor were Protestants the initial leaders of the insurrection. It was not Hollanders but Brabanters and Flemings who first took up arms against the Spanish forces. As John Lothrop Motley's *The Rise of the Dutch Republic* and Pieter Geyl's *The Revolt of the Netherlands 1555–1609* describe, not only the initial confrontation but also most of the revolt's critical battles took place not north of the Rhine, but south of the river in Brabant and Flanders. It was mainly Brabant Catholics (albeit moderate ones) who initially protested against the severe treatment of Protestants. Only after Philip II's harsh repressions led many southerners to flee to the northern provinces did the revolt develop into a conflict in which Dutch Protestants won independence for the seven northern Low Country provinces. Since a winner's perspective drives most of what is written and read about wars, especially ones that gain a country's independence, it is hardly surprising that Dutch and Protestant views have gained general acceptance. The pro-winner perspective of this war—as articulated by many Anglo-American and Dutch authors—obscures the reality that the so-called Dutch revolt did not begin as a conflict between the northern and southern Low Countries and that Dutch Calvinists did not initiate the conflict.

In this war, Spain initially held the advantage; but reluctant and spasmodic help from England, to whom Spain was a threat, helped the rebels persevere. The successive Pacification of Ghent, Confederation of Arras and Union of Utrecht, the last of which formed the basis for the independent Dutch Republic, marked the protracted conflict. While the war did not formally end until 1648, its outcome was clear by 1598. While the cities of Brabant and Flanders had once been the political, economic, artistic and Protestant centres of the Low Countries, even before the end of the sixteenth century the focus of Low Country commercial and cultural life had shifted from Antwerp to Amsterdam, as had most Protestants. Southern Low Country emigrants shaped the development of Holland as a major commercial power and forged its Golden Century.

Philip II aggressively defends royal absolutism and fervent Catholicism

Philip II's introspective personality, autocratic style, fervent Catholicism and persistent persecuting zeal make him one of history's most enigmatic and controversial figures. The intensity of his convictions regarding the grandeur of Spain and the divine right of kings and the fervency of his Catholic faith drove his zealous efforts to suppress the threats from the Reformation and to his autocratic rule. Like other monarchs, he believed that unity of religion was indispensable to preservation of the state and royal rule—a not unreasonable policy in an age when church and state were closely intertwined. Ensconced in his mausoleum-like Escorial, Philip determined to enforce energetically in the Low Countries the Counter-Reformation policies of exiling and executing heretics, practices that the Inquisition was vigorously applying in Spain. In the southern Low Countries, though, the rapid increase of Calvinism, especially in the urban centres, and notably in Antwerp, Brussels, Ghent and Horebeek (near Oudenaarde), combined with a growing detestation for distant, insensitive Spanish rule proved to be too great a challenge. The growing dynamic vigour of Low Country Calvinism provoked a spirited Spanish reaction, which in time split the northern from the southern provinces.

Upon becoming ruler of the Low Countries, Philip's role was initially ambiguous, surrounded as he was by his father's advisers. His long-term impact on the Low Countries proved, though, to be anything but ambivalent. His determination to prevent his Low Country subjects from deserting the one true Roman Catholic faith—as well as dogmatically to uphold the divine right of monarchical rule—proved disastrous. His uncompromising mindset and stubborn reliance on force to cope with the rebels' zealous self-righteousness cost him an expensive protracted war and the northern half of the Low Countries.

Several questions arise from the ironical outcome of this war. How did part of the Low Countries succeed in winning independence from the mighty Spanish empire, then the world's strongest power? Why did the revolt against Spanish rule, of which moderate Catholics from the southern provinces had taken the lead, end in securing independence only for the northern Protestant-led ones? Why did the southern provinces, which had the most Protestants before the revolt, become almost exclusively Catholic after the civil war? Why did the northern provinces that initially had fewer Protestants than the southern ones become the Protestant-led country? How did William the Silent, a noble raised as a Catholic at the court as a favourite of Charles V and later serving Philip II in top Low Country posts, become the leader of the rebel forces?

Many factors contributed to this ironic outcome of a war that split the Low Countries and turned them upside down, in commercial, artistic and religious life. Spain had so long relied on its American gold that it had not developed other resources nor promoted advances in commerce, a syndrome that afflicts many oil rich countries today. Philip faced many other challenges, any one of which, says Diarmaid MacCollogh, 'would have been daunting for a capable ruler: masterminding the peaceful takeover by Spain of the entire Portuguese Empire, facing the continuing threat of Islam in the near East, and devising a strategy to contain or even destroy the growing Protestant power of Queen Elizabeth's England.'[4] The more recently annexed Dutch-speaking northern provinces particularly resented rule by the Spaniards, who administered the Low Countries from Madrid and Brussels. The northern provinces were easier for the rebels to defend: Holland possessed three excellent ports; much of its land could be flooded against the invader and the Rhine provided a defendable frontier. William the Silent, not initially but later the rebel leader, was especially well respected in the northern provinces, where he was *stadhouder* (governor) in Holland, Zeeland and Utrecht. It was the southern provinces, where the Low Country political and commercial capitals were located, that, along with silver from the Americas, provided an indispensable source of the revenue needed to guarantee the loans supporting Spain's many wars and overseas adventures. As the wars came to cost what Spain's resources could not support, bankrupting it, Spain not only found the southern provinces more important and easier to defend, but also found the northern ones more difficult to secure.

Philip II succeeds to a gathering storm

In 1556, a year after turning over the Low Countries to his son Philip, Charles V, wearied with the mounting economic and religious problems confronting his empire, abdicated as King of Spain and as Holy Roman Emperor. While his son became King of Spain, Charles' brother Ferdinand I succeeded him as Archduke of Austria and Emperor. Repeated shocks to the economy, the costs of endless wars, and continuing colonial commitments had forced an almost four-fold increase in the onerous debt from 1544 to 1556. Despite the ordinances issued by Charles against heretics, the Lutherans followed by Calvinists continued to gain ground, especially after 1550. To meet this threat the Spanish escalated their anti-heresy efforts in the Low Countries. While the number tried in ecclesiastical courts averaged thirteen per year from 1521 to 1550, by 1550 the average was sixty per year.

In 1559, Philip left the Low Countries for Spain, never to return, appointing as governor-general his illegitimate half-sister, Margaret of Parma, who had been raised at the court in the Low Countries under the tutelage of Margaret of Austria and Mary of Hungary. He appointed as Margaret's principal adviser Antoine Perronet de Granvelle, a bureaucrat of non-noble background from the Franche-Comté.

Philip returned to Spain despite grave problems in the Low Countries. Protestantism continued to spread even with increasing efforts to subdue the heresy. Discontent among the nobles increased, those in the recently acquired northern provinces were especially upset regarding Low Country centralisation. The States-General sessions in 1556 and 1558 were fiascos. In 1559, in an effort to strengthen the Church and its ability to counter heresy, Granvelle proposed dividing the Low Countries into twelve bishoprics; Philip appointed him as archbishop and primate charged with overseeing the change. The disaffected nobles mobilised opposition, especially in the north where they saw the new dioceses as a threat to their power.

Despite Spanish efforts to curb heresy, Protestantism continued to spread. The Calvinists proved to be more zealous than the Lutherans. A split in the Council of State and Philip II's recall of the Spanish army from the Low Countries to meet problems elsewhere undermined respect for Spanish rule. England's relationship with Spain had deteriorated with the 1558 accession of Queen Elizabeth, following the death of her sister Queen Mary. Philip, who had been Mary's husband, had departed from England in 1557 after he inherited the Spanish throne. By then, since childless Mary was past childbearing age, it was evident that his royal status was a limited asset. The new Queen took steps to develop England's own capacity for making cloth from its wool, measures causing massive unemployment in Flanders and Brabant.

In 1565 a group of moderate Catholic and a few Protestant nobles, led by Hendrik van Brederode and Louis of Nassau, a brother of William of Orange (who only later became known as 'the Silent'), formed the League of Compromise intended to attract all who desired peace. A year later Brederode circulated a vehement denunciation of the anti-heresy decrees and demanded the abolition of the Inquisition. When League members forced their way into the presence of the regent, Margaret of Parma, and presented their 'Petition of Compromise', the count of Berlaymont contemptuously referred to the intruders as *Gueux* (Beggars). Thereafter, the petitioners proudly called themselves by the pejorative epithet. At a banquet of many of the Compromise supporters, Brederode distributed a beggar's bowl and pouch to each guest, an act greeted by the cry '*Vive les Gueux*' ('Long live the beggars').

Efforts to subdue Protestantism instead fuelled the revolt. Outdoor ('hedgerow') preaching sprang up throughout the land. Preachers addressed groups in fields outside the walls of nearly all south-western Low Country towns. The Dutch historian Pieter Geyl describes how the fury extended beyond the 'hedgerow' meetings: 'But the Calvinist community did not let itself be restricted to ...holding of meetings outside churches. They longed for action, in breaking images they found it... A transport of rage suddenly possessed the multitude. Crowds surged into the churches to destroy all the most treasured symbols and ornaments of the old religion. This wave of frenzy swept from village to village ... engulfed town after town. On the 18th, the storm struck Oudenaarde, whence it reached Antwerp on the 20th, Ghent on the 22nd; that same day it swept to Amsterdam...thence to Leiden and Delft; on the 25th to Utrecht, and in the following weeks into Friesland and Gröningen. In the Walloon country the movement was less widespread, but at Valenciennes it displayed peculiar energy...'[5] For weeks, the government took no action. Finally, the Council of State persuaded Margaret to allow the Protestants to meet openly. To calm the situation the Governor-General asked William of Orange to try to reconcile the factions. Neither Spain nor the rebels appreciated William's unsuccessful efforts.

William the Silent and the Duke of Alva

Faced with this news Philip sent a 10,000-man army to the Low Countries. To lead this force he selected his ablest general, the Duke of Alva, a grandee of an illustrious Spanish family with a distinguished military record, who shared with Philip his views on the need for strong measures. Hearing of the impending arrival of Alva many Protestants emigrated. William, Prince of Orange, despite holding large Low Country estates, decided to leave the country and urged a fellow noble, Egmont, to join him. But Egmont, who like William had not supported the heretics, was determined not to abandon his estates. He reportedly bid farewell to William saying 'Goodbye, landless', and William to have replied 'Goodbye, headless'. Alarming as the concerns regarding Alva's coming were, the fears would have been magnified if people had known Philip's instructions: 'try to arrange the affairs of religion in the Low Countries, if possible without having recourse to force, because the means would only imply the total destruction of the country, but I am determined to use it nevertheless, if I cannot otherwise arrange everything as I wish.'[6]

Although disturbances had virtually ceased by Alva's arrival, he lost no time in unleashing a reign of terror. As the final event of a fortnight of festivities, Alva invited the country's ranking nobles to a banquet, during which he arrested those he considered leading Protestant sympathisers. Those taken into custody included Counts Egmont and Horne, despite the fact that they had remained loyal Catholics, renewed their pledges of loyalty to the King, worked closely with Margaret and as members of the Order of the Golden Fleece were immune from charges by anyone other than the king. Recognising that her role as Governor-General had been gravely undermined, Margaret resigned. Philip then appointed Alva to succeed her as govenor-general while continuing as military commander.

Even before the arrest of the counts and Margaret's resignation, Alva organised the Council of Troubles, called by many the 'Council of Blood', to investigate the recent disturbances and punish the guilty. Its staff of 170, according to Blockmans, 'issued 1,071 death sentences and banished 11,136 persons, confiscating their property.'[7] He had Egmont, Horne and others executed in the Brussels Grand-Place. While William was sufficiently wary of Alva to avoid attending the Brussels festivities and escaped, he failed to withdraw from Leiden University his thirteen-year-old oldest son who was taken to Spain as hostage, never to see his father again.

Alva took a number of steps that alienated almost everyone and nurtured the revolt. An attempt to raise funds by levying a sales tax outraged even loyal Catholic subjects. Erection of a statue in Antwerp of Alva stamping on traditional symbols of self-government escalated antipathy to his rule. His reign of terror prompted a second major exodus following the one that had anticipated his arrival. About 60,000 left the country in these early emigrations. Neither repression nor emigration, though, removed the rebel threat, for estrangement from the Catholic Church was deep-rooted and widespread.

At the outset of Alva's governorship, the hopes for armed opposition to Spanish rule were poor. Brederode, leader of the 'Beggars', failed to win William of Orange to the rebel cause, deleted his friend from his will and died dispirited a few months later. Not until William heard of his own condemnation, the confiscation of his property and the abduction of his son did he assume leadership of the revolt. William's aristocratic background and personal qualities served him well as he undertook this role. While William's parents were Lutherans, at the request of Charles V the future rebel leader had been raised in the royal court at Mechelen as a Catholic and remained one until 1566. But he had long rejected the notion espoused by both Philip II and his father that rulers had a God-given mandate to dictate the consciences of those they ruled. William's leadership was enhanced by his positions as *stadhouder* of three northern provinces, the extent of his estates including holdings in Brabant as well as Orange in France and Nassau in Germany, his marriage to Anne of Saxony that connected him with a leading German and energy. His tolerance in religion and public affairs extended to private matters, as shown by his refusal to take action against the man who had an affair with his wife and later fathered Peter Paul Rubens. He was called 'the Silent' not so much for his brevity of speech but for his ability to mask his reactions and to speak without committing himself. The French call him 'the Taciturn', a more accurate description than 'the Silent'. His prestige and access to significant resources, including financial assistance from the Calvinist Elector of the Palatinate and a sizeable number of exiled Low Country nobles, further strengthened his leadership role. Throughout the war, he continued to insist that while he opposed Spanish policies, he remained loyal to the Spanish king. The Dutch national anthem, *Wilhelmus*, memorialises William's professed loyalty by including the words 'to the king of Spain I will always be true'. To this day the anthem is sung regularly at public events in the Netherlands, yet the Dutch appear not to recognise the irony of pledging loyalty to a foreign king against whom a war of independence was won centuries ago.

The conflict escalated in 1568 when William of Orange, finally committed to the insurgent cause, 'risked an invasion of Brabant, a military move that is traditionally considered the beginning of the Eighty Years' War.' Blockmans goes on to report: 'The campaign was unsuccessful, however, as expected popular support failed to materialise and William lacked the money to sustain a long-term campaign.'[8] From 1561 to 1571, only a few bands of Beggars operated in the hinterland and only a few Sea-Beggar privateers conducted raids in the North Sea, using letters of marque issued by William and using English ports as refuge. In 1572, when Queen Elizabeth closed the English ports to the Sea Beggars, forcing them to find an alternative base, they seized La Brielle in Zeeland. Coming when it did in the revolt, this victory unleashed rebel elation and energy. Flushing, Rotterdam, Leerdam, and soon most of the rest of Holland and Zeeland mustered support for the revolt. In the south, the rebels seized Mons and Valenciennes. William the Silent advanced through Gelderland into Brabant, getting as far as Mechelen, which opened its gates. These successes aroused the hopes of the southern provinces, but support waned following a rebel massacre of monks at Gorinchem.

When William's French allies received word of the St Bartholomew's massacre of the French Protestant leaders gathered for the wedding of Henry of Navarre for whom 'Paris was worth a mass' and returned home, the rebels' efforts lost momentum. Alva then launched a counter offensive and with overwhelming numbers he captured Mechelen, where he punished the city for opening its gates to the rebels by sacking it and allowing a massacre. He then proceeded to Zutphen where his troops killed many men, women and children. At Naarden he ordered the killing of every man, woman and child. His advance to Haarlem split the northern provinces into two and dimmed the revolt's prospects. But while the killings in Mechelen and Zutphen demoralised the rebels, the Naarden massacre roused them. When Alva laid siege to Altmar, William was able to rescue the city and thus turned the tide. The Spanish retreat, in October 1573, coincided with a naval victory by the Sea Beggars off the coast of Enkhuizen. Discouraged, Alva returned to Spain.

To replace Alva, the king sent another Spanish aristocrat, Don Luis de Zunga y Requesens—with the assurance from Philip that some concessions were possible as long as there was no compromise regarding religion. Thanks to a Spanish victory at Mookerheide, where two brothers of William were killed, Requesens could afford to make concessions to the States-General without losing prestige. He granted an amnesty, reduced taxes and ended death sentences, but he did not dismiss the Spanish troops. When the revolt leaders refused to negotiate, he laid siege to Leiden. The town was relieved only when William opened the dykes, thus flooding the area, dispersing the Spanish troops, and enabling boats to supply the city. To reward Leiden William offered it a temporary cessation of taxes or a university. Thus Leiden University began.

In 1575, with the German Emperor mediating, representatives of Philip and William met in Breda. But two issues—religion and form of government—proved to be fundamentally irreconcilable. While Philip insisted upon Catholicism as the only recognised religion, William and his colleagues demanded a guarantee of liberty of conscience. While the rebels insisted on limited monarchy with the representative bodies sharing in governance, Philip resisted any encroachments on his royal authority. The war continued.

The Pacification of Ghent, the Confederation of Arras and the Union of Utrecht

When Requesens died in 1576, a Council of State led by moderate Catholics took temporary control of the Low Countries and suppressed the Council of Troubles. But the Council of State could not disband the Spanish troops. Not having been paid for months, the Spanish troops engaged in pillaging raids. The Council felt so impotent that it permitted the States (council) of Brabant to raise its own troops to protect Brussels, Antwerp and neighbouring towns from marauding soldiers. In the power vacuum that followed, Brabant also took the lead in convening the States-General of the Low Countries—the first time since 1477 that one had been called without the concurrence of the ruler. While Holland and Zeeland did not attend, they agreed to co-operate with the newly constituted States-General in driving out the mutinous Spanish troops. While the negotiations were underway, the main body of Spanish mutineers attacked Antwerp, overwhelmed the Brabant troops, and subjected the city to pillage, wanton rape and killing—a rampage remembered as the Spanish Fury.

The Spanish Fury added urgency to negotiations among the provinces. In 1576, the rebel leaders signed the Pacification of Ghent, agreeing to create a union of their provinces and decreeing a general amnesty. While they adopted tolerance in religious matters and allowed

Protestantism in Holland and Zeeland, in other provinces Catholicism remained the sole official faith, all royal edicts suppressing heresy suspended and the practice of Protestantism allowed. The leaders further agreed to unite under the leadership of William to drive out the Spanish troops.

The newly reconstituted States-General indicated willingness to negotiate with the new governor, Don Juan of Austria, an illegitimate son of Charles V, provided he agreed to govern in conjunction with it, send away the Spanish troops and swear to uphold the Pacification of Ghent. Lacking the money and troops to do otherwise, Don Juan generally accepted the terms. But Holland and Zeeland rejected the agreement since it provided insufficient guarantees for the Calvinist faith. There were now three power centres in the war: Don Juan represented the Spanish, Catholic and monarchical cause; the rebel core, led by Holland, espoused Protestantism and autonomy; the Brabant-led States-General attempted to straddle both sides, by compromising with the king, alleviating the rebel concerns and hopefully ending the conflict.

Frustrated, Don Juan fled Brussels and set up headquarters in Namur. William, for the moment at one with the States-General, entered Brussels in triumph. Consistent with his principles of toleration, he tried to advance the cause of liberty of conscience, but he received little support either from the zealous Calvinists, (especially those in Holland and Zeeland) or from the Catholic aristocracy (especially those in Hainaut, Namur, Artois and Luxembourg who, while opposed to many Spanish policies and practices, remained loyal to the Catholic Church and to their legitimate Spanish ruler).

In 1577 Archduke Matthias, a younger brother of Emperor Rudolf II, became the first of a series of royal family members and ineffectual aristocratic adventurers (of Austrian, French and English houses) whom the rebels sought and accepted as their head (nominal or actual) to strengthen their cause. As Peter Wilson states, Matthias 'was completely out of his depth. The rebel leadership simply used him as a face-saving device while they gathered their forces and they expelled him in 1581.'[9] Tripartite negotiations broke down when Holland, Zeeland and many Flemish and Brabant towns refused to budge on the issues of religious toleration or the extent of self-governance, or even on the recognition of Don Juan as Governor-General. When Don Juan defeated the States-General's troops at Gembloux in early

1578 and threatened Brussels, the States-General and William moved their headquarters to Antwerp. By this crushing victory, Don Juan secured the renewed allegiance of the southern tier provinces. With deep reluctance, William recognised that the rebels could no longer achieve the goal of securing a united Low Countries. The battle of Gembloux, says Fisher, was the turning point where it was decided that Holland and Belgium should each 'lead a separate political existence, which, save for their brief and uneasy union between 1815 and 1830, has remained unbroken to this day.'[10]

The growing revival of Spanish power in Namur and Hainaut, coupled with the aversion of the southern Catholic elite to Protestant militancy, further widened the gap between the uncompromising aims of the Holland and Zeeland Protestants and the more modest goals of the southern Catholics. William's proclamation of 'Religious Peace' allowing freedom of practice, though intended to pacify both sides, increased the discontent of both Catholics and Calvinists and further intensified the conflicting objectives of the northern and southern wings of the revolt. Dejected, Don Juan retired to Namur, where he died in 1578. His lieutenant, Alessandro Farnese, heir to the Duchy of Parma and son of Margaret of Parma, replaced him.

The increasing complexity of the struggle escalated the friction between the more radical Calvinists and more moderate Catholics within the rebel coalition. Repeated cruelties committed by zealous Calvinist militants in some communes contributed to many southern Catholic leaders, feeling that William was willing to tolerate excesses of his partisans while paying only lip service to Catholic concerns. This perception led Artois, Hainaut and towns in Walloon Flanders to form the Confederation of Arras in 1579. In response, the seven northern provinces—Holland, Zeeland, Utrecht, Gelderland, Friesland, Overijssel and Gröningen—and Ghent formed the Union of Utrecht.

Throughout the conflict, the rebel leaders beseeched Elizabeth of England for financial and military support. She was the most likely source for assistance because England had a stake in undermining its archrival Spain's hold on the coast so close to its shore, and she wanted to keep the Protestant cause in the Low Countries alive, in part to keep the Spanish king distracted from designs upon England. But Elizabeth firmly resisted becoming directly involved in a war that she feared would strain her treasury and threaten her country—as the Armada later did. Throughout her reign, she walked a tightrope. In 1582, though, she agreed to help by giving funds to the Duke of Anjou, the only surviving brother of the childless French king, to fight the Spanish in the Low Countries. She may have taken this step in part to rid herself of the duke's three-year presence at her court pursuing hopes of becoming her husband. When the States-General asked the Duke of Anjou to lead the resistance, William urged that they grant the Duke the title of 'Hereditary Sovereign'—in order to strengthen his role. 'To make this possible…' Geyl reports, 'the States-General…passed the famous resolution, whereby Philip, on account of his tyrannical rule and his trampling underfoot of the privileges of the country, was deposed from dominion over his Netherland provinces…'[11] The Catholic Duke of Anjou entered into a strange position as lord of a land where its Protestant leadership was waging a war against the imposition of Catholicism.

The northern provinces gain de facto independence

Under the lethargic and incompetent Anjou, the rebel forces were unsuccessful in halting Spanish advances. When Anjou failed to secure further support from Queen Elizabeth, he became unable to pay his troops. Frustrated, Anjou's French soldiers attempted to seize Antwerp but were defeated by the armed citizens in an encounter remembered as the 'French Fury'. Discredited, Anjou left the Low Countries in 1583 and died the following year. While the invitation to Anjou was intended to reconcile the northern and southern leaders and strengthen their coordinated efforts throughout the Low Countries, in fact his appointment had widened the gulf between the factions comprising the rebel forces. A discouraged William abandoned military efforts in the southern provinces and moved to Holland, effectively recognising that the revolt could succeed only in the northern provinces. In 1584, a French Catholic fanatic, emboldened by a reward offered by King Philip for William's demise, shot and killed William at his Delft headquarters. The rebel cause appeared doomed.

By the end of 1585, Farnese had taken advantage of increased support from Spain and the fading resistance in the south to subdue almost every city in the southern provinces, including Dunkirk, Ieper, Bruges, Mechelen and Ghent. Brussels, which had vainly awaited support from the north, finally opened its doors to him the following March. To take Antwerp, Farnese blockaded the Scheldt, forcing Antwerp to capitulate. With these victories Farnese attempted to dictate the terms of peace, specifying that the 'heretics' must leave their cities within two years. In the last two decades of the sixteenth century more than 150,000 (in addition to those who had fled earlier) left the southern Low Countries for religious or political reasons—or simply to escape the ravages, destruction, famine and epidemics brought on by decades of continuous warfare. Combined with the earlier emigrations the impact on southern Low Country cities was devastating. Antwerp lost one-half, Ghent one-quarter and other towns lost significant fractions of their population.

To gain support William the Silent's son Maurice of Nassau, who at seventeen years of age succeeded his father as leader of the rebel forces, turned once again to Queen Elizabeth, who was increasingly concerned with Spanish intentions. While she declined the offer to become sovereign of the rebel provinces, she at last openly allied with them. In 1585, a treaty between the rebels and England effectively established the northern provinces as a protectorate with Robert Dudley, Earl of Leicester as commander of the armies. Frustrated in their desire to secure Queen Elizabeth as their sovereign, a step that the rebel leaders believed would guarantee England's support, they asked the Earl to become their ruler. While the earl had a long-standing interest in the Low Countries and enjoyed the special confidence of the queen, he was handicapped by minimal military and diplomatic experience and little understanding of Low Country politics. When the earl arrived in the Low Countries, he found that the rebels had organised a triumphal progress through the country. For Leicester it was a heady experience recalling his old ambitions of marrying Elizabeth. But when Elizabeth heard that he was being addressed as 'Your Excellency' and had accepted the post of Governor-General, and that the rising costs of the expedition had far exceeded what she had pledged, her worst suspicions about the enterprise were confirmed. She recalled Leicester.

In his preparations for the Armada to invade England, Philip ordered Farnese (now Duke of Parma) to concentrate his troops near Dunkirk. The defeat of the Armada significantly strengthened the rebel cause. Even afterwards, while the failure of the Armada in 1588 might have released these forces, Farnese, instead of returning to the Low Countries, was obliged to fight off French attacks upon his troops. Maurice of Nassau used this opportunity to consolidate rebel gains. While the war continued into the seventeenth century, with an interruption during the twelve-year truce from 1609 until 1621, by the 1590s the seven northern provinces, united in a Holland-led confederation called the United Provinces, had already secured *de facto* independence and begun their rapid development of a globe-spanning commercial empire. Spain, bankrupted by its wars, had begun its decay as an empire. Not until 1648, though, did a treaty signed in the Westphalia town of Osnabruck formally terminate the Eighty Years War between Spain and the United Provinces. The treaty was negotiated in parallel with the treaty signed in nearby Munster that ended the European-wide Thirty Years War, with which the Eighty Years War had become intertwined.

Henry Kamen concludes his biography of Philip II saying he 'was never at any time in adequate control of events, or of his kingdom, or even of his own destiny ... For all his power, he had been unable to stop his realms being sucked into a whirl of war, debt, and decay. The spectre faced him already in 1556. It was still there, larger than ever in 1598.'[12]

Like the ninth century Lotharingian king Lothair II and the fifteenth century Burgundian Duke Charles the Bold, Philip II failed to pass on intact to his heir the Low Country possessions he inherited. Fiscal and related restraints upon the Spanish ability to wage the civil conflict combined with Philip's unwillingness to compromise his anti-heresy policies and his royal autocratic prerogatives, undermined the empire's ability to prosecute the war. Consequently Spain lost the northern half of the Low Countries. The stubborn reaction of the rebels to Spanish obduracy lost them the support of the southern provinces. What the Burgundian dukes and Habsburg rulers had put together, the civil war split asunder. From both points of view, the outcome was less than satisfactory. The division of the Seventeen Provinces set in motion antagonisms that undermined the possibility for a united Low Countries to play a strong role in the balance-of-power politics of modern Europe and left the truncated southern Low Countries vulnerable to the ambitions, invasions and occupations of neighbours for the next three and a half centuries.

The war that ended with the northern provinces gaining their independence depleted the population of the southern provinces, cut off land that had long been integral to the southern Low Country economy, sapped its creativity and left a bitter legacy of countless memories of massacres and broken promises. The hostilities arising from the war and later events continued to corrode relations between the two neighbours—one Calvinist-led and the other Catholic-dominated—for centuries and undermined the prospects for their brief reunification from 1815 and 1830. While Justus Lipsius credits Philip the Good with the founding of Belgium, it was the war that split the Low Countries that nurtured the development of a distinctive southern Low Country common community identity that later drove Belgium's desire for independence. The wars of Louis XIV would further strengthen this sense of Belgian community.

Brussels' Grand Place began as a market in the eleventh century and has evolved as the city's social centre. The 1695 bombardment by the French destroyed most of the buildings, but not the Hôtel de Ville, which was out of range of enemy guns. The rebuilding of the guild houses shown here, which line the square, led to the insolvency of many of the guilds (© Alexey Kuznetsov, istockphoto.com).

The Southern Low Countries

From 1598, when the Dutch had already won *de facto* independence, to 1830–31, when the Belgians declared their independence from the Netherlands, six flags successively flew over the southern Low Countries. From 1599 to 1621, Archdukes Albert and Isabella were its nominal sovereigns. From then to the War of Spanish Succession, Spain directly ruled the southern Low Countries. Austria governed from 1713 to 1795, except during the briefly successful Brabant and Liège revolts. The French under the Directory and under Napoleon governed Belgium from 1795 to 1815. The united Kingdom of the Netherlands, under the newly-crowned William I, ruled a merged Netherlands and Belgium until 1830–31, when the Belgians hoisted their own flag.

For about two centuries from the end of the bitter Eighty Years War, Belgians underwent humbling and humiliating years governed in turn from Madrid, Vienna, Paris and The Hague. A country devastated and demoralised by a long civil war suffered dismemberment and destruction through several wars, ending with the War of Spanish Succession waged by King Louis XIV of France, the War of Austrian Succession and the campaigns of the French Revolution and Napoleon. These wars, plus the conflict that ended with the recognition of Belgian independence, not only defined the present Belgian borders but also promoted Belgians' recognition of their shared sense of extended community and desire for independence.

The Age of Enlightenment, marked by the writings of Locke, Rousseau, Voltaire and Hume, ushered in new thinking, yearning for knowledge and revised perceptions of the individual's place in society. The French Revolution and the rise and fall of Napoleon and his empire sped the demand for change. The industrial revolution quickened the growth of a middle class. The impact of this multi-faceted change was especially dramatic in Belgium where it set the stage for its political revolution and the expansion of political participation that transformed Belgium's nineteenth and twentieth century political, economic and social life.

The 1648 end of the Thirty Years and the Eighty Years Wars marked the start of a relentless march to an era of national hegemony and nation-states, helped by the enshrinement of the concept of sovereignty that Jean Bodin had articulated decades earlier. Blanning points out that by the early nineteenth century: 'in most parts of Europe the claims of the state to a monopoly of legislation and allegiance within its borders were established in fact if not in law. Although there was a rich multiplicity of constitutional forms, ranging from democracy to autocracy, behind them all lay the sovereignty of an abstraction—the state. Political structures unable to achieve that 'monopoly of legitimate force' (Max Weber) lying at the heart of the state, such as Poland and the Holy Roman Empire, became easy prey for those who had read the signs of the times more accurately.'[1] During this six-flags-over-Belgium era, successive southern Low Country rulers renewed the centralisation efforts, developing sources of revenue and a bureaucracy, which would develop exponentially in the nineteenth and twentieth centuries.

Five European-wide events particularly marked Belgium's six-flags era. The end of the revolt against Spain split the Low Countries. The treaty ending the War of Spanish Succession transferred the southern Low Countries to Austria. The French Revolution triggered two Belgian revolts. The treaty ending the Napoleonic Wars merged Belgium with the Netherlands. The 1830 French upheaval inspired the Belgian uprising and independence. How, despite the language frontier, did the southern Low Countries continue developing unifying institutions and a sense of shared community? While Spanish, Austrian, French and Dutch rulers continued to centralise, Belgians strengthened their sense that they were not French, Dutch, or German but Belgian—and their desire for independence.

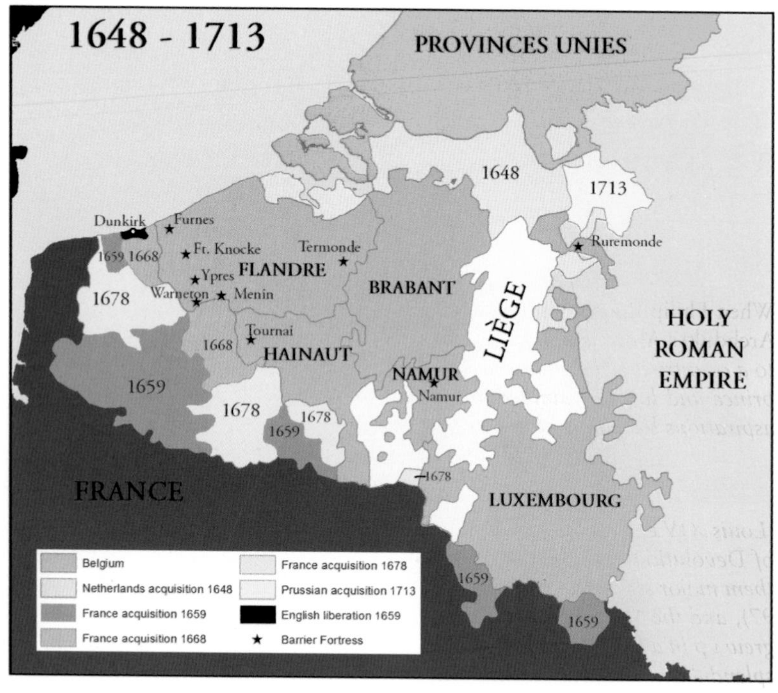

Map 10. The Spanish Low Countries lost land to the Netherlands, France and Prussia from 1648 to 1713.

7

THE SPANISH HABSBURGS RULE AN IMPOVERISHED LAND

1599–1713

When Philip II wrote in the act of cession of the southern Low Countries to Archdukes Albert and Isabella that *'the greatest happiness which might occur to a country is to be governed under the eyes and in the presence of its natural prince and lord, he almost annihilated this very wise concession to Belgian aspirations by adding stringent restrictions.'*[1]

Emile Cammaerts

'Louis XIV engaged in five declared wars, two of them minor affairs—the War of Devolution (1667–68), and the War of Reunions (1683–84), and three of them major struggles—the Dutch War (1672–78), the Nine Years War (1688–97), and the War of Spanish Succession (1701–1714)... This proud monarch grew up in a Europe overshadowed by Spanish power... As a young adult, the splendid Sun King led a France that had become the pre-eminent power on the continent.'[2]

John A. Lynn

From Archdukes Albert and Isabella to Charles II

The revolt that won Holland and other northern provinces their independence turned the Low Countries upside down. Before the revolt, Flanders and Brabant were the Low Countries' commercial, political and artistic centre—and the heart of its Protestant movement. The Dutch secession, accompanied by the flight of Protestants, entrepreneurs, and artisans—and the closing of the Scheldt—moved the focus of Low Country trade from Antwerp to Amsterdam. The Hague became the more important seat of government. Holland replaced Brabant and Flanders as the focus of Low Country Protestantism and artistic life.

Compared with flourishing Holland, the Spanish Low Countries fared poorly. The protracted revolt left the southern Low Countries—in the post-civil war years called the Spanish Netherlands and sometimes the Catholic Netherlands and Belgium—economically devastated and demoralised. Dykes were broken and polders flooded, cultivated land was left fallow and skilled workers were scarce. War, along with epidemics and famine, dominated the Spanish Low Countries to the end of the seventeenth century. While the truce and the leadership of Albert and Isabella supported a glittering court and the glory of Rubens, it was a fading sunset. No longer did an economic and artistic dynamism support and sustain the 'Burgundian' Golden Age. From 1599 to 1621, Albert and Isabella reigned as 'joint sovereigns'; but significant limitations to their rule rendered the land's nominal independence a façade.

Following a 1609–1621 truce, the rebel war against Spain resumed and ran in tandem with the Thirty Years War (1618–48), whose end confirmed the policy of '*cuius regio, eius religio*'. Rulers continued to rule with the presumption that religious conformity was a prerequisite for national unity and governance. Karen Armstrong comments that it was 'impossible ... for an ordinarily constituted man to exist outside of the confines of religion during the seventeenth century.'[3]

From the mid-seventeenth century to 1713, when Austria replaced Spain as ruler of the southern Low Countries, French aggressions preoccupied and ravaged Belgium. Louis XIV's efforts to extend his kingdom, despite the opposition of a Dutch-led European alliance, resulted in the loss of most of Walloon Flanders (now French Flanders). Spain's ability to defend its Low Country possession continued to decline under Philip III, Philip IV and especially the weak in body and mind Charles II, whose demise without issue unleashed the War of Spanish Succession that ended with the transfer of the Spanish Low Countries to Austria.

Saint Carolus Borromeus Church in Antwerp, built in 1615 and decorated by Peter Paul Rubens, has a façade that may be appreciated as a monument to Catholic orthodoxy triumphant over Calvinism. The Counter-Reformation and civil war had, by the early seventeenth century, driven almost all Protestants and many artisans from the southern Low Countries (© R.V. Bulck, istockphoto.com).

Archdukes Albert and Isabella as 'joint sovereigns'

Philip II had promised to send the Spanish Low Countries a royal prince as governor. In 1593, Philip appointed as governor Ernest, his nephew and son of the German Emperor. When Ernest died two years later, Philip appointed Ernest's younger brother Albert as governor. Shortly thereafter Philip II arranged for his daughter Isabella to marry Albert and proposed that the archdukes rule as 'joint sovereigns.' While the arrangement appeared to grant the land its independence with a legitimate Catholic royal monarch, Philip II restricted this apparent gift with crippling limitations. In the event that Isabella had no children, the provinces would revert to the Spanish crown. Secret clauses provided that the joint archdukes obey all orders from Madrid and continue to maintain Spanish garrisons in the principal towns. Philip also reserved the right to re-annex his 'gift' to the archdukes. Philip II died before the marriage took place. Nevertheless the plans proceeded: the cousins married and became the joint sovereigns Philip II had envisaged. Brussels received the archdukes enthusiastically when they entered the capital in 1599. While the new regime excluded Protestantism, this caused little concern. By then most Protestants had left the southern provinces.

In 1600 William the Silent's son, Maurice of Nassau, invaded Flanders. Though failing to rally the Flemish towns to his side, he defeated the Spanish at Nieuwport. The next year Albert successfully undertook the siege of Oostende, which had remained under Dutch control. In 1609, the belligerents declared a twelve-year truce, which recognised the *de facto* independence of the seven northern provinces. MacCulloch points out that 'In practical terms the truce represented a recognition that the Spanish-controlled southern provinces were permanently separated from the independent North,'[4] which aroused in many southern Calvinists a bitter sense of betrayal. By other terms of the treaty the Dutch were allowed to trade with the West Indies, a concession that had been denied to Albert and Isabella's realm, and the Scheldt continued to be blockaded, stopping ships from entering or leaving Antwerp, which consequently lost most of its trade and population.

The twelve-year truce allowed the southern Low Countries to revive slowly, commercially and economically. Grain production began to return to its old levels. The population of most towns and villages grew, but did not return to pre-war levels until mid-century. Antwerp remained handicapped in international trade but began to develop as a producer of lace, diamonds, art and silks. And it continued as an international money market, thus retaining importance as an economic centre. To overcome the blockade of Antwerp, canals were dug connecting Ghent and Bruges with the Oostende and Dunkirk ports.

The curtailed Spanish Low Country economy contrasted starkly with the rapid development of the Dutch Republic, which developed rapidly even before achieving independence. 'In the early years of the seventeenth century,' Pieter Geyl has pointed out, 'Holland was rapidly surpassing all other countries of the world in accumulation of capital. Amsterdam began to rival, and then to outstrip, Genoa and Venice as the great international money market.'[5] Its Dutch East India Company already had a near monopoly of Asian trade when in 1609 it engaged Henry Hudson to discover a new passage to Asia. The North American river he sailed up, in the effort to find a northwest passage to the Indies, now carries his name.

The Eighty Years War recommences

In 1621, Philip III died and Philip IV became king, Archduke Albert died and Isabella continued to govern the Spanish Low Countries but only as governor-General, and the truce ended. The Eighty Years War dragged on until 1648, accompanied by the series of international conflicts called the Thirty Years War, in which the Austrian Habsburgs and German princes and cities, along with Denmark, Sweden, Poland and France, fought over a combination of religious, political and constitutional issues that converted Germany into a cockpit of the European powers.

As the Low Country war continued, Ambrosio Spinola, the Spanish military commander in the Low Countries, captured Breda from the United Provinces, but an apparently politically manipulated disgrace forced Spinola to return to Spain. This allowed the Dutch Republic once more to consolidate its military position in northern Brabant and eastern Limburg, taking Hertogenbosch, Venloo and Maastricht. The fall of Maastricht led Isabella to assemble the States-General in 1632. The long-neglected body took this opportunity to reassert its grievances concerning the abuse of traditional local privileges, the stationing of Spanish troops in the Low Countries and Spanish administrative malpractices. Feeling threatened, the Spanish envoys immediately left the country. After Isabella died, Philip IV recalled the States-General only to dismiss it shortly thereafter. Not until the end of the eighteenth century did another States-General convene.

In 1648 the two treaties ending the Eighty Years War and the Thirty Years War were signed in Westphalia. The treaty between Spain and the United Provinces gave the Dutch almost everything they wanted: their independence was officially recognised; the Scheldt remained closed; and they acquired lands taken on the south bank of the western Scheldt estuary (which ensured them control of Antwerp traffic), north Brabant (which provided a buffer land south of the Rhine) and east Limburg (including Maastricht). While the United Provinces developed rapidly as a flourishing nation-state, the southern Low Countries declined, became economically depressed and remained a land subjugated to a foreign power for 182 more years.

Emigration from the southern Low Countries continued throughout the early seventeenth century. Most emigrants went to neighbouring countries, especially to the new Dutch Republic. A few crossed the

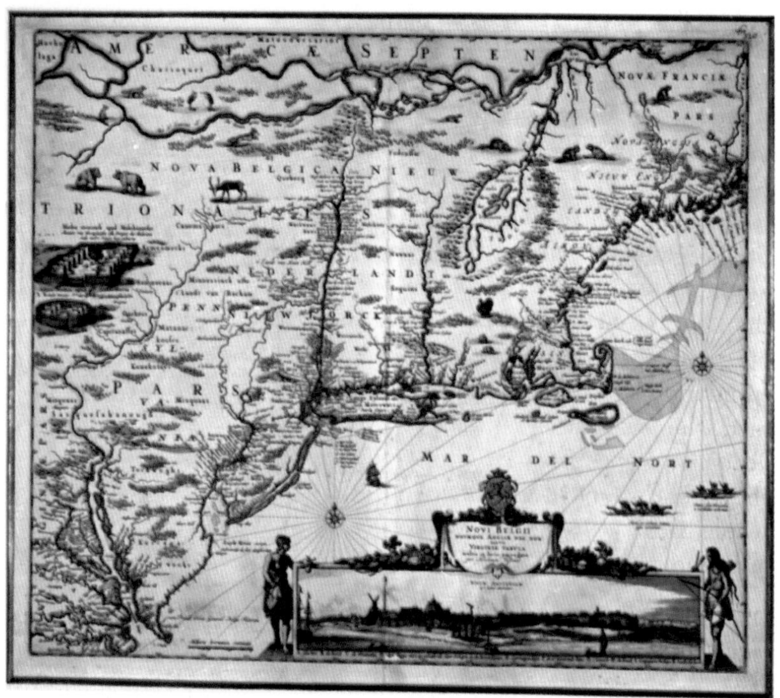

Map 11. 'Novi Belgii'—Nicholas Visscher (c. 1590). Russell Shorto states that it became the 'definitive map' of the American northeast for more than a century and helped imprint Dutch names on many American places.[6] The map applies the term 'Novi Belgii' to the land between the Connecticut and Delaware rivers embracing what is now New Jersey, eastern New York and western New England. The name 'Belgica' (and variants) was long used along with 'Nederlanden' (and variants) for the Low Countries.

Atlantic, after first living in the Dutch university town of Leiden, to settle in New Belgium (or New Netherlands) which a new Dutch company, the *Westindies Compagnie*, claimed to embrace much of what is now New Jersey, eastern New York state and western New England. The company, reports Russell Shorto, 'managed to round up a handful of hale young Walloons—French-speaking exiles from what is now Belgium'[7] to settle on southern Manhattan Island at the mouth of the Hudson. A monument now stands at the foot of Manhattan Island to commemorate their landing. Other Walloon Flemish Protestants later settled in Fort Orange (Albany, NY) and along the Delaware and Connecticut rivers. It was a Walloon, Peter Minuit, who is reputed to have purchased Manhattan Island in exchange for trinkets worth about $24.

Since the term 'Netherlands' continued for many decades to apply to all the Low Countries, and the English long tended to call those from the Low Countries Dutch, it is easy to understand why many today believe that the first settlers of New York were Dutch who emigrated from what is now the northern Low Countries, the Netherlands. In fact, while many early emigrants from Walloon Flanders had lived for years in Leiden (Holland) before being recruited to move to America, they were no more Hollanders than the Pilgrim Fathers, many of whom had also lived in Leiden before sailing on the *Mayflower* to land at Plymouth Rock.

The wars of Louis XIV cost Belgium Southwest (Walloon) Flanders

Following the Eighty Years War, the French under Louis XIV invaded the Low Countries in a series of wars, a part of his many campaigns to expand his kingdom, and a continuation of the centuries long French efforts to integrate (at least part of) the Low Countries into France. The wars contributed to Belgium's long-developed reputation as the 'cockpit of Europe'. The weakened Spanish government, while clinging to its Low Country possession, could no longer defend it against France. The United Provinces, recognising that France, its sometime ally in winning its independence from Spain, was now its major threat, led efforts to thwart Louis XIV's ambitions. Britain later also intervened to prevent France from developing a presence opposite its southeast coast—for England now considered France to be a far greater threat than bankrupt Spain.

In 1643, four-year-old Louis XIV succeeded his father as king of a nation bordered on three sides by countries governed by Habsburg rulers. France, led by Richelieu and then Mazarin, adopted the classic strategy of trying to eliminate insecure frontiers by subjugating the neighbouring lands.

Even before the death of Mazarin in 1661, when Louis took over direct control of his administration, his government had invaded the southern Low Countries, overrunning Artois in a series of battles in the 1650s. The Treaty of the Pyrenees (1659) recognised the French conquest and forced Spain to concede fortified sites along the Belgian side of the Low Country-French border. The treaty also provided for the marriage of Louis with the Spanish Infanta Maria-Theresa 'subject to the payment of a dowry of 500,000 ecus of gold'[8]—which Erlanger, in his biography of Louis XIV, notes Mazarin knew fully well that 'her father's pauperised kingdom would never be able to meet.'

When the Infanta's father Philip IV of Spain died in 1665 and his four-year-old son Charles II succeeded him, Louis XIV claimed part of the Spanish Low Countries in the name of his wife. The French lawyers contrived two grounds for this claim; one, Spain had not paid the dowry of Maria-Theresa; two, as a child of Philip IV's first marriage, she was entitled by Low Country custom to claim Flanders, Brabant, Luxembourg and Franche-Comté. Thus began the War of Devolution (1667–68), which started with French troops invading the southern Low Countries. Lille was the only place where the Spanish put up any serious resistance; French forces advanced to the Scheldt and even as far as Antwerp. Only after the United Provinces, Britain and Sweden joined in the Triple Alliance was Louis stopped. The Treaty of Aix-la-Chapelle that ended the war acknowledged Charles II as ruler of the southern Low Countries; as compensation, France retained several fortified sites, including Douai, Lille, Tournai, Kortrijk and Oudenaarde.

A few years later, in the Dutch War (1672–78), Louis, piqued at the Dutch for interfering in his invasion of the Spanish Netherlands a few years earlier, invaded the Low Countries, advancing along the Meuse and through Germany to capture Maastricht and Utrecht. The Dutch Republic, now led by William the Silent's great-grandson William of Orange—along with Britain, Germany, Spain and Denmark—checked Louis XIV's aggression and forced him to sign the Treaty of Nijmegen, which restored to the Spanish Low Countries some of the fortified towns France had secured earlier, but also confirmed the loss of much of the Artois to France.

In 1683, Louis XIV again invaded the southern Low Countries in the War of the Reunions (1683–84), demanding the return of land once part of France. Lynn notes, 'The treaties of Westphalia and Nijmegen provided the justification for the Reunions…';[9] the treaties, then as now, were notoriously vague, allowing the parties to accept the text more easily because they were accepting their own interpretation of what was agreed, thus generating grounds for subsequent conflicts. The Treaty of Ratisbon (now Regensburg) that ended this brief, brutal war granted France possession of the border towns of Chimay, Beaumont, Luxembourg and a few other border fortifications.

A few years later, in the Nine Years War (1688–97) the Dutch Republic, alarmed by the French threat to the Spanish Netherlands and consequently to its own southern border, supported Spain and enlisted Sweden and Savoy in the League of Augsburg against France. When the Glorious Revolution of 1688 installed William III, *stadhouder* of the Dutch Republic, and his wife Mary jointly in place of her father James II on the English throne, England joined the League against France. Despite French victories in 1690, 1692 and 1693, the League with William III's leadership rebuilt its army and in 1695 took Namur. With the League forces engaged at Namur, the French invaded Belgium with 70,000 troops, marched to Brussels, took positions on the Molenbeek Heights, and bombarded the city for thirty-six hours, destroying 4,000 houses and most of the Grand Place, but not the historic Hôtel de Ville that was just out of range of the French batteries. Subsequent League victories, though, enabled the allies to negotiate the Treaty of Rijswijk that returned to Spain the border fortresses granted to France under the earlier treaties.

In 1700, the death of the long-frail (in mind and body) Charles II of Spain without an heir ignited the War of Spanish Succession. In designating his heir, Charles chose between two grandnephews, one Bourbon and French and the other Habsburg and Austrian. Determined that the empire built up by his ancestors be preserved, his will left the the crown of Spain and its possessions to his grandnephew, Philip of Anjou, Louis XIV's second grandson, with the hope that this heir, with the aid of France, would be capable of holding the Spanish empire intact. The Habsburg Emperor refused to accept this pro-French settlement. The Spanish Low Countries Governor (the husband of a niece of Charles II), succumbing to French promises to appoint him ruler of the semi-autonomous Low Country protectorate, allowed French troops to enter the country unopposed. The former allies again combined forces, but not until 1706, with the Duke of Marlborough at the head of their forces, did they secure a victory, routing the French at Ramillies. While the Belgians initially welcomed Alliance troops, their harsh actions caused such indignation that several towns, including Ghent, opened their doors to the French. Finally, the Alliance defeated Louis XIV at Oudenaarde and Malplaquet.

Rivalries between the Dutch Republic and England delayed the peace negotiations until 1713, during which time the Dutch Republic administered Belgium. Meanwhile Archduke Charles, who had been disappointed in his hopes to become king of Spain, upon the death of his brother without heirs succeeded to the Austrian throne as Charles VI. In compensation for his loss of the Spanish throne, the Treaty of Utrecht (1713) awarded what had been the Spanish Low Countries to the new Austrian ruler. France restored Tournai and the portion of west Flanders beyond the Yser including Ieper to what was now the Austrian Low Countries, but France kept Artois and border portions of Flanders, Hainaut and Luxembourg. The Dutch secured the continued closure of the Scheldt and acquired 'barrier' forts at eight towns including Namur, Tournai and Ieper. The Dutch and British insistence on securing these forts arose from their concern regarding Austria's ability to defend its Low Country possessions. Success in securing these forts demonstrated the southern Low Countries' status as a pawn of European politics.

The War of Spanish Succession, like the War of Austrian Succession which followed, although ostensibly a dispute over royal succession was in reality fought over terriory not only in Europe but also elsewhere. For example, the War of Spanish succession was fought in colonial North America as King William's War and the War of Austrian Succession as King George's War.

The southern Low Countries, which the Treaty of Utrecht secured for Austria, were devastated by war, depressed economically and dismembered of most of what was once Walloon Flanders and was now largely French Flanders. The closure of the Scheldt and the presence of Dutch, French, German and Liège customs barriers suffocated southern Low Country trade. Despite its rich mineral resources and agricultural potential, the land continued to languish. Adrienne de Meuss described this era saying, 'Every form of novelty seemed fraught with peril. True wisdom consisted in holding on to what one already possessed and making the best of the situation in which one was vegetating.'[10] The land was hardly a promising candidate for social, industrial or political change that the Age of Enlightenment would introduce.

Map 12. The Austrian Low Countries, also called the Austrian Netherlands, continued to be divided by the prince-bishopric of Liège. Based on a map from Shepherd, William R., *Shepherd's Historical Atlas*, New York, Harper & Row, 1976.

8

THE AUSTRIAN HABSBURGS REACT TO THE ENLIGHTENMENT

1713–1794

Passing from the Dutch Republic to the Austrian Low Countries in the mid-1700's '*was like stepping from modern times into an earlier period.*'[1]

E. J. Kossman

Joseph II '*as a man has the greatest merit and talent; as a prince he will have continued erections and never be satisfied*'[2]

Charles Joseph, Prince of Ligne, a Belgian noble, distinguished soldier and diplomat, intimate friend and counsellor of the Emperor Joseph II, as reported by Andrew Wheatcroft

Charles VI, Maria-Theresa and Joseph II react differently to the Age of Enlightenment

The Treaty of Utrecht (1713) ended the War of Spanish Succession and gave the Spanish Low Countries to the Austrian branch of the Habsburgs. While the Austrian Emperors—Charles VI, Maria-Theresa, Joseph II, and then briefly Leopold II and Francis II—ruled with institutions similar to those of their Spanish cousins, the Supreme Council was now in Vienna, not Madrid, and the new masters had no experience in dealing with their new subjects; neither did they have any appreciation of their subjects' long struggle for self-governance. Austria took over a land, Kossman says, 'dominated by the traditional and seemingly well-established powers of nobility, clergy, and corporations. The economic and social strength of the nobles was unbroken. They possessed greater wealth than any other group except the clergy...'[3]

The return to peaceful conditions, except for the War of the Austrian Succession (1740–48), facilitated economic progress in the southern Low Countries. While the Austrian rulers did not deliver the country from the economic sanctions imposed by the treaty of Westphalia and confirmed by the Treaty of Utrecht, they encouraged development. The beginning of the industrial age began to turn Belgium, which had long been essentially agricultural, into an industrial power. The Age of Enlightenment facilitated the beginning of the transition from absolutism, where monarchs ruled with what was considered a God-given mandate, to representative government, in which rulers were at least nominally responsible to an electorate.

Joseph II's attempt to reform the governance of Belgium failed; and subsequently Austria lost its Low Country possessions. Inspired by the spirit of the Enlightenment, Joseph intended to improve governance by doing away with many of the traditional customs and privileges that had long encumbered local and central administration. But his style contrasted with that of his mother, who had urged him to be patient and accept local customs and ceremonies that were vital to maintaining the difficult balance between local pride and prerogatives, and sovereign rule and loyalty. Conscientious and dogmatic, Joseph was an enlightened despot whose myopic stubbornness doomed his progressive vision of what he considered best for his subjects. He strove vigorously to implement his vision but took inadequate account of the views of subjects. While impressed with the enlightened philosophy that emerged in the eighteenth century, he considered his autocratic role justified, because reforms introducing reasonable and just government should not be subjugated to popular whims and parochial wilfulness. Joseph fervently believed that he was right and that his vision justified his vigour. Just as Philip II in his efforts to save men's souls lost the northern Low Country provinces and bankrupted Spain, so Joseph II in his efforts to improve men's lives lost the southern Low Countries and undermined the Holy Roman Empire. The modernisation of the governance of the southern Low Countries had to wait until the French Revolution and Napoleon, whose ruthless imposition provided no opportunity for opposition.

Charles VI, Maria-Theresa and the War of the Austrian Succession

Charles VI faced problems of civic unrest in his new Low Country possessions as soon as he became emperor. The recent war, military occupation, continued closure of the Antwerp port, corollary unemployment and poverty increased the number of restless youth and the readiness of the guilds to provoke trouble. Having found old charters recording self-governing rights in the Grand Place ruins left by the earlier French attacks, Brussels' guilds opposed newly imposed regulations inconsistent with these traditional rights. Led by Frans Anneessens, the artisans refused to pay taxes and rioted. Since the only police force was the Burghers' guard, which was not sympathetic to Austrian rule, revolts broke out in Brussels, Antwerp and Mechelen. The situation quickly got out of control. The Austrian government, feeling obliged to exert its authority, arrested the leaders and decapitated Anneessens.

Despite minor setbacks, the economy gradually revived. To attract more Atlantic-bound traffic from Germany the government built an internal network of roads, which increased paved road mileage from thirty-seven in 1715 to 620 in 1789. The mining industry took off after 1725 when steam engines were first used to pump water and the installation of new equipment facilitated digging faster and deeper. Coal borings in northern and southern Belgium increased tonnage from 400 in 1762 to 21,000 in 1785. Modern commercial practices took root at the same time. Bruges and Ghent organised chambers of commerce in 1729. In Ghent, a commercial academy was established in 1781. Belgium, like England, had begun to industrialise, laying the ground for the nineteenth century when it became a leading economic power.

To develop its international trade, the government supported the founding in 1723 of the 'General Company of the Indies to trade in Bengal and the extreme East' (generally known as the 'Oostende Company'). Soon eleven ships sailed between Oostende and the east India and south China coasts. But England and the Dutch Republic forced the emperor to close the company down, as a condition for their acceptance of the Pragmatic Sanction, the intent of which was to ensure the succession of Charles' daughter to the Austrian throne. Dynastic concerns again superseded southern Low Country ones.

Despite the Pragmatic Sanction, the accession of Maria-Theresa upon Charles' death touched off the War of the Austrian Succession. The forces of Prussia, France, Spain and Poland united against her succession. Britain and the Netherlands joined to support Austria. A British landing in Oostende warded off a French invasion in the first year of the struggle. But in 1744, French troops once again invaded and attacked Brussels, which after a month's siege surrendered. Meanwhile the Dutch occupied Antwerp and several other cities. For two years warfare continued, during which the Austrian, British and Dutch forces sustained losses on land but won victories at sea. The Treaty of Aix-la-Chapelle that ended the war returned Belgium to Austrian rule. But while the Dutch regained their barrier fortresses on the Austrian Low Country side of the French-Low Country border, the futility of these forts in the recent war made these Dutch bases in the southern Low Countries even more detested than before. Their presence, along with the continued closure of the Scheldt and the termination of the Oostende Company, further entrenched the already bitter animosity towards the Dutch and antipathy to Austrian rule that had proved ineffective in protecting the Low Country borders.

Once the 1744–46 conflict ended, the Low Countries were uninterrupted by war, even escaping the turmoil of the Seven Years' War whose impact was felt as far away as Asia and North America. The British won from the French most of their Indian possessions and deprived France of Canada in what Americans call the French and Indian War. While Maria-Theresa was a firm believer in autocracy, she tempered this with recognition of the diversity of the states, races and constitutions comprising her empire. Under the southern Low Countries governor-general, Charles of Lorraine (the brother of Maria-Theresa's husband, the Emperor), respect for noble privileges and lavish entertainment obscured the lack of social, economic and political progress, leaving the land largely unprepared for the era of Enlightenment and reforms proposed by Joseph II.

Joseph II attempts to modernise

In 1780, upon the death of his mother Joseph II succeeded to the Austrian throne. He had been elected Emperor upon the death of his father in 1765. His education, which included the study of Voltaire and the Encyclopaedists, encouraged his zealous belief in the power of reason and the reasonableness of his own reasoning and thus could not appreciate that his philosophy-based rational plans could meet with what to him were irrational, parochial heated opposition.

Early in his reign, he made what was intended as an incognito visit to the Low Countries. Giving his name as Count Falkenstein, clad in a suit of coarse cloth, accompanied by a single aide, and staying at local inns, he made rapid visits to barracks, schools and factories. But he disappointed many, once his identity was known, by refusing invitations to receptions prepared in his honour. Joseph returned to Vienna convinced not only that reforms were necessary, but also that they would be accepted. While sufficiently progressive to appreciate and advocate reform, he was not sufficiently modern to recognise the importance of gaining sufficient popular support to implement them.

Joseph attempted to promote Low Country economic development. When the Dutch-British alliance broke down during the American Revolution, Joseph demolished the barrier forts and forced their Dutch garrisons to depart. In an effort to reopen the Scheldt, Joseph challenged the Dutch by sending a small brig downstream. When the Dutch fired upon it, to prevent the so-called 'Cauldron War' from breaking out, the French King mediated a treaty, which recognised the elimination of the barrier fortresses but maintained the Scheldt closure. Joseph's Low Country subjects perceived that his failure to gain more in the treaty indicated not only his incompetence but also a sell-out of local interests.

The country that Austria ruled from an indulgent distance 'represented for Joseph a potential asset but a practical liability.'[4] While its resources were sufficiently large that Joseph considered attempting to incorporate it into his monarchy, he recognised that the European powers would object strenuously. Instead in 1784, as Bryce notes, Joseph 'proposed to the Elector of Bavaria to give him the Austrian Netherlands except the citadels of Luxemburg and Limburg, with the title of King of Burgundy, in exchange for his Bavarian dominions, which Joseph was anxious to possess. The Elector consented, France (bribed by the offer of Luxemburg and Limburg) and Russia approved; the project was only baffled by the Frederick the Great promptly forming a League of Princes to preserve the integrity of German territories.'[5] Joseph's bid demonstrates that his dynastic interests trumped his Low Country ones.

Joseph's reform efforts included laying the basis for revising the fiscal and legal system, dissolving many monasteries, creating several schools and developing numerous factories; but he continually intervened and interfered at all points. By announcing steps that affected local customs and festivals as well as the church and government institutions, he lost the vital support of not only his officials, the nobles, and the clergy but also the people. He undermined his standing with the public by fixing only one day of the year for the celebration of all local festivities, a step that prevented villagers not only from celebrating their own cherished holidays, but also from taking part in the holidays in neighbouring towns. He alienated the clergy by issuing from 1781 to 1786 a series of edicts proclaiming freedom of worship for all, authorising mixed (Catholic and Protestant) marriages, suppressing clerical seminaries, closing 'useless' convents and monasteries and altering parish borders. He cancelled payments to public officials, 'pensions' that Blanning describes as thinly veiled bribes that had been 'a vital lubricant oiling the cogs of Habsburg influence ...'[6] He lost the support of the merchants as well as the nobles by proposing to replace the provinces (with their time-honoured borders and rights) with nine 'circles,' each under an emperor-appointed *intendant*, with new boundaries and to replace all courts (provincial, municipal, ecclesiastical, university and corporate) with sixty-four ordinary tribunals, two appeal courts and one court of revision. Perceiving these steps as abolishing privileges won and defended through centuries of struggle, the clergy, nobles and merchants united in their efforts to frustrate his plans. The combination of far-sighted grand plans and petty meddlesome direction brought his realms to a state of crisis. His heavy-handed approach to reform drove the southern Low Countries from hostility to revolt.

Joseph II's reform efforts provoked opposition not only in his Low Country possessions but also in other parts of his multi-national empire. Hungary was in open revolt and in other countries there were peasant uprisings. A sick Joseph II, isolated even by his ministers, rescinded his reforms in January 1790. One month later he died, to be succeeded by his already sick and dying brother, Leopold II, whose son Francis inherited the troubled situation in 1794. The Brabant revolution with its short-lived United Belgian States, the Liège revolution, and conflicts between French and Austrian forces (see the next chapter) interrupted Austrian rule. French invasions and the subsequent occupation and annexation ended it.

'Joseph II interfered with everything great and small ... isolation was his weakness,' says A. J .P. Taylor in assessing his rule. 'His revolutionary policy did not have the support of a revolutionary class. Napoleon came after a great revolution and could base his support on the French peasants.'[7]

Three centuries of Habsburg Low Country rule ended with the French occupation and incorporation into the French Empire. The French revolutionary government, and especially Napoleon, promulgated changes, which made those proposed earlier by Joseph II appear exceedingly modest.

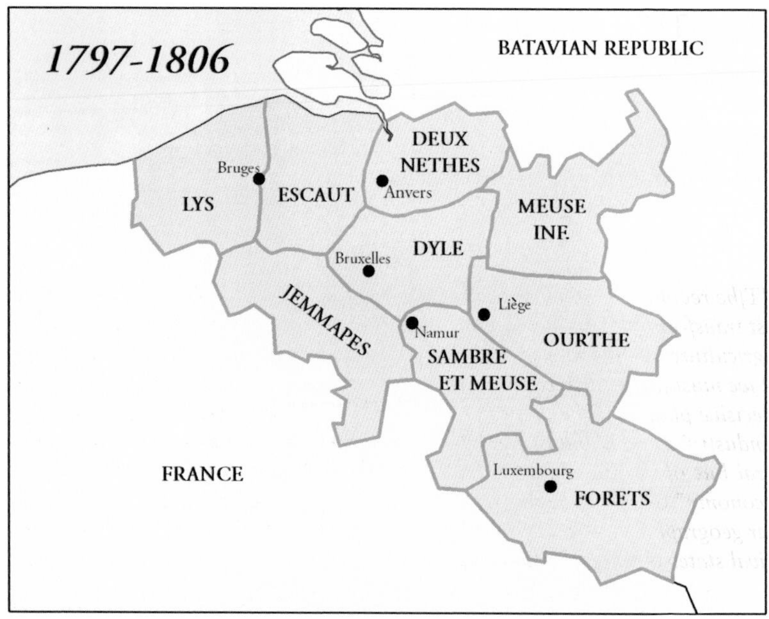

Map 13. The southern Low Countries under French rule as reorganised in 1797 into nine 'departments' with names and boundaries that differed significantly from those of the old provinces. Based on a map in Duby, Georges, *Atlas Historique*, Paris, Larousse, 1987.

9

TWO REVOLTS, FRENCH OCCUPATION AND UNION WITH THE DUTCH

1789–1830

'[T]he revolution which broke out between 1789 and 1848… forms the greatest transformation in human history since the remote times when man invented agriculture and metallurgy, writing, the city and the state … But in considering it we must distinguish carefully between its long-range results and its early and decisive phase … The great revolution of 1789–1848 was the triumph not of 'industry' as such, but of capitalist *industry; not of liberty and equality in general but of* middle class *or 'bourgeois' liberal society; not of "the modern economy" or "the modern state," but of the economies and states in a particular geographical region of the world …whose centre was the neighbouring and rival states of Great Britain and France.'*[1]

Eric Hobsbawm

The French Revolution, Napoleon and William I end entrenched practises and privileges

A 'combination of many factors and forces—the growth of literacy, the increase in the number and circulation of journals, the rise in population and incomes, the spread of technology and industry, the diffusion of competing ideas—and, not least, by the actions of great men,'[2] writes Paul Johnson, drove the Age of Revolution. The French political and social revolutions and the English industrial and political revolutions prodded the world through a decisive period. Wedged as it was between Britain and France, Belgium incurred revolts in 1789–91 and 1830–31. The combination of the political and industrial revolutions set in motion trends that later extended the suffrage to the middle class and even later to the working class as well.

To appreciate the dramatic impact of this revolutionary age, compare the early nineteenth with the late twentieth century life-styles. In the early nineteenth century, land owning served as the primary basis for wealth and field-labour, the almost universal occupation. Transport by horse and boat was slow, expensive and limited to the wealthy: almost everyone walked. Only a few travelled anywhere—or thought about anything—beyond their local communities. In 1800, only about twenty European cities had more than 100,000 inhabitants: one was Brussels. This age of successive, symbiotic revolutions spurred the emergence of rapid transport and instant communication, the shift from physical labour to mechanical power, the move from farms to villages and cities and from rural unskilled to urban skilled labour.

In a few tumultuous decades, the industrial revolution hastened industrial development in Belgium, transforming the country from a highly socially stratified, rural economy into an urban one with a growing entrepreneurial and professional class. The age of revolutions radically changed the way people lived, worked and thought—and how states could and should be governed, and how people could and should participate in their governing. The revolts against Austria, the French invasion and occupation, the French Revolutionary Directorate's and Napoleon's discarding of outdated feudal traditions and the Congress of Vienna's merger of Belgium with the Netherlands provided the backdrop for the successful Belgian revolution of 1830–31. While for centuries merchants and artisans had exercised more political power in Belgium than in most other parts of Europe, those who owned the land continued to play a significant role in the political and economic scene while those who worked the land continued to be ignored.

The short-lived United Belgian States

The ideas and spirit underlying the 1789 French Revolution directly inspired two revolts in what is now Belgium. One began in Brabant and attracted the support of other Austrian Low Country provinces. The second occurred in the prince-bishopric of Liège. The failure of both revolts led the Liège and Brabant leaders to combine their efforts and encourage French forces to help free Belgium from Austria. The dual revolution, industrial and political, nurtured an expanding middle class that later transformed social as well as economic and political life.

The Brabant revolt began when Jean François Vonck and Hendrik Van der Noot, influenced by the revolutionary mood in France, reacted to Joseph II's latest reform edicts by convincing the States of Brabant to refuse payment of taxes. The Emperor did suspend his most recent decrees, but he sent an envoy with dictatorial powers and armed troops to enforce tax collection. He continued to suppress clerical seminaries and close 'useless' convents and seminaries, steps that led to riots in Leuven, Mechelen and Antwerp. When the States of Brabant again threatened to withhold taxes, the Emperor dissolved it and aimed his guns at the Grand Place in Brussels. By the summer of 1789, widespread opposition to Austrian rule had mounted. Vonck and Van der Noot gathered 3,000 volunteers on the Dutch side of the Austrian Low Countries border, crossed the frontier and defeated a small Austrian force at Turnhout. The victory, followed by the Austrian retreat, led to popular uprisings throughout the country. The Austrian general, deserted by his troops, fled to Luxembourg, the only Low Country town that remained loyal to Austria.

Van der Noot and Vonck triumphantly entered Brussels and called a meeting of representatives of the provincial governments comprising the Austrian Low Countries. Except for Luxembourg, they formed a government called the *Etats Belgiques Unis* (United Belgian States), thus adopting the name Caesar had given this land, and one that distinguished it from its northern Dutch neighbour. The representatives developed a constitution providing for a confederation with a congress given a limited role in defence, foreign policy and commercial affairs, one that resembled the weak American Articles of Confederation ratified in 1781 more than the federal constitution adopted in 1787. While the French Revolution had inspired the Brabant revolt, it did not permeate the spirit that shaped the governance of the short-lived United Belgian States. The early Belgian constitution, written mainly by upper class Brabanters and Flemings who deliberated and wrote their reports in French, reflected and preserved the local prerogatives of the provincial States, the nobles and the clergy, and included no proclamation of the 'rights of man'.

When Leopold II succeeded his brother in 1790, he reopened negotiations with the Belgians, promising a complete amnesty, the suppression of reforms and the nomination of only Belgians to top posts. When the Netherlands, Prussia and Britain (the latter only after abandoning, along with Russia, its war against the Ottoman Empire) supported the Emperor, the Austrian army had no difficulty reoccupying the country. The lack of support from the major powers doomed the short-lived Brabant-led confederation.

The Liège revolt

Unlike the other southern Low Country principalities, the prince-bishopric of Liège, while part of the Holy Roman Empire, was not a personal fief of the Habsburgs. While the Austrian Low Countries under Charles VI, Maria-Theresa and Joseph II experienced only limited economic progress, the prince-bishopric of Liège was prosperous. The presence of liberal nobles and industrial magnates, coupled with less restrictive medieval guild and corporate regulations than those that long affected the Austrian Low Country provinces, had spurred industrial development. In the prince-bishopric of Liège and particularly in Verviers (a new city founded as recently as 1651) a deluge of new inventions, ideas and technical progress, combined with the area's natural resources, had put their factories, workshops and collieries in the first rank of the emerging industrial revolution.

In the 1780s the French revolutionary spirit spread to the prince-bishopric. From 1784 to 1789, Liège frequently welcomed French revolutionaries such as Mirabeau. Its residents followed with interest the events leading to the fall of the Bastille. A movement was organised that proclaimed the people's sovereignty and indicated willingness to follow the example of the Paris insurgents. In August 1789, shortly after the fall of the Bastille, when the prince-bishop closed a Spa gambling hall, workingmen viewed this action as an intrusion upon the 'rights of man'. They stormed the Liège town hall, took control of the city and forced the prince-bishop to recognise the revolution. To avoid Austria sending troops to counter the revolt, the Liège revolutionaries asked the Prussian king to send troops and he did. For nearly two years, the Austrian Emperor dallied with regard to the deteriorating situation in Liège. When the British, Dutch and Prussian governments withdrew their support of Liège at the same time as they stopped support for the Brabant revolt, the Prussian troops returned home and Austrian forces reoccupied the prince-bishopric without opposition.

The collapse of the Brabant and Liège revolts prompted the leaders of both revolutions to work together. Impeding their cooperation was the fact that for almost a thousand years the prince-bishopric had maintained a separate identity from the rest of the Low Countries. The repeated subjection and brutal repression exacted by the Burgundian dukes had left bitter memories. Different ideals, traditions and contrasting memories led each side to detest one another. The ideological differences between the more progressive Liège and more traditional Brabant leaders added to the friction.

Driven by their revolutionary spirit and recognition of a common goal, the revolutionaries from both sections of the southern Low Countries united in viewing France as their only prospect for driving the Austrians out. By 1791, Brabant and Liège refugees had fled to France and begun forming themselves into armed bands. When the Austrian government took action against the bands on the frontiers, the refugees met in Paris and formed the Committee of United Belgians and Liégeois, a foreshadowing of the merger of Liège into modern Belgium. In April 1792, the committee called for a war of Belgian independence and developed a proposal for a constitution. Its anti-Austrian propaganda helped sway French opinion. Whereas in the days of Louis XIV those in the southern Low Countries had opposed French aggression, now the Belgians asked for and supported a French invasion as an act of liberation. Once again, they collaborated with one European power to liberate themselves from another, and once again, they succeeded only in trading one foreign yoke for another.

The French Revolution enforces centralisation and uniformity

Initially the French revolutionary government had little interest in intervening in the southern Low Countries, but with Belgian encouragement, French forces invaded the land. In the fluctuating military successes in the 1790s neither side gained a decisive advantage. While Austrian imperial troops repulsed the first attacks, a major French victory at Genappes (November 1792) opened Belgium to the French army. Within a week Brussels had fallen, within a month most of Belgium had followed suit. The French commander declared that his soldiers were coming as friends and allies. Liège, Mons, Brussels, Ghent and Bruges received him so joyfully that he failed to recognise how superficial the welcome was. Even his efforts to organise elections encountered opposition. When the Austro-Prussian war machine finally did start to move early in August, at first it carried all before it. When Austria defeated the French at Neerwinden (March 1793), Austria again occupied Belgium.

The ensuing fourteen months (1793–94) of Austrian rule coincided with the period of Robespierre's ascendancy in France. Belgians thus generally escaped the ravages of the Reign of Terror, which sent many French priests and aristocrats to the scaffold or into exile. Most of those who had fled Belgium eventually returned. There was relatively little long-term emigration or confiscation of property of the former governing classes. Some of the elite not only kept their estates but also increased their fortunes—by buying church properties at cut-rate prices—and thus increased their pro-property conservative perspective. The sale of church land at low prices stimulated the growth of a merchant and industrialist class and spurred the economy.

Threatened by the reaction of the conservative powers to their revolution and the humiliation of their king, the French mobilised their economy with a *levée en masse*. In 1794 at Fleurus the French beat Austria, whose leaders faced with other French attacks in other parts of Europe were losing the will to defend their peripheral Low Country possessions. The French reoccupied Belgium and then invaded the Netherlands. Arbitrary government and widespread poverty accompanied the military occupation. Despite protests, in October 1795 France annexed the Low Country provinces including Liège, using the rationale that France needed to extend its borders to what it had long considered its 'natural' frontiers—thus to the Rhine.

The French applied throughout Belgium the French legal system, changed street names, enforced the Republican calendar and replaced religious festivals with secular events. More significantly, they reorganised Belgian internal administration as they had already organised France, replacing the old provinces with nine *départements* (administrative divisions whose geographic boundaries differed from the old provinces and whose new names reflected landscape features). The reforms swept away long-entrenched distinctive parochial traditions, abolished internal tolls and customs duties, terminated many traditional aristocratic privileges and hereditary rights, introduced population registers, authorised divorce and introduced compulsory education. The French imposed these comprehensive changes so rapidly that there was little opportunity for discussion, or opportunity for piecemeal modification or resistance.

In 1796, the French government aroused the ire of the Roman Catholic clergy and their communicants by abolishing most religious orders, shutting down monasteries, closing churches and confiscating their property. In 1798, the government required all priests to pledge an 'oath of hatred' against the royalty; most refused. Even in this time of 'closure' of religious institutions, however, the church continued to celebrate mass and wield influence, albeit clandestinely.

Not until 1801, when France signed a concordat with the Holy See, did Catholicism regain its status as a state church. To support its many military campaigns throughout Europe, the French revolutionary government raised tax levies six fold. In 1798, the French imposition of military conscription, coming on top of the anticlerical and tax measures, triggered the Peasants' Revolt that began in Flanders and soon spread to Brabant. France quickly suppressed these disturbances.

The French government, says Kossman, 'quite unlike the Austrian, had a purposeful linguistic policy and just as it combated the dialects of French proper so it drove Dutch, which until 1795 was used in local administration ... out of public life.'[3] French was the language of governance and instruction in universities and secondary schools. Not only did everyone in Wallonia speak French, or a Walloon variation of it, so did the patrician classes in northern Belgium, where the working class spoke one of the Flemish dialects of Dutch.

Napoleon systematises Belgian governance

By *coup d'état* in 1799, Napoleon made himself First Consul, then in 1804 Emperor. His victories throughout Europe led to the crushing December defeat of the Austrian and Russian forces at Austerlitz. The treaty which Napoleon imposed on Austria following this defeat humiliated the Habsburg Empire by excluding its presence from western Germany and the Low Countries. Napoleon then forced the abolition of scores of minor German principalities. Under Napoleon, sixteen of the larger German states absorbed their smaller neighbours in this maze of long entrenched principalities, formed the Confederation of the Rhine with the French ruler as its 'protector' and supported the Napoleonic campaigns. Napoleon declared defunct the 1,000 year-old Charlemagne-created empire, which the Habsburgs had ruled as its elected head—with few interruptions—for six centuries. In 1806, the last Holy Roman Emperor formally abdicated this title, substituting the title of Austrian emperor.

The Treaties of Lunéville and Amiens secured for Napoleon Austrian and British recognition of the incorporation of the southern Low Countries as a 'permanent part of France'. Reacting to the confusion and inefficiency under the Directorate that had inspired his coup, Napoleon centralised the political system. His reforms supplanted the last remaining vestiges of feudal customs, noble privileges and disparate laws affecting governance. Throughout his empire, he developed a pyramid of authority directly responsible to him, appointing in each *département* a prefect with unrivalled local power and prestige (*un petit empereur*), in each arrondissement a sub-prefect and in each commune a mayor. The entrenched bishops, abbots and nobles could no longer interfere with the administration of the realm. He introduced a system of direct and indirect taxes. The Napoleonic Code which he introduced has survived as the basis of modern European jurisprudence. Given Napoleon's preoccupation with his endless wars, his civil administration achievements were remarkable. As with Charlemagne and Charles V his military achievements have overshadowed his civil accomplishments, whose impact remains to this day.

In the southern Low Countries Napoleon promoted industry and the use of French. In Brussels, he demonstrated his ecumenism by setting aside the *Eglise de Musée* (which now adjoins the Royal Library and is often called the Chapelle Royale) for Protestant worship. Napoleonic rule adversely affected intellectual and artistic life as well as general morale throughout the southern Low Countries. When the victorious allied armies entered Belgium after the victory at Leipzig (October 1813), the Belgians welcomed them. But the enthusiasm waned when in August 1814 Belgium came under the administration of the Dutch leader, William of Orange, a seventh generation descendant of William the Silent.

After the Allies entered Paris and Napoleon abdicated in April 1814, the Allies exiled him to the island of Elba. The first Treaty of Paris placed Louis XVIII, the oldest surviving brother of Louis XVI, on the French throne. To negotiate the complexity of post-war issues, the Allies held a Congress at Vienna, whose actions the Prince de Ligne described as: 'Le Congrès danse, mais ne marche pas.' While the powers dithered in long protracted, parties-abundant, decision-delaying sessions and struggled to carve up Europe and ensure a peace, Napoleon escaped from Elba. Within 100 days of his lonely landing at Antibes on 1 March, Napoleon won over Marshal Ney, who had been sent to 'bring him back in a cage', and entered Paris in triumph. Louis XVIII fled. Napoleon recruited an army and moved north to attack the forces of the Allied coalition, which included the British, Dutch and German troops under the command of the Duke of Wellington. On 16 June at Ligny, Napoleon defeated the Prussians commanded by the seventy-two-year-old Field Marshal Gebhard Blucher who nevertheless retreated with some of his troops in good order. In the early morning of 18 June, Napoleon's forces attacked the British and their allied forces south of Waterloo. Led by Wellington, the Allied forces resisted the repeated French charges in a day of slaughter. The late arrival of Blucher's Prussian cavalry, having escaped the French at Ligny, enabled the Allied forces to win the day.

Having defeated Napoleon again, the allies resumed deliberations regarding France's fate and Europe's future. The 'Hundred Days' led the allies—principally Britain, Russia, Austria and Prussia—to revise the earlier peace settlement in a second Treaty of Paris. With the aim of insuring against another French invasion, Belgium was merged with the Netherlands to constitute a buffer state. Prussia gained scattered non-contiguous possessions in western Germany; so its western half extended on both sides of the Rhine from Cleves to Koblenz, bordering the united Netherlands and thus strengthening Prussia and, ostensibly, its ability to protect the Low Countries from another French invasion. The treaty shifted Prussia's interest to the west, with fateful consequences for its western neighbours in the early twentieth century. In 1818, the major powers added France to the Concert of Europe that was intended to guarantee continental peace and stability.

The Congress of Vienna creates the United Kingdom of the Netherlands—merging Belgium with the Netherlands

The Spanish Low Countries and the United Provinces, separated since the Dutch gained their independence, shared the fate of French annexation during the Napoleonic Wars. After the French revolutionary forces had overrun and occupied the Austrian Netherlands, they also invaded the United Provinces and forced its leader, the Prince of Orange, into exile. With the cooperation of some anti-Orange leaders, the French created the Batavian Republic as a client state. In 1805, Napoleon converted the republic into the Kingdom of Holland with his brother Louis as King; then in 1810 he annexed the country to France as he had Belgium earlier. When the Allies forced France to abandon the Low Countries, Zamoyski notes, the British foreign minister Castlereagh encouraged the Prince of Orange to occupy Belgium 'and discreetly extend his rule over it. Having been assured by the Prince that the Belgians would welcome Dutch rule, Castlereagh … foresaw no problems.'[4]

A major concern of Castlereagh at the Congress of Vienna (1814–15) was the creation of a strong Low Countries buffer state across the channel from Britain. The 300-year-old British fear of France, a concern driven by the colossal cost of the campaigns it had just waged in America, Asia and Europe, and the desire to secure access to coastal ports led him to convince his colleagues at the Congress to unite Belgium with the Dutch Republic to form a united Kingdom of the Netherlands, capable of defending itself against France.

By this treaty, the allied powers pleased almost everyone. England kept France away from the coast opposite its southeast corner. Prussia gained territory along the Rhine. Austria and Russia were happy to have a buffer state checking the ambitions of France and Prussia, and William of Orange became a king—William I of the new Kingdom of the Netherlands, that united the Low Countries. In theory, fusing these two lands made sense. They shared much history. Combining the two lands created a sufficiently large buffer country capable of defending itself. The new constitution provided for two capitals, Brussels and The Hague, and a legislature with equal representation for each part.

Who complained? The Belgians did. They resented the shotgun marriage. Despite their long demonstrated desire for independence, the Allies had not even consulted them. For two centuries, fuelled by totally different experiences from the Dutch, Belgians had developed a distinct sense of collective community and identity and had drifted further and further apart from them in character, habits, ideas and more significantly in religion. The animosity stemming from the atrocities committed in the war that split the Low Countries, the continued closure of the Scheldt, the collapse of Antwerp as a port and other deprivations had fuelled hostility towards their northern neighbour, an animosity comparable to the antagonism France had provoked earlier by its repeated interventions and invasions. The Dutch regarded Belgium as an annexed territory, awarded as a reward for losses sustained in the recent wars. While the Belgians outnumbered the Dutch three million to two million, each had the same number in the united country's Estates-General, which was largely advisory. Only one member of the seven-man cabinet was Belgian and the overwhelming majority of senior officials were Dutch. Many Belgians did not want to be absorbed into a country headed by an arrogant, Protestant king.

William I was a hardworking, narrow-minded man whose role model was Frederick the Great, the Prussian 'benevolent despot' who had significantly expanded his kingdom. William, convinced he had a mandate from the European powers to assure the fusion of the Belgians and Dutch, was confidant these powers would back him if problems arose. The Dutch monarch disdained the British parliamentary system and escalated existing animosities with his dictatorial obstinacy. Like Joseph II, he focused on administrative, financial and economic development issues with a single-minded vision. William was so sure that he was right that he took little advice and made little effort to gain the support of his Belgian subjects who regarded him as a foreigner. William I staffed the civil service principally with those speaking 'proper Dutch', that is the Dutch spoken north of the Rhine, not one of the often mutually incomprehensible Flemish dialects of Dutch. He insisted that Belgians conduct all government business in 'proper Dutch'. These actions alienated the Flemish-speakers as well as the French-speaking Walloons and the French-speaking elite in Ghent, Antwerp and Brussels.

William incurred the hostility of both the conservative and the less conservative anti-clerical Catholics. He alienated the anti-clericals by censoring and closing journals and prosecuting a writer who attacked government policy. He antagonised the conservative Catholics by imposing state control over education, closing seminaries, placing the Catholic University of Louvain under state control, founding two new state-controlled secular universities (at Ghent in 1816 and Liège in 1817) and setting up state primary and secondary schools throughout the land. To counter these moves, especially threatening because a Protestant king had undertaken them, the Catholic hierarchy authorised the development of parish schools to challenge the state ones. A diplomat noted: 'The Belgian hates the Dutchman; the Dutchman despises the Belgian and considers himself greatly the superior.'

William's industrial promotion efforts, though, did prove helpful. He removed the Scheldt embargo, thus allowing Antwerp to double its tonnage from 1818 to 1829. He supported the construction of new canals and the creation of banks, including the Société Générale. He partnered with John Cockerill, the son of the English inventor and manufacturer William Cockerill, in constructing at Verviers the first wool carding and spinning machines in continental Europe and a factory at Liège to manufacture these machines. Their partnership built the biggest steelworks on the continent at Seraing near Liège. He invested heavily in a new state company, the *Nederlandsche Handelsmaatshappij* that revived the East Indies trade.

To support these efforts he helped created a credit system to fund new industries, thus ensuring the investment necessary for Belgium's progress. The mining and export of coal were critical to the development process. The effort to assure adequate capital and cash flow kept wage levels low. These steps helped make Belgium the first country on the continent to experience the Industrial Revolution. Dutch trading prowess, Belgian agricultural and industrial potential, and the market opportunities provided by the Netherlands overseas possessions improved Belgium's economy, so that it ranked first on the continent and second to England as an economic power. Nevertheless, from 1828 an economic downturn led to unemployment and unrest that contributed to the 1830 uprising, the beginning of the events leading to Belgian independence.

The humiliating and traumatic experiences of the Belgians under French occupation, Blanning observes, 'ensured that they would not succumb meekly to rule by the Dutch after 1815.'[5] The long yearning of Belgians, at least of many Belgians, for freedom from foreign rule was about to be realised, helped not only by widespread antipathy to King William's rule but also by his diffident and dithering efforts to cope with the early stages of the Belgian revolt. The irony of Castlereagh's hard-fought-for creation of a buffer state to defend against the French was that in fifteen years Belgium won its independence, and it was the Germans, rather than the French, who became the major threat to European peace.

Clear datelines do not mark history. Els Witte points out: 'Even the 1830 revolution, an obvious point of departure, was not the clear-cut watershed to mark the birth of a nation. It is beyond doubt though that the revolutionary days of September and October 1830 marked a turning point in the relations between the North and the South of the United

Kingdom of the Netherlands. They were proof that the policy of assimilation imposed by King William I was a failure, even though the causes of this political debacle by far preceded these heady autumn days. It made one thing painstakingly clear: the historic, social and cultural development in the North and South differed so much that it made integration, or even absorption of the South by the North impossible.'[6]

The Royal Palace, working headquarters of the Belgian monarch (© Franky De Meyer, istockphoto.com).

Belgium

While foreign rulers had nurtured common institutions of governance for the southern Low Countries, resentment of foreign rule and aggression had fostered a collective community identity—and a yearning for independence. The nineteenth century world in which Belgium won its independence and developed its nation-state differed dramatically from the one existing a few decades earlier. The Age of Enlightenment spawned ideas upon which the Age of Revolution grew. Political, industrial and social movements transformed the governance of Europe. Over the course of the nineteenth and twentieth centuries three critical, concomitant phenomena fuelled this transmutation: a significantly increasing electorate; a rising sense of national consciousness; and the growth of nation-state institutions. All, or almost all adults, gained the right to vote, eroding the power of the long dominant elite. Enhanced transport, travel, trade, literacy and communication facilitated social and economic community interaction and cultivated a sense of national community. The expanding electorate and rising sense of national community spurred the growth of the nation-state, whose nation-building efforts included promoting a common language, nurturing a shared history (and heroes and myths) and constructing transport and social systems, as well as the strong centralised bureaucracies and revenues to support these efforts.

Proximity to the French socio-political and the British industrial revolutions, and the rejection of the merger with the Netherlands, propelled the growth of Belgian political, economic and social life. New mines, mills and railways promoted prosperity and provided the setting in which independent Belgium evolved in the nineteenth century. Not until the rise of the Flemish movement was the French-speaking elite's political dominance challenged. It was the Francophone propertied, professional class that organised the government. They established one that reflected their common interests. The elite wrote the constitution in French, limited voting to less than one per cent of the population and prescribed French as the language for parliamentary and judicial affairs. As in other countries, the Belgian propertied class dominated public affairs, not doubting that what was good for their interests was what was best for the country. Today's trickle-down theory is a modern incarnation of this mindset.

Hardly considered were the interests of the workers, especially the Flemish-speakers. Despite continuing discrimination and repeated agitation throughout the nineteenth and early twentieth centuries, the Belgian Francophone elite passed few laws addressing language discrimination issues and gave only lip service to the few enacted. For most of the nineteenth century, the principal political battles were over the extent of church control of education. Not until the end of World War II did successive governments directly confront the language issue. Not until the late nineteenth and early twentieth century did the pressure for expanding voting rights affect Belgian politics. Initially a coalition Unionist grouping governed the country, and, by the latter part of the nineteenth century a two-party system emerged. By the end of the century a third party developed. These changes profoundly affected cabinet formation. Not until the latter part of the twentieth century did the language issue develop sufficient momentum to divide parties along language lines, make politics more frenetic and frustrating and fracture the Belgian polity.

How, despite the fact that so many Belgians spoke Flemish, did the upper-class French-speaking leaders of independent Belgium continue to ignore Flemish and worker interests for so many decades? The Francophone propertied elite remained dominant until the increase in literacy, the growth of the middle class and the gradual extension of the suffrage abetted not only the civic-mindedness of what has been the underclass but also the growth of language driven sectionalism that fundamentally altered the political priorities of nineteenth and early twentieth century Belgium.

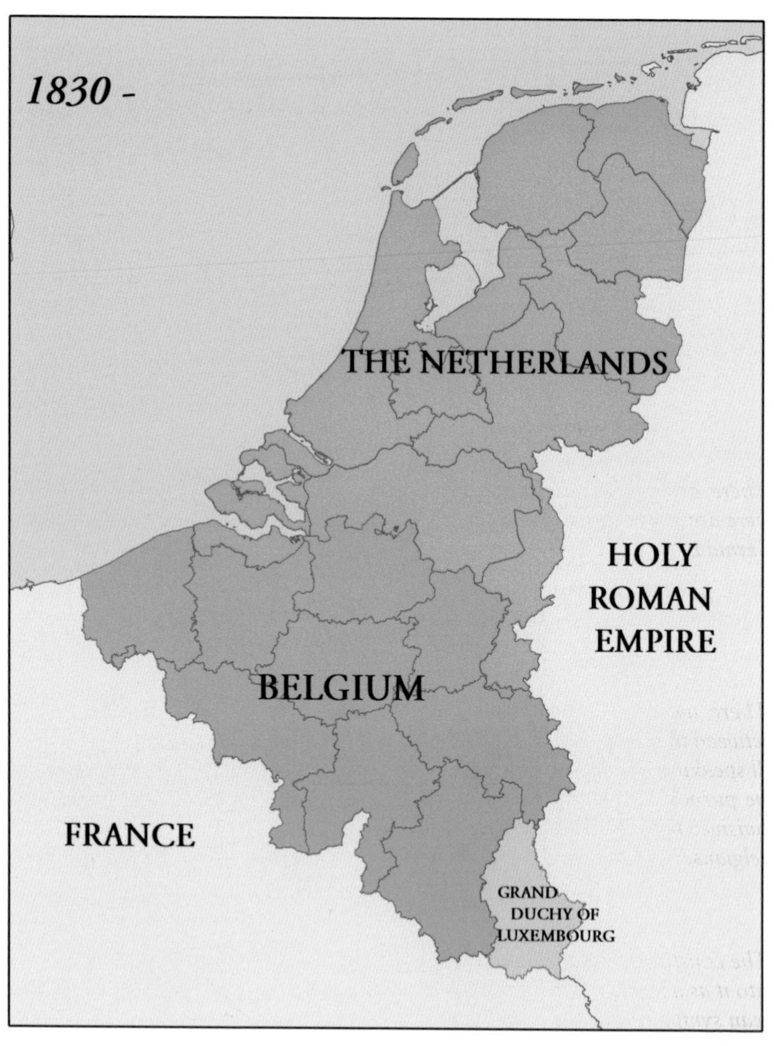

Map 14. The Kingdom of Belgium, the Kingdom of the Netherlands and the Grand Duchy of Luxembourg after Belgium won its independence.

10

A FRANCOPHONE ELITE WINS BELGIUM ITS INDEPENDENCE

1830–1865

'There are no Belgians, there never have been, and there never will be: there are Frenchmen, Flemings or Dutchmen (which is the same thing) and Germans'[1]

Charles Maurice de Talleyrand, the French Foreign Minister, whose comment in 1830 stemmed from centuries-long French claims to at least part, if not all, of Belgium.

'There was less opposition between the Flemish and the Walloons than between the Catholics and the liberals. All belonged to the same social milieu, all speaking the same language, French, all devoted to the same cause, and for the purpose of creating a common nationality, all careful to avoid anything divisive; the members of the assembly wanted only to be and were only Belgians.'[2]

Henri Pirenne, describing the first Belgian National Congress

'The constitution was essentially republican. The monarchy had been written into it as a symbol and an ornament, simply for the purpose of winning European sympathy for the young state; and it had been conceived in such a manner that the monarch had no real powers ... However, there was one important article in the constitution that had not been fully appreciated, and which enabled Leopold to re-establish his authority: the article providing that the sovereign should be head of the army ... Directly after his accession Leopold assumed the role of generalissimo and thus exercised real power.'[3]

Adrien de Meeus

Leopold I, the establishment of a state and the emergence of a two-party system

Belgium finally gained its independence in 1830–31, but only with luck and pluck. Following an outbreak by restless youth, more moderate and established citizens asserted control and asked for an autonomous administration. While the Dutch King temporised, frustrated Belgian leaders proclaimed their country's independence, wrote a constitution, organised a government and secured Leopold of Saxe-Coburg-Gotha as their king.

Belgium's revolt was successful—despite the opposition of most of the great powers, who had merged Belgium and the Netherlands at the Congress of Vienna in 1815. The support of Britain and uprisings in Russia, Austria and Prussia played a vital part in achieving this aim. Despite the fact that the Great Powers created Belgium and most of them opposed Belgian efforts to secure independence, modern separatists claim that Belgium is an artificial state cobbled together by the great powers. With the achievement of independence, Belgium began the complex process of state building. The minute Francophone elite proceeded to develop public institutions and transform the country into an industrial power. Belgium's government, inspired with its newfound national independence and consistent with nation-building efforts in other European countries, organised an army, civil service and diplomatic corps. A Unionist coalition initially formed the government, but within a few years the anti-clerical liberals formed a separate party. While almost all Belgians were at least nominal Catholics, those who were concerned about the extent of church control of schools formed an anti-clerical Liberal faction that brought them into conflict with the more clerical-supportive Catholics. While the Liberals challenged the Catholics in the 1850s regarding the Church's dominance of education, not until the 1870s did the issue erupt politically. Until the mid-twentieth century it was the principal *raison d'être* of the Liberals. Catholics and Liberals dominated Belgian politics until challenged by the Workers' Party in the twentieth century. The Enlightenment and the Age of Revolutions had sown the seeds that expanded voting rights, promoted popular (or populist) nationalism and spurred the Flemish movement from the late nineteenth century.

Théâtre de la Monnaie, built on the site of a former mint, is where the outbreak occurred that led to the revolution winning Belgium its independence (© Michael Palis, istockphoto.com).

The Belgian Revolution begins

On 25 August, one month after the July 1830 revolution in France, Brussels planned to honour King William I of the united Netherlands with a festival. While the authorities cancelled the fireworks for fear of incidents, they proceeded with an event scheduled at the Théâtre de la Monnaie. The performance was Daniel Auber's opera *La Muette de Portici*, which recounts the story of a fisherman during the Neapolitan revolt against Philip IV of Spain in the mid-seventeenth century. Its highlight, the Amour Sacré de la Patrie (Sacred Love of Country) aria, 'Amour sacré de la patrie, rends-nous l'audace et la fierté, à mon pays je dois la vie, il me devra sa liberté' (Sacred love of my country, give us courage and pride, my country gave me life, I will give it freedom)—roused those attending the performance. The fervour quickly spread to many gathered outside the theatre to hear fragments of the opera. Many restless youth began to demonstrate. As their activities spread, they burned homes and ransacked shops. The burgomaster's absence compounded the next day's confusion. The Brussels garrison, overwhelmed and with no orders, retreated to their barracks. Rioters wandered at will through the city. With the situation out of control, leaders from the propertied class formed a committee to regain order. As news of the events spread, committees of civic leaders were organised in Liège, Verviers, Huy, Leuven, and Namur as well as Brussels.

King William reacted to the outbreak by sending his son, Prince Frederick, to Brussels with 6,000 men. The prince, warned before reaching Brussels that barricades were set up at key street intersections, did not march his troops into the city. Instead he went ahead to appraise the situation. Upon entering the city, the prince met an angry and armed mob. Alarmed, he withdrew with a promise to plead the rebel cause with his father; an act that appeared to legitimise the revolt. Volunteers began to pour in from all over the country and from as far as Poland to aid the cause.

A newly formed committee of civic leaders initially asked not for independence but for autonomy within a federation; but William stalled, promising to assemble and consult with the parliament of the united country. The departure of the Belgian deputies for the parliament in early September left the field clear for new leaders to assert themselves. Prominent among the emergent leaders was Charles Rogier, who had earlier founded a journal promoting Belgian nationalism. In September, he arrived in Brussels with 300 armed volunteers from Liège and quickly asserted leadership, seizing control of the ministries and transforming the resistance into a national movement.

King William, preoccupied with the marriage of his daughter, underestimated the gravity of the situation. He temporised by appearing to accept the idea of limited autonomy. By doing so he effectively postponed confronting the issue, for to grant limited autonomy required an election and thus the preparation of new electoral registers. More important, allowing limited autonomy required the consent of the guarantor powers. With his troops at the gates of Brussels, disturbances occurring in Brussels, Louvain, Liège and Verviers and many of the wealthier families either supporting him or keeping clear of the conflict, the autocratic king dithered. Thinking he could avoid compromise, he set aside the petitions of those moderates who hoped to secure only limited autonomy. Meanwhile, the parliament voted in favour of limited autonomy by the enormous majority of 81 votes to 19, with many Dutch delegates supporting the Belgian ones in passing the motion. In late September, though, many less moderate insurgents lost patience and seized the Brussels town hall. Anarchy followed.

Prince Frederick, following events closely through spies, announced that he would march into the city the next day and many Brussels residents fled. On the morning of 23 September, Netherland forces entered Brussels with their bands playing the overture to *La Muette de Portici*, the melody that had triggered the August revolt. Expecting no trouble, the troops marched down the Rue Royale. Despite snipers unexpectedly shooting from rooftops, the troops continued their advance. If the Dutch had taken the Royal Palace (at the south end of the Park Royale), they would have controlled the upper town and thus the whole capital, but upon reaching the north end of the Park Royale, the troops took cover before re-forming and continuing the attack. That evening, upon recognising that snipers on rooftops threatened his troops, the commander ordered a retreat under the cover of darkness. Not until morning did insurgent scouts discover that the troops were gone.

At this point Rogier took the lead in forming a provisional government, thus transforming the Belgian uprising into a national, and regime-changing, effort. When Belgian soldiers deserted William's army, the Dutch retreat became a rout. The provisional government soon controlled most of the country south of the Rhine, except for the Dutch-controlled citadels in Antwerp, Maastricht and Luxembourg. The latter two holdings later affected the final borders of Belgium. On 4 October 1830, the provisional government quickly proclaimed independence, called for the election of a congress to adopt a constitution and began to fill the administration with its supporters.

To elect a congress the provisional government nominated a single slate of candidates. Many who tried to stand encountered obstacles and of the limited number of opposition candidates who succeeded in filing, few were elected. Of the limited electorate, only a little over one per cent of the total population, more than a third abstained from voting. Most of the abstainers were *Orangists*, men whose economic and anti-clerical interests led them to prefer a Belgian-Dutch federation to independence. Internal opposition, principally from the *Orangists* who supported the Dutch King's son, the Prince of Orange—did not cease until King William signed the 1839 treaty. Thereafter the *Orangists* generally supported the Belgian Liberals.

Securing international recognition

Confident of the support of the guarantor powers, which had negotiated the 1815 Congress of Vienna Treaty creating the united Netherlands, William appealed to them to restore the situation. The Dutch bombardment of Antwerp in October removed any hope for reconciliation. Britain, Austria, Prussia, Russia and France called for an armistice, telling each belligerent to withdraw its forces behind the boundary that divided their lands before the 1815 creation of the merged kingdom. The autocratic powers, Prussia, Austria and Russia, opposed the Belgian desire for independence. For many in their capitals 'the threatened dissolution of the united Netherlands ... appeared only as the first stage in a revolutionary process that might again engulf Europe',[4] especially since secession would have set an ominous precedent for their restless subordinate parts, including Russia's Poland, Austria's Italian possessions and Prussia's territory along the Rhine. The Belgian provisional government thus confronted an urgent challenge to secure international recognition. To meet this challenge the Belgian leadership hastened to enact a constitution and recruit a king. Meanwhile, the Dutch reinforced their hold on Zeeland, Flanders, Antwerp, Maastricht and Luxembourg—sites that strengthened their positions for the conflicts and boundary settlements that followed. Belgium was not prepared to defend its historic borders.

Domestic outbreaks in other parts of Europe contributed significantly to the Belgian efforts to secure their country's independence. Revolution in Poland, troubles in Italy and the intervention of the British foreign minister, Lord Palmerston, prevented a concerted effort by autocratic Russia, Austria and Prussia to intervene on behalf of King William. In January 1831 at the urging of Britain, the guarantor powers reluctantly agreed to let Belgium separate from the Netherlands. While William was ready to accept the initial 'Basis of Separation', the Belgian leaders refused to accept an agreement that did not explicitly recognise their independence. When the terms were revised as 'the XVIII Articles Treaty' to recognise Belgian independence, William not only did not accept them but also unleashed the 'Ten-Day Campaign' in which Dutch military forces drove deep into Brabant. Only French help stopped the Dutch invasion. The Belgian humiliation led the London Conference to impose a new, and much tougher, treaty on Belgium. By the terms of this 'XXIV Articles Treaty', the Netherlands gained Zeeland, Flanders and eastern Limburg including Maastricht, and William I gained the eastern part of Luxemburg province, including the city of Luxembourg, as an independent Grand Duchy. Recognising Belgium's vulnerability due to its small size and loss of defendable frontiers, the major powers included in the treaty a section guaranteeing Belgium's 'neutrality'. A later German Chancellor called this provision a 'scrap of paper'. Not until 1839 did the Dutch government under William I approve the 'XXIV Articles Treaty'. One of its provisions opened the Scheldt, thus granting Antwerp access to the sea, but the traffic remained subject to tolls. While Belgians gained independence, the treaty dashed their hopes of recovering frontiers and people that they had long considered theirs.

Adopting a constitution and securing a monarch

While the great powers worked to resolve the crisis and Belgian diplomats tried to influence its outcome, the provisional government rushed to write and adopt a constitution that presented the great powers with a *fait accompli*. An ad hoc committee prepared a draft constitution that the provisional government approved and presented to the Congress when it opened on 10 November 1830. The constitution adopted by the Congress was, for its time, a progressive one. It provided for a parliamentary form of government with a cabinet responsible to an elected parliament, albeit the electorate was limited to one per cent of the population. The constitution, while it essentially limited the role of the monarch to that of a ceremonial head of state, allotted him royal prerogatives that included heading the armed forces and appointing and dismissing ministers. Leopold I, and later Leopold II, exploited these provisions.

Despite the initial spirit of the 1830 revolt and the progressive character (by early nineteenth century standards) of the constitution, the mindset of the members of Congress reflected their propertied, professional and Francophone backgrounds, and hence conservative interests. While many of those who wrote the constitution and formed the government were from Flemish and Brabant towns, most spoke French as their first language. The constitution, written in French, stated that the official versions of acts of parliament and royal decrees were those in French. The electoral law passed by the Congress limited the franchise to about 46,000 men, that is about one person in ninety-five, about the same as it was before the separation from the united Netherlands. While more progressive than that of other European countries at that time, the limited suffrage assured more support for national economic development interests than for social and egalitarian ones.

The National Congress, after declaring the House of Orange deposed, was determined to establish a constitutional monarchy. Neal Ascherson writes 'The constitution they drew up for Belgium was republican and libertarian, fencing in the executive power and proclaiming that "All powers emanate from the Nation" ...(T)hey chose to head it with a King ... because the rest of Europe associated a Republic with social—not just political—revolution, and because not even Palmerston or Louis Philippe, let alone the more conservative monarchies of Europe, could have tolerated such a challenge to the spirit of the Congress of Vienna. And the middle-class revolutionaries themselves, though most of them were noisy young men in their twenties, were equally nervous about social change.'[5]

The Congress considered several possibilities for the kingship. The conservative powers favoured the candidature of the Prince of Orange, whom the Orangists supported. Others suggested the Duke of Leuchtenberg, a relative of Napoleon; but King Louis Philippe of France made it clear that he would not tolerate a Bonapartist. A few moderates backed the second son of the French King, the Duke of Nemours; Louis connived to secure the offer. When by a narrow majority the Belgian Congress voted to offer the French prince the throne, Britain threatened war unless the French King declined the offer. The British pushed the candidature of Leopold of Saxe-Coburg, who until his wife's death had been the British presumptive prince-consort.

Finally, the Belgian leadership offered the throne to Leopold of Saxe-Coburg, the eighth child of a German Lutheran family who had lost its principality in the Napoleonic wars. He had married King George IV's daughter and heiress apparent, Princess Charlotte, but within a year of their marriage, she and their child died at childbirth. With Charlotte's death, Victoria, the daughter of the British King's brother and Leopold's sister, became the heiress. In February 1830 Leopold tentatively accepted the Greek throne, but by setting difficult conditions he in effect rejected it. Shortly afterwards, with British support, he was offered and accepted the offer of the Belgian throne. The offer was facilitated by his willingness to marry the daughter of the French King and, despite his Protestant faith, his pledge to bring up his children

Catholic. Curiously the Belgians secured their independence from a Protestant king only to replace him with another Protestant, albeit a more moderate one.

Leopold accepted the monarchy despite his reservations about its constitutional limitations, but he did not intend to be limited by them. While he generally left domestic policy to his ministers, he enhanced his power base through his military, diplomatic and ministerial selection and dismissal prerogatives. Since the disastrous 'Ten-Day Campaign' had revealed a military vacuum, the new king seized the opportunity to assert a strong royal role in foreign and defence matters based on his own diplomatic connections and the implicit mandate he had received to organise the nation's defence. By September 1831, he was devoting his time to reorganising the army. He took advantage of his prerogatives as head of the armed forces to establish the tradition of appointing a general as minister of war, thus virtually ensuring a minister sympathetic to his pro-military views. Leopold made it a practice to appear in public dressed as a lieutenant general, spent time with his fellow officers and rewarded them, thus assuring that they provided support for the monarchy.

Leopold kept in direct touch with the sovereigns and ministers of Europe, often upstaging the minister of foreign affairs, earning in the process the sobriquet *roi diplomatique*. In time, and by precedent, he consolidated his constitutional powers, including the right to remove ministers from office, to dissolve Parliament and to defer indefinitely the signing of documents that displeased him. To free himself from fiscal constraints, he built up an immense fortune through use of inside sources of information and apparently lucky speculation. This fortune later enabled his son Leopold II to help finance the exploration and initial colonisation of the Congo.

The Liberals split from the clerical-supportive Catholics

For centuries, the Catholic Church dominated political and everyday life as well as religious practices in the southern Low Countries. The clergy established the observances and rituals marking life from cradle to coffin, set the rules governing education and controlled it, defined the major holy days (holidays), inspired art and literature and guided government policy. The pervasive clerical dominance of public affairs began to wane, though, in the eighteenth century when the Age of Enlightenment helped the spread of secular philosophy and undermined the role of the Catholic Church. The French Revolution and the subsequent annexation of Belgium by France accelerated the decline of its influence. Freemasonry, which dates back to 1721 in Wallonia, gained ground during the French occupation, under united Netherlands rule and after independence with the support of Leopold I and the founding of the Grand Lodge of Belgium. A feature of this change was the 1834 founding of the freethinking, anti-clerical Free University of Brussels (ULB) to provide a counterpart to the Catholic University of Louvain (KUL).

In the early days of the independent kingdom, Catholics and liberals worked together in a 'Unionist' alliance. The Catholic faction, composed generally of rural landowners and small-town residents, tended to be conservative as well as supportive of the church establishment. The liberal faction generally comprised the bourgeoisie of larger towns and tended to be more progressive, supportive of transport and financial infrastructure and critical of the strong role of the clerical hierarchy in public affairs. The extent of church control of education was the major political issue dividing these factions. The term 'liberal' derives from the Latin word 'liber' meaning 'free'. To the liberal faction this meant free, above all, from clerical control of schools. Thus the term does not convey the progressive meaning as understood in the English-speaking world.

This uneasy partnership between the clerically supportive Catholics and anti-clerical liberals held together only as long as the Netherlands remained hostile. As soon as relations with the northern neighbour calmed, the period of Unionism ended. Xavier Mabille has written: 'The period that extends from the end of Unionism until 1884 witnessed a distinct bipolarisation of political life ... The opposition of the liberals and Catholics on all questions caused the relations between the church and the state to dominate political life...'[6]

The fact that Belgian Catholicism, with its strength in the rural areas, was making considerable strides around 1839 added to the tension between these two factions. From 1830 to 1846, the number in religious orders more than doubled. The influence of liberalism increased when it began to resist the growing power of the clergy in Belgian society and politics, which included almost complete control of the educational system. The Catholic Church then controlled about half of the primary schools, including almost all the rural ones, as well as the majority of secondary ones, with the state paying the teachers' salaries.

The Free University of Brussels, founded in 1834 by the anti-clerical Liberals, provided an alternative to Catholic education. 1960s linguistic tensions divided the university into the French-speaking *Université Libre de Bruxelles* (ULB) and Dutch-speaking *Vrij Universiteit Brussel* (VUB). This is the main building of the pre-divided university, now ULB (© Roby, Wikimedia Commons).

Liberal attempts to gain some influence over secondary schools failed in the 1830s and again in 1840–41, when an anti-clerical leader briefly headed the cabinet. In 1842 the cabinet was once more led by the Catholic faction, which, recognising the need for more firmly establishing the system, secured the passage of an education bill that codified the church-state partnership in education and granted the Church significant control over teaching in the public schools.

Aroused, the Liberals under Rogier began to organise in 1846. They drafted a party doctrine favouring the extension of voting rights and a declericalised modern state, and won the election of 1847. While Rogier was prime minister, the party's leader was Hubert W. Frère-Orban, a lawyer of modest origins married to a wealthy Orban family heiress from Liège. As minister of finance, he initiated the founding of the National Bank and implemented free-trade policies.

In 1850, the Liberals took steps to create a state-run secondary school system to compete with the Catholic one. The effort provoked a major political confrontation. The clergy viewed the Church as the guardian of humanity and denounced the move as an attack on the traditionally dominant role of religion. This was the major issue in the 1852 elections that returned to power a Catholic government, which passed legislation confirming clerical control of most schools and mandating that all teachers must be Catholic. When the Catholic government then proposed the so-called 'Convents Bill', strengthening the funding of clerical schools and placing the administration of the charities supporting education under the clergy, serious unrest led the government to prepare for the sending of troops to quell the expected riots. While the bill was dropped, the clerical-secular controversy regarding the role of the Church in education persisted. The Liberals came back into power in 1857 and stayed in office until 1870, but their earlier defeat discouraged them from renewing the push for new school legislation. Agitation regarding the extent of church control over education persisted, with periodic flare-ups, until the latter part of the twentieth century.

Liberals and Catholics developed social and commercial support institutions. Ascherson describes the impact of the Liberal-Catholic schism: 'There were Catholic butchers, bakers, chemists, and doctors and there were Liberal butchers, bakers, chemists, and doctors: the customer shopped with his own sort. Liberal processions went through the streets with blue flags and cornflowers in the buttonhole, while

Catholic processions used pink flags and poppies. The priest on one side and the Freemasons on the other aroused this football-crowd clamour to frenzy at local and national elections. In the towns, where Liberals were strong, resolute atheists with walking sticks attacked religious processions; in the villages, the religiously faithful broke up civil funerals and desecrated coffins. Polling days became signing-on ceremonies in a petty spoils system, as vote-papers were marked and registration lists altered.'[7]

While according to the 1846 census 57 per cent of Belgians were Flemish, they were, except for the elite who spoke French, excluded from public life. Only one article of the constitution, the one proclaiming the equality of languages while installing French as the official language, even noted their existence. While the parliamentary districts in Flanders were, in principle, equitably represented in the national legislature (115 out of 200 seats), 'In fact, the combination of electoral qualifications and eligibility tended to the election in Flemish constituencies of leading Francophones.' Jean Sigmann goes on to say: 'The gallicization of the bourgeoisie, begun curiously enough in the seventeenth century by the centralizing activities of the House of Austria, was continued in the times of the Revolution and the Empire had not been checked by the Netherlands regime. After 1830 the Belgian "political class" was in agreement to ensure the triumph of the French language throughout the country; in Flanders it was not only the language of the social elite but also that of the administration of the courts and of the army.'[8]

Helped by the ripple effects of the 1848 Paris insurrection that overthrew the French King, Louis Philippe, the Liberals passed legislation modestly extending the suffrage from 59,000 to 79,000. Aided, perhaps, by this token accommodation, and more critically by the fact that socialism and Flemish nationalism had not yet in 1848 gained momentum, Belgium escaped the impact of the wave of crises that affected many European countries at that time. The critical extension of suffrage and the accompanying rise of the labour and Flemish movements would over the course of a few decades, alter the party landscape and shift the focus of partisan battles.

Industrial growth and changing social structure

In its early decades of independence, Belgium underwent several economic crises. Severance from the Netherlands not only deprived it of the valuable Dutch and Netherlands East Indies markets but also cut off the commercial trade with Germany that had relied upon access to the Scheldt and Rhine. The flax-spinning and linen-weaving cottage industries, not being able to compete with England's mechanised industry, declined. A severe crop failure in the 1840s caused a famine. At mid-century, a million people, almost a quarter of the Belgian population were receiving charity. Many of the working class had migrated from the rural areas to the cities where they joined the labour surplus, thus imposing downward pressure on wages.

By the mid-nineteenth century, nevertheless, the Belgian economy had taken steps that led to Belgium developing as the first industrialised country on the continent. The Scheldt was reopened in 1839 and tolls were eliminated in 1869. Alternate transport routes were and developed. Belgium built the Meuse (Maas)-Scheldt canal, and developed a railway network that by-passed the Netherlands and linked with Germany, with branches connecting Liège, Verviers, Brussels, Antwerp and Ghent. On 5 May 1835, the first Belgian train—and the first continental one—left Brussels for Mechelen. By 1843, railways connected the major cities of Belgium. In the late nineteenth century, Belgium had a more railway lines per square mile than any other country.

The development of railways supported and depended upon the existence and expansion of industry, particularly in the Liège and Charleroi regions. John Cockerill set up the first coke-operated blast furnace at Seraing (near Liège), the success of which made the area prosperous. The growth of the economy led to the establishment of a *Bourse* (stock market). As the economy industrialised and urbanised, the growth of the middle class accelerated. Many ambitious and able 'new men' became lawyers, clerics, bureaucrats, military officers and engineers—the professions that led to prosperity, power and prestige. The 'new men' mixed with the aristocracy, expanding the class providing most of the country's leaders in the nineteenth century.

Belgium's capacity to finance its rapid industrial expansion from 1830 on was due in part to the concentration of wealth in the hands of a few. The industrial revolution made many rich and the rich richer; but wealth did not trickle down to the workers. Els Witte, a leading Flemish historian, has noted, 'the capitalist system was pyramidal to the extreme and it was next to impossible to move up the ladder from the lower social ranks ... While some were going up, the industrial proletariat was going nowhere.'[9] Industrialists, taking advantage of unemployment, kept the wages of the labourers low. Consequently, workers suffered from crowded quarters and inadequate food, and died young. Despite these conditions, the 1848 revolution in France, followed by ones in other European countries, did not spread to Belgium. The few strikes that did occur, in 1848, 1857 and 1859, were repressed. Not until the 1880s did workers succeed in focusing political attention on social reforms and an expanded suffrage.

Devoted as most nineteenth-century Belgian leaders were to constitutional government and an elected parliament, they continued to exclude almost all males (and all females) from voting. But by the later decades of the nineteenth century, continuing economic and educational development had spurred increasing political pressures for further enlarging the electorate. The workers increased their intolerance of the elite political monopoly. They demanded change. Rising aspirations set the stage for expanding voting rights, the advent of the Socialist Party and the rise of the Flemish movement. In time these developments transformed Belgium by undermining the wealthy Francophone political hegemony through extending the suffrage to working class and Flemish-speaking voters.

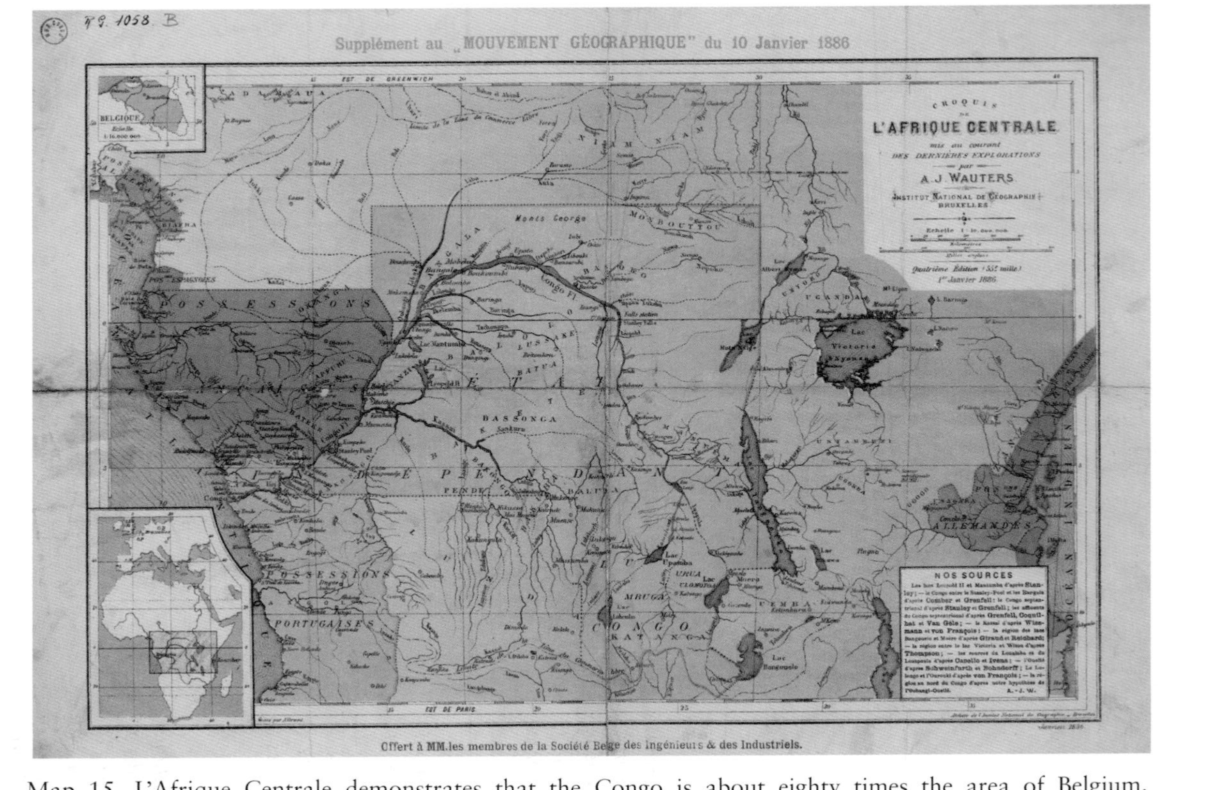

Map 15. L'Afrique Centrale demonstrates that the Congo is about eighty times the area of Belgium. (A. J. Wauters prepared this map in 1886 for the Belgian Society of Engineers and Manufacturers). Courtesy of the Musée Royal de l'Afrique Centrale.

11

LABOUR AND FLEMISH MOVEMENTS BEGIN TO DEVELOP

1865–1914

Leopold II's '*quest for colonies has been described in innumerable books and in many different ways. To some this is the crowning glory of an energetic and idealistic genius who showed his complacent nation the mission she had to fulfil in the primitive world of Africa. To others it is a story of plunder, unlimited greed, and ambition.*'[1]

E.J. Kossmann

'*Around the turn of the century, the pace of social and economic change suddenly picked up, affecting all sectors of society and the population at large. The expansion of democracy over that period was one of the most fundamental political transformations in Belgian history. It created the basis of Belgian society as we know it and the developments of one century ago still determine politics to this day.*'[2]

Els Witte

'*Nationalism is an intellectual concept. The man who cannot read or write speaks a "dialect"; this becomes the "national language" only on the printed page. The national movement sprang from peasants; it could not embrace them so long as they were illiterate, capable only of describing themselves as "men from here." … Nationalism broke in when the peasants, able to read and write, wished to read newspapers and when emancipated, they wished to go to law.*'[3]

A. J. P. Taylor

Leopold II and the emergence of labour and Flemish movements

In the latter half of the nineteenth and beginning of the twentieth century the age of revolutions continued to transform Belgium industrially, socially and thus politically. The industrial revolution that made Belgium into a leading commercial power expanded the urban middle and working classes and loosened the rigidity of the highly stratified class structure. The growth of an urban working class increased the pressure for expanding suffrage, paving the way for the rise of the Socialist Party and empowering the Flemish movement. While clerical control of education was the principal issue dominating Belgian partisan politics for the first half century of independence, once the School War of 1879–84 ended attention shifted to workers and Flemish issues.

Leopold II became king in 1865 and continued his father's strong activist monarchical role. Concerned with competing with France, Britain and the Netherlands, he took steps to found and develop an African colony whose resources would complement and support Belgium's industrial and trading prowess—as well as his personal resources. Until near the end of his life, Leopold ruled the Congo Free State as a personal possession, exploiting its resources with a ruthless tenacity. While in every country many loyally resist the urge to judge the inhumane practices of an earlier generation of their countrymen, the documented horror of the Congo atrocities indicates how repugnant and excessive the abuses were by any standard.

The growth of the Belgian economy and the wealth generated by the exploitation of the Congo supported the development of Belgian cities, especially Antwerp and Brussels. The role played by Leopold II in this era earned him the accolade '*roi bâtisseur*' (the constructor king).

Anti-clerical liberals challenge the Catholics: the 1878–84 School War

From the 1840s on, the Liberals developed their organisational and electoral strength. The Catholics, threatened by the rise of the Liberal anti-clerical secular policies, asserted their conservative theological dogma and economic philosophy more forcefully. Polarisation around the issue of religion, particularly the extent of church control of schools, helped the Liberals to return to power in 1878. They passed the Primary Education Act of 1879, which excluded the teaching of religion from public primary schools and authorised the establishment of a public school in every commune. In 1881, the Liberals passed a similar act for secondary education. Both bills aimed to provide parents a choice regarding where to send their children to school. The Catholic hierarchy reacted vigorously, by threatening to withhold communion from anyone who supported public schools, proposing the building of a free Catholic school opposite each new state school and succeeding in raising most of the funds required. The controversy launched a bitter ideological conflict, not only between the parties but also within the Catholic one. The moderate Catholics braced for a fight with the pro-Vatican 'ultramontane' conservatives for control of the party. But the death of one pope and the new Pope's strategic decision to back the moderates, in order to increase the prospects of an 1884 Catholic victory, undercut the ultramontane faction.

The prospective cost of the Liberal government's educational programme required such a large tax increase that the Catholics won an overwhelming victory in 1884. They ditched the Liberal proposal, ending the most bitterly fought political conflict of the nineteenth century. The confrontation did increase the number of schools and supported a growth in literacy from 47 per cent in 1866 to 70 per cent in the 1880s. Riding on the strength of their 1884 victory and a stronger organisational structure, the Catholics won parliamentary majorities and governed without a coalition partner in every election until World War I (see Appendix 3, which demonstrates the long dominance of the Catholic Party, participating in every cabinet from 1884 until 1945 and holding the prime ministership in every cabinet except from 1937 until 1939). The Church continued to control the teaching of 80 per cent of the student population. For both sides the first School War intensified party loyalties and partisan animosity. Many who resented what they considered clerical strong-arm tactics stopped attending church services. The bitterness of this confrontation sharpened the divide between pro-clerical Catholics and the anti-clerical Liberals. The victory of the Catholics pushed the school controversy off the top of the Belgian political agenda. For the next several decades, pressure for expanding the suffrage supplanted the school conflict as the issue dominating the Belgian political scene.

The rise of labour

The labour movement evolved slowly, first as a social movement and later as a political force. Flemish workers, inspired by the German workers' movement, founded a political party in 1877. The more militant Walloon workers, on the other hand, tended to focus on organising strikes. The Flemish and Walloon groups finally merged in 1885 with the establishment of a unified Belgian Workers' Party, carefully avoiding the word 'socialist' in the hopes of attracting Catholic workers.

In the late nineteenth century, Workers' Party members organised supportive 'pillar' organisations. They not only bargained through unions, but also bought at socialist co-operatives, saved and borrowed at socialist banks and read socialist journals. To compete, Catholics further developed their own 'pillar' institutions. Carl Strickwerde notes 'People came to identify with a political and ideological group that, to a certain extent, cut across horizontal class lines ... the form that pillarisation took in Belgium by the twentieth century [was] largely working-class socialism, a middle-class liberalism, and a multi-class Catholicism...'[4] which created a network of loyalties. By the early twentieth century, the Workers' Party had evolved as a major political force in Wallonia, especially in the cities.

In 1886, an economic crisis increased unemployment. Frustrated by the lack of government action, trade unions initiated strikes in Liège and Charleroi. When these led to riots, the government headed by Catholic Prime Minister August Beernaert tried to conciliate labour by the passing the first social legislation regulating working hours for women and children and introducing insurance benefits and pensions.

More strikes broke out in 1892, followed by a massive general strike and rioting. To calm the masses, in September 1893 Beerneart tackled the problem of universal suffrage, which had baffled the parliamentary politicians: he accepted the principle, yet ensured that it did no harm. As Els Witte points out: 'He was one of those prescient conservatives who saw that socialism needed to be contained and kept out of government.'[5] The law he succeeded in passing was an exercise in electoral geometry that far exceeded in ingenuity and impact the voting distortions of 'rotten boroughs' in England and 'gerrymandering' in the United States. The law granted all men over the age of twenty-four the vote. To mitigate the impact of the suffrage extension, the law provided for plural voting: men aged thirty-five and over with a family and living in a taxable home received a second vote, and men owning property or having professional qualifications obtained a third vote. The number of electors thus rose from about 136,000 to about 1,360,000 but the total number of potential votes, due to 'plural voting', rose to over 2,000,000. Of these votes, the poorer and younger voters with only one vote numbered about 850,000, which compared with about 1,240,000 votes cast by those with two or more votes. Also introduced was compulsory voting, a provision intended to assure the turnout of the less concerned, and thus presumably less radical, voters. In the next election (1894), since the socialist vote was more geographically concentrated and the Liberal electoral support more dispersed, the 'first past the post' single member district electoral system facilitated the Belgian Workers' Party becoming the major opposition in the parliament, winning twenty-eight seats to the Liberals' twenty. Feeling more threatened by the Workers' Party than by the Liberals, in 1899 the Catholics passed legislation adopting the list system of proportional representation (PR), a proposal they had rejected in 1893. In the next election, the Liberals regained their role as the party with the second largest delegation in the lower house of Parliament, and kept it until 1919.

The Flemish movement gathers momentum

The Flemish movement traces its beginning to the early years of the monarchy when it reacted to the ruling elite mindset, which sanctioned French as Belgium's only official national language. The French-speakers' disdain for Flemish (which they considered a peasant patois—much as they also considered 'Walloon'), the fading French dialect spoken by the lower classes in Wallonia—aroused various groups of intellectuals, especially in Ghent and Antwerp. Their claims seemed modest enough, for in fact they were prepared to continue to recognise French as the state's official language. Yet at the time, their claims appeared too radical to the political elite for any significant response.

Not until near the end of the nineteenth century, when suffrage significantly expanded, were even modest steps taken to meet the demands for alleviating discrimination against Flemish-speakers. While in 1873 Parliament passed an act providing for the use of Dutch in criminal cases and in 1898 passed an act guaranteeing equality of the languages, discrimination continued. For example, a Dutch version of the civil code did not appear until 1961. At the local government level, though, the use of Dutch made some progress. By 1866, Antwerp conducted its municipal business in Dutch. By 1900 many more Flemish towns did the same, but not Brussels, which by this time was already well on its way to being transformed into a French-speaking enclave entirely surrounded by Dutch-speaking northern Brabant.

The emergence of Flemish literature spurred the growth of Flemish consciousness and pride. In Flanders the challenge of developing a literary language, and an accompanying Flemish consciousness, was at first easier than in many other parts of Europe; it was not a task of forging a literary language but of putting the already existing literary language of the Netherlands to the service of the Flemish movement. Hendrik Conscience (1812–83) pioneered writing in Flemish. His book *De Leeuw of Vlaanderen* ('The Lion of Flanders'), published in 1838, gained him a reputation as the man who 'taught his readers to read.' More important, he encouraged the Flemish to consider their language as more than second-rate. As Flemish literacy and literature developed, writers had to choose in which of the various spoken Flemish dialects of Dutch to publish. The patois spoken in the provinces of West Flanders and Limburg, and points in between, had evolved so differently over the centuries that many had difficulty understanding those from other areas. To meet the challenge, writers chose to publish in the variant of Dutch used in the Netherlands, which already had a long literary history.

On the other side of the linguistic frontier was Albert Du Bois, an aristocratic Walloon, who wrote *Belges ou Français?* and *Cathéchisme Wallon*. He argued that, because the Walloons were French-speaking they shared France's race, language, history and religion with the French. His thinking influenced Jules Destrée, later leader of the Walloon separatists.

The spirit unleashed by the age of revolution, with its socio-economic and political ramifications, fuelled prosperity, dramatically increased literacy along with the number of primary and secondary schools, and extended the suffrage. An expanded electorate and increasing Flemish and working class pride increasingly enhanced Flemish political power.

Leopold's Congo venture

By the late nineteenth century, the scramble for Africa had escalated. France, Britain, Portugal, Spain and Germany were anxious to found colonies that would assure them raw materials and gain them markets for their manufactured products. Searching for a way to make money as well as frustrated with the limitations of being king of only a small country, Leopold II determined to secure overseas possessions that could provide raw materials and markets. At different times Leopold sought openings for Belgian interests in Mongolia, Manchuria, Siberia, Korea, Siam (now Thailand) and other places in East Asia.

In 1876, while much of sub-Saharan Africa remained *terra incognita*, Leopold pursued his ambitions by hosting a conference of geographers and others concerned with exploring Africa and suppressing the slave trade. The conference endorsed the founding of the International African Association as a scientific and philanthropic body; after serving as a cover for Leopold's entrepreneurship, it never met again. Its successor was the Comité d'Etudes du Haut Congo, the medium through which Leopold secured Henry Morton Stanley to lead an exploration expedition to the Congo basin and conclude treaties with native chiefs. Within five years, the committee had brought under its aegis a region eighty times larger than Belgium. In 1879, the King replaced the Comité with the Association Internationale du Congo, his private commercial enterprise through which Leopold asserted his control over this huge territory. In 1884–85 while attending the Berlin Conference, which was meeting to establish guidelines for future intervention in Africa, Leopold secured international recognition of the land he claimed (based on the treaties secured by Stanley) and thus was recognised as the ruler of the Congo Free State. An undertaking that began with international backing to abolish the slave trade had metamorphosed into an autocratic reign of relentless greed supported by ruthless human servitude and oppression. The United States, persuaded by forceful lobbying, was the first government to recognise the Congo as a sovereign state.

In exploiting the Congo, the King exerted absolute control. To run the colony he relied largely on seconded army personnel, whom a Belgian professor has described as 'too young and incompetent; they are sent out, without knowing the native language, without a probation period, to a distant place where they are usually alone.'[6] (In that era colonial officers of Britain, the Netherlands, France and other colonial powers may be similarly described.) Leopold's administration ruthlessly conscripted and abused natives to achieve the maximum return from the Congo's rich resources, which were initially mainly ivory but from the 1890s on were mostly rubber. In order to meet the ever-increasing demands, military detachments went into villages and forced their men to go deep into the forest to gather their monthly quota, often holding women, children and chiefs hostage. Many natives died from overwork. With few able-bodied men left in the villages to harvest food, hunt or fish, many women and children starved. Even more natives died as large numbers moved throughout the country, bringing new diseases to people with no resistance to them. The brutality imposed on the native labour included whipping, cutting off of hands and killing. Not surprisingly, the population plummeted. The Belgian historian Daniel Vangroenwegh has estimated the death toll as about 50 per cent of the pre-colonial population of the country; others believe 20 per cent is more accurate. But despite the severe and cruel measures taken to secure large revenues from ivory and rubber, the funds were insufficient to fund Leopold's increasing expenses, including his industrial investments, the promotion of new edifices that continue to distinguish Belgium and his and his many mistresses' expensive tastes.

Leopold's extravagances forced him to borrow funds from the Belgian government in 1891 and 1895. On the latter occasion, he offered the Congo to the Belgian government, which refused the offer. Continuing financial pressures led the King to exploit the Congo even more ruthlessly, accentuating the abuses and protests. In 1903 Roger Casement, an Irishman who was serving as a British consul in the Congo, prepared a report calling the Congo Free State 'hell on earth' characterised by 'wholesale oppression and shocking mismanagement'. The report scandalised Europe and inspired E. D. Morel's Congo Reform Association. These reports sharply contrasted with Leopold's carefully cultivated humanitarian reputation. In 1904, Leopold agreed to send a Commission of Inquiry. Its detailed report described the extent of extensive brutality. Continuing investigations and widespread condemnation by the Belgian, British, American and other governments led Belgium to annex the Congo in 1908. The Belgian government enacted a Colonial Charter that was intended to lay the foundations for a 'model colonial regime', but as a recent publication prepared for the Royal Museum for Central Africa notes, while the charter prescribed reform, what action was taken was long in coming. The report paved the way for legislation that 'for example, outlawed compulsory labour ... [but] this provision was not implemented until the 1930's. Freedom of press, the right to hold meetings and the right of association did not come into effect until 1959.'[7]

The hostile reaction of many Belgians to Hochschild's 1998 book *King Leopold's Ghost*—even though its description of atrocities is consistent with the narrative by other authors such as Bouda Etamad, Daniel Vangoenweghe, Ndaywel e Nziem—indicate continuing Belgian sensitivity regarding the issue. Hochschild's book includes discussion of the role of several European nations and the United States in facilitating the beginning and continuation of the Congo regime. The subject of colonial and minority oppression continues to be difficult to consider without emotion. The particularly brutal severity of forced labour, brutality and the drastic loss of population in the Congo remain particularly touchy subjects in Belgium today, where many feel the need to view the atrocities in the context of earlier times and the conditions in the 'the dark continent'. How many countries and people strong enough to assert their will on those weaker have not resisted, at least for a generation, acknowledging the cruelties and crimes they have inflicted on those peoples they considered inferior?

Gerlache's Antarctic adventure

Another foreign venture launched from Belgium in the late nineteenth century was headed by Baron Adrien de Gerlache de Gomery, who in 1897–99 led the first international scientific expedition to the unknown Antarctic. His crew included Roald Amundsen, the Norwegian first mate who later was the first to reach the South Pole, and Dr Frederick A. Cook, the American ship's doctor, anthropologist, and photographer, who was the first to claim, albeit fraudulently, to be the first to reach the North Pole. Gerlache secured sufficient donations—including one from the Belgian government—to undertake the expedition. His ship, the *Belgica*, left Belgium in August 1897 and reached the Antarctic in early 1898 (the Antarctic summer). When he pressed further south than any explorer had gone before, his ship became ice bound, forcing his ship to be the first to spend winter in the Antarctic.

During the course of the voyage, Gerlache mapped and named islands and other sites along the western side of the Antarctic Peninsula after donors, friends and places. Three islands and a bay were named after Belgian provinces, and an island for Ghent; these were the Osterrieth Mountains, the Solvay Mountains, and Andvord Bay, Brialmont Bay,

Buls Bay and Cape Renard were named in honour of expedition supporters; an island named after Cook's home city, Brooklyn; another after Brooklyn's mayor, Van Wyck; Wilhelmina Bay was called after the Dutch queen; and the passage between the peninsula and larger islands along its coast was named the Belgica Strait (now Gerlache Straight). Gerlache named nothing after King Leopold, who had rejected the explorer's request for an audience to solicit support for the expedition. Gerlache's achievements inspired subsequent expeditions by Scott, Amundsen, Shackleton, Byrd and other explorers.

Industrialisation and the 'Roi Bâtisseur'

The last decades of the nineteenth century and the first of the twentieth were times of peace, prosperity and progress. The 'Gilded Age' witnessed the introduction of such Second Industrial Revolution products as the telephone, electric light, automobiles, motion (if not talking) pictures, air flights, manufacturing advances and dramatic improve-

Arcade du Cinquantenaire in Brussels, begun in 1880, was completed in 1905, in time to celebrate the seventy-fifth anniversary of Belgian independence. The Parc Cinquantenaire was created in 1870 to celebrate the fiftieth anniversary (© Veniamin Kraskov, istockphoto.com).

ments in weapons (that shaped how World War I was fought). Walloon-based mines and mills as well as Congo profits spurred Belgian prosperity.

New industries contributed to the economy. Coal mining and steel firms flourished in the Ardennes. Prominent among the other industries was one begun by Ernest Solvay, who invented a process for the industrial production of soda in 1861, leading to the formation of one of the world's leading chemical firms. The Delhaize brothers developed one of the world's wealthiest supermarket companies, trading in Europe, North America and southeast Asia. So successful was Belgian industry that by the end of the nineteenth century, Belgium ranked seventh in the world in GDP per capita. While behind the United Kingdom, the United States, the Netherlands and Switzerland, it ranked ahead of Germany and France by more than 20 per cent.

Increasing prosperity spurred the building of public buildings, new corporate offices and mansions throughout Belgium. In this regard Alexander Murphy has noted, 'The overall character of the central Brussels landscape owes much to the processes that unfolded during the early decades of the reign of Leopold II ... The city emerged as the dominant urban area in Belgium, encompassing more than ten per cent of the country's population and sprawling out over the surrounding countryside. Moreover, the city acquired many of the trappings of a significant turn-of-the-century European capital: broad avenues, great monuments, splendid parks, and pretentious public buildings. One of the driving forces behind these changes was the desire of the (largely Francophone) aristocracy and upper middle class to promote urban growth and to build a capital city in the image of Paris.'[8]

The King promoted the development of Avenue Louise, by excising a strip of land from the commune of Ixelles, one of the nineteen municipalities comprising greater Brussels, to connect the city downtown with the extensive Bois de la Cambre, a forest then on the city outskirts but now almost surrounded by built-up areas. At the foot of this new boulevard, on the edge of what was then the city, was built the massive Palace of Justice. In the northwest of the city another major boulevard was built to link the Place Rogier with Koekelberg. At its end the King determined to build a monumental basilica, but its foundation stone was not laid until the late 1920s and the structure not completed for forty-four years. Many landmarks were constructed in the centre of the city, one of which was the Bourse (the stock exchange). The King also promoted the development of a major route to Tervuren, at the beginning of which was constructed the Parc du Cinquantenaire, which celebrated the fiftieth anniversary of Belgian independence and, at the end, the African museum. Among the efforts outside the capital was the development of Oostende and the other seaside towns from Knokke-Heist to De Panne and their connection by a rail line.

This was the period of Art Nouveau, the distinctive architecture of late nineteenth and early twentieth century Belgium. In particular the work of Victor Horta led to his international recognition as an architect, first with the private houses at the beginning of his career, but more significantly for the execution of the many public buildings constructed later. These included the Hôtel de Eetvelde, the Palais des Beaux Arts and the Gare Central that put his stamp on the historic centre of Brussels.

Growing European unrest

Yet, amid this absence of conflict and evidence of wealth and development, signs of unrest permeated Europe. Increasing ethnic consciousness spurred nationalist fervour among minorities who felt trapped within multi-national empires ruled by 'outsiders'. Disputes over trade and tariffs, envy regarding colonial possessions, the rise of socialism and the continuing enmity between Germany and France, still embittered by its 1871 defeat in the Franco-Prussian War and the consequent loss of Alsace and Lorraine, further fostered international stresses.

The tensions—coupled with indications that in the event of war German troops would avoid the terrain and fortifications along the French-German border by invading France via Belgium—deprived Leopold of any faith in the 1839 treaty guaranteeing Belgian neutrality. During the long period of armed peace in the late nineteenth and early twentieth centuries, two sets of major European powers formed up sides: the Triple Entente (Britain, France and Russia) and the Central Powers (Germany and Austria-Hungary), with Belgium caught in the middle. As Germany's aggressive policies became evident, Belgium only slowly reinforced its defences, despite the desperate efforts of a few political leaders and the King.

Although neutral, as required by the treaty establishing its independence, Belgium looked to Britain, as it had so many times in the past. Serious co-operation would have required Belgium joining the Triple

Entente, an option the government avoided because of concerns that Germany would consider such a step as a violation of the neutrality principle, giving it an excuse to invade. Lacking a foreign protector, Belgium took steps to strengthen its defence. The government built two bridgeheads, one at Namur and one at Liège, and passed a law introducing armed services conscription, which King Leopold signed three days before his death in 1909. In 1913, with the strong pressing of Albert, who had succeeded his uncle, Belgium passed a bill to increase the army to 340,000 men, but by 1914 the army had only been able to recruit 200,000.

Leopold II's grand vision for the development of Belgium included founding a colony supporting its economic growth and constructing edifices that glamorised its cities. To pursue this vision he continued the efforts of his father to develop a dynasty capable of sustained national leadership. He considered it essential to securing financial resources that were private and not dependent on parliament. To achieve this goal, Acherson points out, 'he mastered and used with unique skill the techniques of colonial exploitation and trust capitalism.'[9] In an era of strengthened democratic institutions and politics, his actions fostered scepticism regarding the role of the monarchy.

During this era, the working class began to exert political power and force change. Els Witte has noted, 'The expansion of parliamentary democracy was the result of two opposing forces at work. The working class had come of age and shed its inhibitions and it demanded political power to improve its lot in life. The ruling classes wanted to safeguard capitalism from social revolt and a steady, supervised integration of the working class into the political processes was their safest bet.'[10]

These late nineteenth century economic, social and political dynamics began a process that transformed twentieth century politics. A portent of the future was Jules Destree's 1912 *Lettre au Roi* which he began, 'Sire, allow me to tell you, there are no Belgians.'[11] He went on to deny the existence of a Belgian sense of community and pleaded for a Belgian federation. In the next decades both Albert and Leopold III faced the challenge of how a constitutional monarch provides leadership to a country confronted with invasion and internal strife.

Map 16. The German invasion through Belgium in 1914 occupied all of the country, except for its small western corner that the Allies defended at a high cost throughout the war. The line of 'trench' warfare, extending from the North Sea to Switzerland, changed little through the war. Based on a map from Shepherd, William R., *Shepherd's Historical Atlas*, New York, Harper & Row, 1976.

12

TWO GERMAN INVASIONS AND A DEPRESSION SPEED CHANGE

1914–1945

'*Before August 1914, Belgium had been the world's sixth ranked industrial power, but the Germans plundered so thoroughly that it never regained its former place.*'[1]

Larry Zuckerman

'*The three main areas of tension were already established before the war. The social divide had turned into a battle between pressure groups and parties seeking to increase their parliamentary representation and decision-making powers. The School War highlighted the Catholic-anticlerical divide between public, neutral education and private, Catholic institutions. The lopsided relations between Flanders, Wallonia, and Brussels marked the language division. The introduction of the one-man one-vote system changed the complexion of each of the three conflict areas.*'[2]

Jan Craeybeckx

[Speaking of Leopold III] '*With the Weygand plan obviously stillborn, his front beginning to crack and defeat looming ahead, he had become increasingly preoccupied with the choice he knew he must make: Whether to leave Belgium with his ministers or stay with his army and his people...The sole question was: what was his duty to his country? In this he had a clear precedent. During the 1914–18 War King Albert had always declared that he would never leave his country, even if the Germans overran it completely, for he considered, as one of his ministers recalls, that to do so "would be tantamount to treason".*'[3]

Roger Keyes

Transition from a Francophone elitist hegemony to one-man one-vote suffrage

Two wars and the intervening depression increased the threat to the political hegemony long exerted by Belgium's Francophone, propertied and professional elite. Major economic, social, and political changes—fostered by two invasions and occupations and the severe depression—forced the pace of change in the political dynamics of Belgium. Extending the suffrage increased the need for the government to respond to two long ignored, overlapping groups: workers and Flemish-speakers. The advent of universal suffrage after World War I strengthened the role of the Workers Party. The presence of three major parties, Catholic, Liberal and Workers, introduced an era of unstable coalition governments. The increase in suffrage spurred the continuing rise of Flemish and Walloon movements, and the corollary fermenting of separatism. The rapid rise in literacy, hastened by the spread of education and an increase in journals and books (including the growing number in Flemish), combined with the expanded suffrage to erode the long-entrenched elite Francophone domination of Belgian politics, brought three long submerged divides to the surface. The Flemish-Walloon language schism, the clerical-secular split and the economic cleavage combined to complicate political strife, erupted to divide the political parties and began to fracture Belgian unity. A major depression highlighted the economic distress and motivated the political assertiveness of the workers.

The divisive policies and draconian practices of both German occupations fuelled friction between Flemish-speakers and French-speakers. The wars forced two Kings, Albert I and Leopold III, to make difficult choices. While Albert gained the reputation of a gallant 'knight-king', Leopold lost his throne—and the role of the monarchy suffered.

World War I

The long-prepared von Schleiffen plan for the invasion of France called for Germany invading France through Belgium. On 4 August 1914, the German ambassador to Belgium delivered a twenty-four hour ultimatum demanding the right of transit for German armies through Belgium to France. The bullying demand demonstrated German contempt for Belgian sovereignty, whose neutrality had been guaranteed by the major powers in the 1839 treaty, which the German Chancellor now dismissed as 'a scrap of paper'. When Belgium summarily refused the ultimatum, German forces immediately invaded.

Memories of the more recent World War II invasion and occupation of Belgium have tended to overshadow the horrors of the World War I invasion and subjugation. From the outset of the 1914–18 invasion and occupation, the atrocities were manifold and exceptionally brutal. With the objective of cowing any resistance, German troops committed countless outrages, burning towns and killing civilians, claiming that civilians firing on their troops provoked retaliation. In the city of Dinant, the Germans killed 612 men, women and children. In Tamines, the invaders rounded up 400 Belgians and machine-gunned them to death. In Louvain, the historic library of the university was burned along with much of the city. The invaders intended these acts to discourage hostility; but instead they aroused resistance. Many refused to work. Others were active in the resistance, some managing escape routes and intelligence networks. The Germans executed more than 1,000 Belgians, eight of whom were women. The execution of Edith Cavell, an English nurse who had used her Brussels clinic to shelter Allied soldiers, generated severe criticism and sympathy in Britain.

By 20 August 1914, the German forces entered Brussels. Four days later, they entered France. The Belgian government fled to Le Havre and formed a coalition government in exile. Led by King Albert, the small Belgian army fiercely resisted the German invasion. After the fall of Liège and Namur, Albert withdrew his army to fortifications around Antwerp, diverting the German forces from their attack on French and British troops defending France. The race to the sea began in mid-September, with both the Allies and the Germans rushing troops to the Belgian coast. Despite a determined resistance, which gave the British forces time to move into Flanders, Antwerp fell in early October. The Belgian forces then joined with British troops landed at Oostende in a retreat that ended beyond the Yser River in the south-western corner of Belgium.

King Albert stayed with his troops for four years, defending the western end of the Allied line, which extended from the Belgian coast through France to the Swiss border. Describing the horror of the Ypres Salient Winston Groom wrote, 'It was in this small confine of Belgium from 1914 to 1918 that a million soldiers were shot, bayonetted, bludgeoned, bombed, grenaded, gassed, incarcerated by flamethrowers…'[4]

The Ypres Salient in Belgian Flanders was the most notorious and dreaded place in all of the First World War. Flanders was, in effect, a giant corpse factory. Hundreds of thousands died there for ground where gains were measured in mere yards. This is where the Germans introduced the flamethrower and poison gas. Its horror inspired Major John McCrae, a Canadian doctor later killed in action, to write the poem that begins 'In Flanders Fields the poppies grow—Between the crosses row on row.'

The German occupation was outrageously brutal, economically disruptive and devastating and politically divisive. The Germans seized machines, raw materials, money and food to support their war effort. Winston Groom reports that the occupiers deported 'nearly 700,000 Belgian men to take the place, on farms and armaments factories, of Germans who had gone to war.'[5] The loss of farm labour and agricultural produce led to severe food shortages. Already by the autumn of 1914, according to Zuckerman, 'more than a million people were said to be on the bread line, and the country had a three-week supply at most ...'[6] Wartime relief efforts led by Herbert Hoover only partially alleviated the problem.

The Germans imposed *Flamenpolitik* policies—with the intent of encouraging Flemish collaboration. The occupiers in March 1917 divided Flanders and Wallonia with the northern half governed from Brussels and the southern from Namur. They transformed the University of Ghent into a Dutch-speaking institution, fulfilling an important pre-war demand of the Flemish movement; but many professors resigned in protest, including a number of Flemish professors. The new university was unsuccessful and short-lived. Some Flemings so bitterly resented the pre-war lack of significant progress in reducing discrimination that they took advantage of the *Flamenpolitik* opportunities offered by the Germans and cooperated with the occupation. A few Flemish people continued many decades later to tell passionately how uneducated working class Flemish boys who did not understand French had been expected to carry out orders given by Francophone officers speaking only in French. Flemish protests spawned the formation of an illegal Flemish Front Movement that infiltrated army units and organised demonstrations, and developed a political agenda that included Flemish autonomy and monolingual Flemish and Walloon regiments. Although quickly squelched, the Front Movement attracted wide attention. With the coming of peace, though, it became apparent that the extent of the '*flamangant*' activism had set back the cause by pressing so hard while the country was still at war. Their demands for an autonomous Flanders were, however, now firmly on the Belgian political agenda.

When Allied forces checked the German spring offensive of 1918, Germany and Austria crumbled. When the warring countries signed the armistice on 11 November, the final line of battle crossed the fields of Flanders in front of Ghent and Tournai. The Treaty of Versailles awarded reparations to Belgium, annexed the German-speaking eastern border areas of Eupen, Malmedy and Sankt Vith to Belgium, and gave Belgium a mandate over the former German colonies of Burundi and Rwanda. The invasion and the occupation significantly affected post-war politics, bringing the Workers' Party into the government, increasing pressures for an equitable suffrage and arousing sectional tensions.

Between wars: an enlarged suffrage, a multi-party system and the depression

Albert emerged from the war as a popular 'knight-king'. Immediately after the signing of the armistice, he invited prominent economic and political leaders representing the three major parties—but not the more right-wing tradition-bound politicians or the more activist Flemings, to his Loppem headquarters near Bruges to consider and initiate major institutional changes. Barely ten days after the armistice a Catholic-led three-party coalition was formed, which pushed through a one-man one-vote suffrage, even ahead of the constitutional revision that should have preceded the change. To secure Catholic acceptance of this electoral change, the Liberal and Workers Parties granted concessions regarding Catholic education.

The introduction of the one-person one-vote suffrage ended the essentially two-party system which had governed Belgium since the Liberals had broken with the Unionist Alliance eight decades earlier. While the Catholics remained strong in Flanders, the Workers' Party became predominant in Wallonia. Each of these two parties received about one-third of the national vote with the Liberals and various splinter groups sharing the rest. For the next five decades, that is until the parties split along language lines, these three parties competed and dominated the political scene. Coalition governments were the norm, with the Liberals as the weakest of the three.

In this trisected political environment, voters rarely switched party affiliation. Each party redeveloped its 'pillar' associated agencies, not only trade unions, schools, banks and co-operatives but also mutual aid associations, social groups, philanthropic organisations, literary societies, journals and radio stations. These networks constituted the 'pillars' which strengthened ties within the Catholic, socialist and liberal communities, and separated each community from the others. Little social intercourse existed between Catholics and Liberals, and almost none between Catholics and socialists. Strengthening these pillars enhanced party cohesiveness and increased the ability of the party leaderships to exert power.

The World War I aftermath and the depression changed the socioeconomic dynamics of the class structure and the political balance of power among parties in Belgium. The expanding suffrage and the emergence of a three-party system significantly enhanced the impact of the working classes and Flemish-speakers in politics. It reduced the political influence of the clerical hierarchy; no longer could the Catholic Party expect to govern without entering into coalitions. The changing political alignment and the pressing economic issues of the decades between the wars shifted the major arena of political conflict to socioeconomic and language issues. The school issue gained prominence briefly in 1932 when the Liberals called for a discontinuance of the increased subsidies for Catholic education that the three-party coalition had introduced in the immediate aftermath of the war.

The 1929 Wall Street Crash triggered the worst depression of modern times. Deflation led to cuts in wages, pensions and unemployment benefits. By 1932–33, more than 22 per cent of the Belgian labour force was unemployed. Strikes occurred in Wallonia in 1932. The political consequences were dramatic. As social and economic problems became especially critical in the depression years, the unions, especially in Wallonia, and the sectional movements, first in Flanders then in Wallonia, became increasingly aggressive.

The rise of sectionalism

From the late 1920s the Flemish movement developed as an influential political force. Immediately after the war, a few ex-servicemen who had been active in the Flemish Front Movement during the war founded a new political party called the *Het Vlaamsche Front* (The Flemish Front) whose ideology Kossman has described as 'so capricious that left-wing sentiments and democratic convictions could be transmuted into fascist authoritarianism without too much intellectual tension being experienced.'[7] But in the early post-war period, the movement had little support, in part because many of its adherents had been collaborators lured by German promotion of Flemish separatism. Dissatisfactions fuelled by the depression strengthened Flemish activism. The Flemish movement divided between those who chose to work within established parties and those with a more radical agenda. In 1931, the radicals founded the League of Dutch-speaking Partisans of National Solidarity (Verbond van Dietsche Nationaal-Solidaristen: Verdinaso). In 1933 a fascist-leaning Flemish National League (Vlaamsche Nationaal Verbond: VNV) was formed to unite the various Flemish nationalist organisations. By 1939, it had increased its representation in the 202-member lower house of parliament to seventeen. The Flemish movement did secure a few legislative gains in the inter-war period—a 1930 act endorsed 'bilingualism in the public service'; in 1936 parliament introduced simultaneous translation; in 1938 the army organised monolingual regiments—but such steps were few and their implementation haphazard.

A Walloon movement had already arisen in the late nineteenth century in reaction to Flemish efforts at undermining the rights of French-speakers in Flanders. Jules Destrée, one of its leaders, had drawn attention to growing sectional tensions with his famous 1912 *Lettre au Roi* in which he stressed the differences between Wallonia and Flanders and advocated a Belgian federation. World War I, however, postponed the consideration of any concept of federalisation. In part as a reaction to the growth of Flemish nationalism, in 1936 Léon Degrelle led the formation of the Rexist Party. Martin Conway points out that the party 'briefly won support for its populist message of authoritarian political reform...'[8] that moved Rex towards an explicitly pro-Nazi strategy and rhetoric. The Walloon Movement had sufficient momentum after the war for the National Walloon Congress to hold a vote to decide which of four options to support for Wallonia: union with France, independence, a continued unitary Belgian structure or federalisation. In the second ballot, where the choice was limited to union with France and federalisation, the majority chose federalisation.

Opportunities for employment for French-speakers grew in government bureaucracy and business. French-speaking Belgians and Dutch-speakers determined to learn French migrated into the capital region.

While the Dutch-speakers who moved into Brussels initially tended to form Flemish cultural islands, in time they merged culturally and linguistically into the French-speaking environment. As the percentage of French-speakers, by heritage or learning, in the expanding Brussels metropolitan area increased, the government used the decennial census figures to determine which Brussels suburban communes to designate as dual-language ones. As even more French-speakers moved into the Brussels and its suburbs, the government enlarged the Brussels metropolitan region to include several nearby suburban, once-Flemish communes that now were attracting many French-speakers. Tensions between Flemish and Walloons escalated.

Following World War I Belgium abandoned 'neutrality' and joined a number of pacts designed to strengthen its national security. It joined the League of Nations and despite Flemish protests, the government negotiated a defensive agreement with France. The government joined in a Belgium-Luxembourg Economic Union in 1921. In 1925, Belgium negotiated the Locarno Pact with France and Germany by which each power mutually guaranteed their common borders. The Kellogg-Briand pact and the disarmament conference, which began in Geneva in 1932, gave hope that the post-Locarno spirit was bearing fruit, but hopes were shattered by the world depression, the rise of Hitler to power in Germany in 1933, the German renunciation of the Locarno Pact, the German reoccupation of the Rhineland, the Italian intervention in Abyssinia (Ethiopia) and the League of Nations' failure to act with regard to these interventions. Belgium embarked on a delicate balancing act, announcing a policy of 'active neutrality'; but with the 1920 military agreement with France virtually abandoned, the possibility of effective co-ordinated action against a German attack was lost.

In 1934, during this time of rising sectional and international tensions, Albert died in a mountain climbing accident; his son Leopold III succeeded him. Shortly afterwards, Leopold's beloved Queen Astrid died in an automobile accident, leaving three children: Josephine-Charlotte (later married to Jean, Archduke of Luxembourg), Baudouin and Albert.

Leopold conducted his kingship differently from his father. Appreciating that the assertive role of the first two Leopolds was less appropriate in the rising democratic atmosphere of the 1930s, Albert had been more cautious in the exercise of his powers. Leopold III, though, was more assertive. Aronson points out, 'And not only in this notion of a strong, positive monarchy did Leopold differ from his father but in his handling of his ministers he was not nearly so tactful ... where Albert had been long suffering, Leopold was impatient ... the King's ministers began to resent his independent and badgering tone. Relations between the King and cabinet became steadily worse.'[9] The ministers bristled at his lectures urging preparation for war.

World War II

In September 1939 when Germany invaded Poland, the Belgian coalition government expanded to include all parties, declared its neutrality, mobilised the army and rushed to construct defensive works. The eight months 'silent war' ended on 10 May 1940 when, without declaring war, German aircraft flew in at dawn, destroying Belgian planes on the ground. German parachutists quickly seized key bridges and the major fortresses. 20,000 Belgian soldiers died in the eighteen-day Belgian resistance to the German blitzkrieg. German Panzer divisions led by Rommel broke through the French positions at Sedan, and by 20 May reached the Somme, forcing the British to begin evacuating their forces from Dunkirk.

When the invasion began, the Belgian cabinet left for France and ordered Leopold to leave. Instead, Leopold chose to do what his father had done: stay with his troops. When the Allies recognised the need to begin the Dunkirk evacuation, the French commander, General Maxime Weygand, asked Leopold to fall back on the line of the river Yser, as the Belgian army had done in 1914. Robert Jackson notes, 'Leopold promised merely to consider Weygand's proposals ... according to the Belgian premier, M. Pierlot—who saw Leopold a few minutes later—"the king considered the position of the [his] armies in Flanders almost, if not quite, hopeless."'[10] Factors undermining his army's effectiveness included the lack of supplies and crowded conditions of the roads, which were jammed with refugees. When the Dunkirk evacuation began Leopold, appreciating his army's plight, told the British his army could not hold out longer. Without consulting his cabinet, as commander-in-chief the king surrendered on 28 May. On 4 June, apparently responding to a French suggestion 'that Leopold was to be made a scapegoat whether unfairly or not'[11] for surrendering his army and exposing our whole flank and means of retreat, Churchill rebuked Leopold in the House of Commons, in effect condemning Leopold for not defending—down to the last Belgian—the evacuation of British troops from Dunkirk.

Surrender presents no heroes; instead it presents scapegoats along with many after-the-fact second-guessers. No one wants to surrender, or to admit failure. Everyone looks for a villain. In Poitiers, the cabinet refused to sanction surrender. Many accused the king of capitulating too soon, without coordinating with the Allies. Months after the caption of France the Catholic Prime Minister Hubert Pierlot, the Belgian Workers' foreign secretary Paul-Henri Spaak and others formed a government-in-exile in London. Not until the Allies signed the Atlantic Charter in 1942 did the Belgian government-in-exile formally commit to the Allied cause.

The trauma of Belgium's rapid defeat and Britain's perilous state, which so depended on the Royal Air Force (RAF) (as Winston Churchill once said: 'so much owed by so many to so few'), created dismay and doubt regarding the future of Europe. Divisiveness within Belgium served the Nazi cause. Germany imposed a ruthless occupation with a racist ideology and a ready-made *Flamenpolitik*. Its cause attracted many opportunists from Belgium as well as from many other conquered countries.

Once again, as in World War I, Germans played off Flemings and Walloons against one another. As in 1914–18, the Germans initially established a military government served by Belgian civil administrators. By 1942, though, the Nazis had replaced most civil officers with Rexist or Vlaams National Verbond (VNV) collaborators. Long-ignored anti-discrimination language laws were enforced. The Nazis imposed Flemish-speakers on the civil service. They released some Flemish prisoners-of-war shortly after the surrender, but not Walloon and Brussels ones unless they could prove Flemish descent. The occupation enforced strict economic controls, seized food supplies, imposed harsh rationing, re-established the World War I division of Belgium into Flemish and Walloon regions and deported a massive number of labourers to German factories.

Actions taken against the Jews were especially horrifying. At the war's outset, the Nazis forced Jews to register and wear yellow stars. Later the Nazis gathered them into holding centres, in Mechelen and elsewhere, and sent them in boxcars to concentration camps where most were killed or died of malnutrition and sickness. That they were sent as labourers, as the round-up announcements stated, was clearly a ruse, for very old persons and young children were included. Of the approximately 25,000 Jewish men, women and children deported from Belgium to Auschwitz only 1,206 survived. Of the pre-war Jewish population of 90,000, over 50,000 perished. In 2007 a group of Belgian historians described the sorry saga in *La Belgique docile*, a book that documented the extent of Belgian bureaucrat cooperation and general passiveness of the population. Alexandra Fanny Brodsky's book *A Fragile Identity* tells the story of a Jewish family during the occupation.

The German occupation forces, with the help of Belgian collaborators, dealt harshly with those suspected of resistance. Many suspected of resistance were summarily executed; many others were imprisoned in places such as Fort Breendonk run by the SS, the Nazi regime's especially feared troops. Most prisoners were forwarded to concentration camps in Germany and beyond. Of the approximately 3,500 prisoners who spent time in Fort Breendonk, more than half did not survive the war. Within the fort, the guards, many of whom were Belgian collaborators, practiced systematic degradation through starvation, hard work, torture and executions.

Some Flemish and Walloons collaborated for opportunistic and ideological reasons. Disgruntled by memories of continued linguistic discrimination and enamoured with the concept of a '*Groot Nederland*' (embracing not only Flanders but also the Netherlands and the once Flemish-speaking part of northern France), some Flemish repeated the collaborative path they had taken in World War I. Particularly tempted were members of the separatist and fascist VNV in Flanders and Rexists in Wallonia. Volunteers from both groups served with the Nazis in Belgium as local militia and guards in prisons. Others, reasoning or rationalising that Nazism was a 'lesser threat' than Communism, enlisted with the SS to fight on the Russian front. Hugo Claus's book *The Sorrow of Belgium* describes the complicated mix of emotions and motivations that led some Flemings to collaborate.

Several resistance organisations developed, including the Armée Secrète sponsored by the exile government, the left-wing Front de l'Indépendance and the Mouvement National Belge. Not until the last stage of the war, though, did the resistance develop significantly.

Following the Allied landing on D-Day, 6 June 1944, British troops crossed the Belgian frontier on 2 September 1944 and liberated Brussels two days later. By 3 November, German troops had retreated from

Belgium. When the Allies repulsed the German counter-offensive in the Battle of the Bulge, victory over Germany was assured.

With the war over, the government-in-exile returned and faced the urgent need to rebuild the country's economy and political fabric. Two wars and a major economic depression had set in motion societal changes, which over the coming decades changed the dynamics of the party system and exacerbated the Flemish-Walloon schism.

The disputed wartime role of Leopold III added to the tensions setting Walloons against Flemish, socialists against Catholics, and ministers against the king, jeopardising the continuance of the monarchy and presaging the sectionalism marking the last decades of the twentieth century.

European Parliament Building, Brussels (© Ziutograf, istockphoto.com).

Flanders and Wallonia

By the mid-twentieth century an enlarged electorate, two world wars, a depression, an increasingly inter-active global economy and a growing social consciousness had eroded the dominance of the Belgian Francophone propertied and professional elite. This set the stage for the economic, social and political dynamics that dramatically transformed the Belgian political environment for the following decades.

By the eve of World War II Belgium was the only country, in addition to Britain, where agriculture and fisheries employed less than 20 per cent of the population. Two World Wars and post-war prosperity reduced the more striking class differences; the contrast was particularly evident in housing, dress, transport and communication. Universal suffrage increased governmental responsiveness to the heretofore politically excluded and virtually ignored segments of society.

The post-war rise of nationalism abetted not only the independence of many former European colonies in Africa and Asia, but also the rise of sectional forces espousing separatist aspirations within Belgium as in other European countries.

Just as external threats once abetted Belgian togetherness, the development of NATO and the EU, by minimising military and mercantile threats, undermined its internal cohesion.

The balance of power shifted among the Belgian parties. The extension of the suffrage increased labour and Flemish political power and enabled the socialists to become Belgium's second largest party, and the strongest in Wallonia. The presence of no longer two, but three major parties frequently required unstable coalition governments. In Belgium as in many other north Atlantic countries, the nature of the political leadership changed, relying less on the 'old families' and more on 'new men'. While those in office continued to exert extensive political power, they no longer enjoyed the limited suffrage that assured their predecessors a near monopoly of power. The decline of mines and mills in Wallonia strengthened its militant unionism and socialism. Wallonia's decline contrasted with the rise of Flemish trade, manufacturing, confidence and prosperity. The language-divisive German occupations in two World Wars, conflicting perceptions of World War II collaboration and post-War prosecutions of collaborators, and contrasting opinions regarding Leopold III's retention of the throne and continuing language discrimination fostered increasing Flemish-Walloon tensions.

Following World War II, Belgium helped found NATO and what has become the EU. The combined anti-clerical stance of the Liberals and Socialists undermined the political role of Catholic hierarchy, whose extensive control of Belgian education was again challenged in the School War of 1958. In the latter decades of the twentieth century, aroused Flemish-Walloon passions unleashed the long politically submerged language and related cultural and ideological schism, divided the major parties along language lines, encouraged separatism and split the land into an asymmetrical federation of two sets of autonomous parts.

Post-war ideological conflicts masked the economic problems that emerged in post-war Belgium. The country experienced a rapid post-war economic recovery, in part because its infrastructure was left relatively undamaged, but as neighbouring countries rebuilt their infrastructure, Belgium no longer competed effectively. When the country hosted the 1958 World Exposition, its economic problems were already surfacing.

How, after the language issue had remained politically benign for so many centuries, did it finally erupt in the final decades of the twentieth century to fracture Belgium? Universal suffrage, the cultural and political emancipation of Flemish society, and the rapid growth of Flemish prosperity and Walloon stagnation propelled the rise of sectionalism, reoriented partisan priorities and split the parties. Despite successive efforts to accommodate sectional tensions, the Belgian polity fractured.

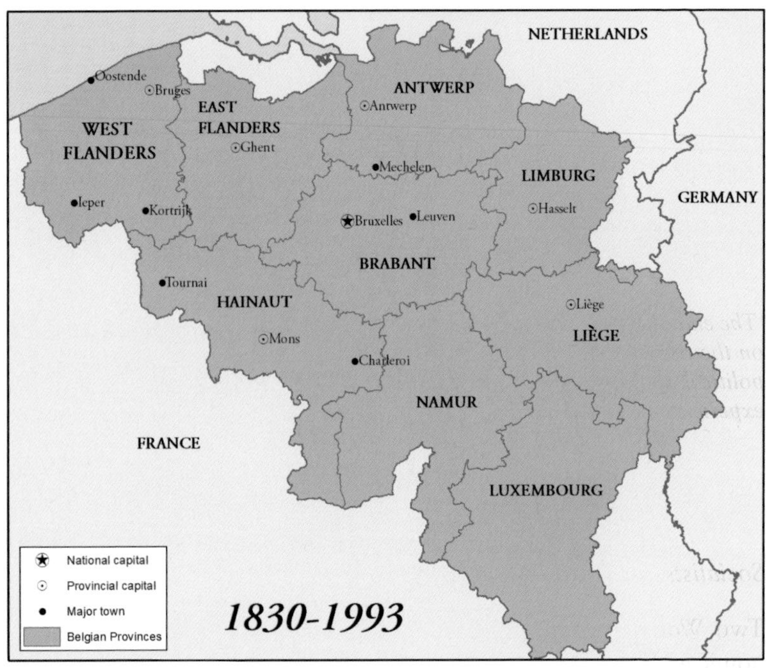

Map 17. The nine Belgian provinces before the 1993 reforms were West Flanders, East Flanders, Antwerp, Limburg, Brabant, Hainaut, Namur, Luxembourg and Liège.

13

THE FRANCOPHONE, PROPERTIED AND DOMINANT ELITE ERODES

1945–1968

'The end of World War II also liberated a new political spirit. Democracy was on the rise, patriotism was on a high, and a drive for renewal dominated the political agenda as soon as the victorious tanks had crushed the fascist war experience.'[1]

Els Witte

Socialists and Catholics contest post-war policies

Two World Wars dramatically hastened the pace of political, economic and social change. The Soviet threat and the drive for economic resurgence propelled European integration. The post-war egalitarian spirit, a growing Socialist Party and an increasingly militant Flemish movement fuelled a more socially conscious electorate which strove for greater equality of opportunity and increased educational opportunities and developed a welfare state. Striking evidence of the tide of social change was the fact that there was a significant increase in the number who bought ready-made clothes, washing machines, refrigerators, toys, telephones, TVs and even cars. These trends were concomitant aspects of the societal metamorphosis that weakened the long-existing almost rigid social structure, and the long protracted erosion of elite class hegemony.

Almost immediately after the cessation of hostilities, renewed political spirit led to a 'social pact' by which the employers won guaranteed labour peace in return for a state-organised comprehensive social security system. The 'Royal Question', the controversy regarding the return of Leopold III to the throne that ended with his abdication and the accession of his son Baudouin to the throne, transformed the role of the monarchy and its relations with the government. The impact of the war and its aftermath affected the balance of power among the parties. After the war (not for the last time) each party rebuilt its structure, redeveloped its 'pillar' organisations and reoriented its mission in an effort to strengthen its appeal. The changes after the war were followed by even more dramatic ones half a century later when the parties were challenged by electoral crises. While in the initial post-war years the wartime activities of some '*flamangants*' limited the appeal of the Flemish movement, later it developed as a powerful political force. The re-emergence of the school controversy sharpened the schism between the Catholics on one hand and the Socialists and Liberals on the other, but the compromise negotiated in 1958 sufficiently alleviated the issue to remove it from the top of the national political agenda, to be replaced by the Flemish-Walloon schism.

Increasing economic disparity aggravated Flemish-Walloon tensions. While Belgium's nineteenth century industrial revolution had flourished in Wallonia, the post-World War II decline of the coal and steel industry precipitated its economic doldrums. In contrast, northern Belgian cities prospered, attracting industry and trade. Demographic changes reflected the dichotomy between the two economies: while French-speaking Wallonia grew about 10 per cent from 1947 to 1991, the Flemish region grew 28 per cent in the same post-war decades. These economic and other changes combined with the linguistic tensions to fuel regional acrimony and split the parties, and later to enact the constitutional changes transforming Belgium into a federation with two sets of parts. Sectional tensions mounted, with *separatists* striving for a complete break-up of the country; *autonomists* preferring to devolve power to constituent jurisdictions; and *unitarists* wanting to make only incremental changes and retain a unitary state.

Belgium aligns with the West and loses a colony

Since its founding as an independent country, Belgium had played a neutral and rather passive role in international policy-making. World War

II led it to adopt an activist policy. In 1944 the Belgian government-in-exile formed a Benelux customs union that later became an economic union. Belgium was a founding member of the Council of Europe, the Organisation for European Economic Co-operation (OEEC) founded to co-ordinate Marshall Plan efforts and the United Nations (UN), whose General Assembly elected Belgium's Paul-Henri Spaak as its first President. In April 1949, in response to Soviet actions that led Winston Churchill to talk of the Iron Curtain, Belgium joined with other Western European and two North American countries in establishing the North Atlantic Treaty Organisation (NATO). In 1967, after France forced NATO to move its headquarters from Paris, Belgium provided sites for the NATO secretariat in Brussels and its SHAPE military headquarters in Mons.

Driven by the desire to promote economic prosperity as well as avoid another European war, Belgium, France, Germany, Italy, the Netherlands and Luxembourg founded three international organisations in the 1950s, the European Coal and Steel Community (ECSC) in 1951 and, by two treaties negotiated in Rome in 1957, the European Atomic Energy Community (EURATOM) and the European Economic Community (EEC). In 1967 the ECSD, EURATOM, and the EEC merged to become the European Community (EC), which in 1992 was folded into the European Union (EU). With the offices of the EU Council of Ministers, its Commission and most of its bureaucracy located in Brussels, and the European Parliament meeting in Brussels as well as Strasbourg, Brussels has become, in effect, the 'Capital of Europe'.

The growth of these organisations has led to Belgium sharing many of its critical military, economic and monetary decisions with its NATO and EU partners. The march of the EU to 'ever closer union', and increasing globalisation, have forced a reconsideration of the traditional concept of national sovereignty. Earlier European empires—the Roman, the Merovingian, the Carolingian, the Habsburg, the French and the German ones—by force of arms or by the arms of marriage had included Belgium, but this time Belgium entered the enlarged continental polity voluntarily.

In the aftermath of World War II, 'a wind of change', to quote Macmillan, swept the colonies of Africa and Asia and gained the endorsement of the international community, forcing Belgium to reconsider its role in the Congo. A 1956 popular manifesto demanded self-rule for the Congo. Except to allow municipal elections, little was done to prepare for its independence. One indication of the lack of preparation was that by 1960 no more than seventeen Congolese had earned university degrees. In the period of nationalist unrest that followed, many ethnic Congolese political organisations sprang up. The hesitancy of Belgian reforms contrasted with the pace of independence movements in other African countries. When riots broke out in the Congolese capital Leopoldville, later renamed Kinshasa, the native leaders pressured the Belgian government to grant independence on 30 June 1960. With Prime Minister, Patrice Lumumba, and President Joseph Kasavuba contending for power, the new independent Congo grew more violent. Moïse Tshombe declared Katanga independent. A Force Publique mutiny on 5 July convinced Belgium to intervene with military force. The severity of the crisis led the UN Security Council, on 14 July 1960, to ask Belgium to withdraw its forces, which a multi-national contingent replaced. In the years of civil war that followed, many areas of the Congo refused to acknowledge any central authority. In 1965, Mobutu (a non-commissioned officer whom Lumumba had appointed as head of the Force Publique) seized power, named himself president, and subsequently renamed the country Zaire, enriched himself and his cronies and economically devastated the country.

Post-war recovery

Economic recovery, the 'Social Pact', the post-war collaboration trials and the 'Royal Question' dominated the post-war domestic political agenda of Belgium. Despite its losses, the country made a remarkably fast recovery. It avoided inflation, the widespread post-war affliction, in part by introducing new francs to replace the wartime ones, a step that effectively rendered wartime black market profits worthless and restored faith in the currency. By the summer of 1947, industrial production was up by 15 per cent over pre-war levels. Belgium became a major producer of most of Europe's essential needs, especially iron and steel products, a situation that lasted until the 1950s. This export income facilitated Belgium becoming a relatively wealthy nation and a major lender to other European countries.

In February 1945, even before the end of the war, the Catholic, Liberal, Belgian Worker and Communist parties formed a coalition government led by the Belgian Worker prime minister, the trade union leader Achille Van Acker, with his socialist colleague Spaak serving as foreign minister. The new government secured the passage of a series of reforms stemming from the 'Social Pact' negotiated between labour and employers during the war. The legislation introduced a welfare state, with guarantees of a minimum standard of living in case of accident, illness or old age. These reforms, which provided workers a share in the economic prosperity and assured business of strife-free labour conditions, reflected a major shift in the relations between classes. Together with the rapidity of the recovery, these reforms helped the country meet new economic challenges. Almost all the mines in the Sambre-Meuse area closed down in the post-war period, directly and indirectly causing almost 200,000 jobs to be lost. The shift in economic power to Flanders exacerbated Flemish-Walloon relations.

In September 1945 the government began to investigate more than 400,000 persons accused of collaboration. The government prosecuted almost 100,000 persons, of whom the courts sentenced more than 1,000 to death; 242 were executed. The trials and the severity of the sentences generated Flemish-Walloon tensions that remain acute decades later. Some still argue whether the pro-German collaborators were fairly treated. Many Flemings argue that some collaborators were attracted more by '*flamangant*' principles than by Nazism or opportunism, and thus the sentences were overly severe. Many Walloons retort that as many Walloons were sentenced and executed as Flemish.

The 'Royal Question'

The 'Royal Question', whether the government should allow Leopold III to return to the throne, aroused national passions, disrupted political life, threatened the continuation of the monarchy and cost Leopold his throne. The issue, even many decades later, remains complicated by emotions. Defeat demands scapegoats, military occupations pose cruel dilemmas, politics rewards populism and the passage of time encourages second-guessing. Following the strong monarchical example of the first two Leopolds, Leopold III had strained pre-war relations with leading politicians, in part by aggressively pushing rearmament.

Leopold's surrender, refusal to go into exile and what many perceived as compromising conduct during the occupation undermined his public support. A major complaint levied against Leopold included the allegation that he had prematurely surrendered to the Germans in 1940, thereby jeopardising British and French troops at Dunkirk. The issue requires consideration of the extent to which the king's roles as commander-in-chief and constitutional monarch were dependent on the will of his cabinet. Leopold's predecessors had used this ambiguity to their advantage. Many criticised Leopold's decision to remain in occupied Belgium rather than go abroad as his cabinet and Queen Juliana of the Netherlands, did. Leopold was also accused of being unduly friendly with the occupation authorities and enjoying unusual benefits for a 'prisoner of war' (including marriage in 1941 to a commoner of a wealthy, bourgeois Flemish family), a honeymoon in Nazi-occupied Austria, and a meeting with Hitler (even though ostensibly for humanitarian purposes). Clandestine newspapers in Wallonia attacked him viciously. Furthermore, many of those from Wallonia felt he was too tolerant, or at least insufficiently critical, of Flemish collaboration. While the problem could have brought about a constitutional crisis over the monarchy itself, party leaders limited the discussion to Leopold's personal qualifications for the office.

A less evident issue fed the attitudes that ignited the crisis. Many political leaders resented the autocratic character of Leopold III, who had continued to exert the strong role that earlier predecessors had played—a characteristic that appeared increasingly out of place in mid-twentieth century politics. Albert's shy manner, his appearance of diffidence often accented by his thick pince-nez, and his image as knight-king stemming from his stand along the Yser River in World War I had generally sheltered him from such criticism. Leopold's pre-war clashes with the cabinet regarding strengthening the military and his wartime conduct did not. The Royal Question thus provided an opportunity to tame the monarchy. While the question was debated, Leopold remained in exile in Geneva. Prince Charles, the King's younger brother who had participated in the resistance during the war, served as regent from 1944 to 1950.

Public opinion rapidly divided along linguistic lines. When a March 1950 referendum on whether to allow Leopold to resume his throne returned a vote of 57.7 per cent in his favour, the king felt vindicated, but the sectional disparity in the vote undermined the result. While in Flanders 72 per cent voted for his return, only 42 per cent in Wallonia and 48 per cent in Brussels supported him. To protest against his return as king, mass demonstrations, strikes, and violence broke out in Wallonia in which the Workers' Party led by Spaak played a major role. Leopold refused to apologise and stubbornly insisted on not accepting a more restricted constitutional role. The anti-Leopold drive forced the King in 1950 to appoint his son Baudouin to rule as Prince Royal and to abdicate on 16 July 1951. Baudouin, feeling his father was condemned unjustly, never forgave those, including Spaak and Churchill, who had maligned him.

The post-war parties redevelop their structures and reorient strategies

After World War II, the parties redeveloped their structures and redirected their strategies in the light of post-war challenges. The Communists, having gained support by their wartime resistance efforts, emerged strengthened from the war and participated in five post-war governments. However, the outbreak of the Cold War adversely affected their image and the party faded. The Flemish movement only slowly regained support in the post-war years, in part because many of its adherents had collaborated. Not until 1953 did a Flemish separatist party, the Volksunie (VU), emerge.

The wartime collapse of the union movement, the associated decline of the socialist 'pillar' groups and the initial post-war gains of the Communist Party, initially undermined the Belgian Workers' Party after the war. To meet this challenge, the party adopted a more moderate social democratic platform focusing on securing a comprehensive social security system. It also developed an individual membership base, rebuilt its 'pillar' social associations and economic enterprises including banks and insurance companies, and renamed itself the Socialist Party, to be consistent with other European parties with similar aims and adherents. As a consequence the renamed party won a plurality of seats in the next election and led a coalition government from 1945 until 1949.

The Catholic Party faced the challenge of reconciling supporters from its progressive and conservative wings. The party's endorsement of women's suffrage represented an opportunistic joining of these two wings: the progressive wing were in favour of extending the suffrage because it granted women the vote; the more traditional members saw the move as advantageous for Catholics since women more regularly attended church and supported the Catholic Church's values. The party also renamed itself, as Christian Democrat, and strengthened its 'pillar' organisations. After the Catholic Party regained the plurality in 1949 it participated in every cabinet until 1999 and named the prime minister in all cabinets in these years except those in 1954–58 and 1973–74 (see Appendix 3).

The Liberal Party, although less troubled by intra-party differences, floundered after the war and rarely gained an electoral base over 10 per cent. Initially it continued its pro-business and anti-clerical ideology. Not until 1961, in the aftermath of the School War of the 1950s did the party drop its anti-clerical stance. At the same time, it also changed its name to the Party of Liberty and Progress (PVV in Flemish, and PLP in French) but continued popularly to be called the Liberal Party. The changing strategies and renaming of these three parties presaged the later split of each of them along language lines into three pairs of rival parties. Since under proportional representation (PR) the party leadership determines those placed on the party's electoral list—and in what order—and therefore those who get elected, party leaders can and do exert strong party discipline, a phenomena that effects intra- and inter-party chemisty.

The Second School War

From the creation of an independent Belgium, its parties fought over the extent of church control of education. As has been noted, opposition to the extent of church dominance of the educational system, which had been a major factor leading to the formation of the Liberal Party, provoked political conflict in 1852, the first School War in 1879, and renewed negotiations in 1919 and 1934. The post-war surge in demand for secondary education revived the long-standing clerical-secular conflict. Whereas before World War II few working class children went on to secondary school, after the war the demands of industry and trade increased, and so did the demands for secondary education for all classes. The Socialists and Liberals wanted to respond to the demand by increasing the number of public secondary schools to meet the needs of the working class, who could not afford Catholic school tuition fees. Post-war socio-economic changes helped revive the clerical-secular conflict and fuelled the turbulent 1952–58 School War.

In 1950 the Christian Democrats, having gained electoral support from their stand on the 'Royal Question', won a majority of the seats in the lower house of parliament for the first time since the introduction of universal manhood suffrage thirty-three years earlier. Governing without a coalition partner, they took advantage of their majority to introduce a bill giving Catholic schools substantially increased subsidies for church schools and control of religious teaching in state ones. The Socialist and Liberal parties, both led by free-thinkers who supported state schools, attacked the plan and gained sufficient support in the 1954 election to form a Socialist-Liberal coalition led by the Socialist Achille Van Acker. The coalition proposed legislation that provided an alternative to Catholic religious instruction and set strict limits on the amount of money spent on Catholic education. In a society in which the church still exerted significant political influence, this move led to an outbreak of strikes, demonstrations and boycotts of firms run by free thinkers. When the Christian Democrats led by Gaston Eyskens returned to power in the 1958 elections (first as a minority government, then in coalition with the Liberals), the parties negotiated a compromise: the School Pact of 1958. In effect, the new law created a free market educational system in which the schools competed for students with state support linked to enrolments.

The new pact did relieve the country's religious and ideological tensions but did not undermine the extent of the parties 'pillar' organisations. Pillarised educational institutions, trade unions and mutual-aid societies continued to flourish. The alleviation of the long-standing, divisive school issue helped raise the language issue to become the paramount problem driving the Belgian political agenda.

Economic issues and sectional disparity

Economic trends further affected the sectional tensions. From the 1950s successive Belgian governments took many steps to promote growth. Most focused on encouraging investment, loan guarantees and so-called interest subsidies, steps that generally favoured capitalism and the so-called unearned income, but these efforts were undermined by a recession in 1958–59 that hit Wallonia's coal, steel and textile industries hard.

In 1960, industrial leaders pressured the Christian Democrat–Liberal coalition to introduce measures to reduce the budgetary deficit, which the depression had significantly increased. 'The infamous "Unity Law—Loi Unique—Einheidswet for economic expansion, social progress and financial recovery" called for a sizeable increase in indirect taxation and a decrease in social spending which included cuts in security benefits and subsidies for coalmines.' Alain Meynen goes on to say, 'During the winter of 1960–1961 it provoked one of the most serious class confrontations in Belgian history.'[2] In December 1966, the Socialist public sector union began a strike in which 700,000 workers confronted the government. Socialist mayors in Wallonia supported the strikers and refused to carry out central government directives; but the Catholic archbishop primate of Belgium condemned the strike movement, demonstrating the clash of ideologies. The government took steps to suppress the strikers, mobilising not only the police but also army units to break up picket lines and guard key buildings and sites. The strike exposed the contrasting stances of the trade unions in Wallonia and Flanders. In Wallonia, the unions opposed the cuts in social services and wanted reforms in public economic policies; but the failure of the Flemish union movement to support the Walloon union cause intensified sectional tensions. The feeling of betrayal led to the founding of a Walloon sectional party, the Mouvement Populaire Wallon (MPW).

While the Flemish and Walloon labour movements underwent sectional strains, the Flemish nationalists continued their recovery from their post-war setbacks. The continued lack of effective steps to reduce linguistic discrimination, and the ongoing French-speaking influx northward into the Brussels metropolitan area, aroused the Flemish. A Christian Democrat-led coalition passed legislation establishing what its sponsors hoped would be a permanent language border between the Flemish and French-speaking parts (a line that extended from the North Sea through Brabant province a few miles south of Brussels to the German border) with the intent that this border would no longer be adjusted with each census. At the same time, the bilingual Brussels region was expanded to include suburban communes that had once been overwhelmingly Flemish-speaking, but whose residents were now more likely to speak French than Flemish, as more French-speakers and non-Dutch speaking-foreigners moved there. While many foreigners spoke some French, or were willing to learn, only a few of those moving to the Brussels area spoke any Dutch or made any effort to learn the language.

Sectional stress escalated in the late 1960s. The gains of the separated and separatist parties reflected and affected a rise in tensions. In 1968, Flemish students at the Catholic University of Louvain led a demonstration demanding that the government convert the university into a Dutch-speaking one. Following riots, in 1970 the government divided the university into two. While the Dutch-speaking Katholiek Universiteit Leuven (KUL) retained the traditional campus, the French-speaking Université Catholique de Louvain (UCL) built a new campus a few kilometres south at Louvain-la-Neuve. At the same time, the government split the French-speaking Free University of Brussels (founded by anti-clerical Liberals in 1834) into a Dutch-speaking Vrij Universiteit Brussel (VUB) and a French-speaking Université Libre de Bruxelles (ULB). The two now occupy adjoining campuses. In a related action, the government divided the ministries of education and culture, with one set dealing with French-speaking Wallonia and the other with Dutch-speaking Flanders. Whereas control and financial support of education had once united the Liberals (and later the Socialists) nationally, now language set the Francophone parts against the Dutch-speaking parts. Whereas the former divided the country along ideological lines, the latter split it along its language frontier—a more politically threatening political schism because it left less room for accommodation and compromise.

Increasing economic disparity between Flanders and Wallonia further intensified the sectional schism. While continuing decline in the coal and steel industries contracted the Walloon economy, the northern part of the country prospered. As the members of the European Community integrated their economies, Flanders benefited from the reduction in tariffs and other trade barriers. The government expanded the ports at Antwerp, Oostende-Zeebrugge and Ghent, developed a limited access highway network and took steps to attract more foreign investment. These efforts, together with the well developed multi-lingual skills of many Flemings and the low cost of housing and office space, attracted substantial foreign direct investment, which helped Flanders develop as an international trade and manufacturing centre. By the end of the century, Antwerp developed as a leading centre of the chemicals industry, especially in plastics. Flanders also became a major centre of vehicle assembly, with major Opel (a GM subsidiary), Volkswagen, Volvo and Ford plants located there.

The decline of Walloon industry led not only to less economic interdependence between the regions but also to increasing political sectionalism, with each part developing its own competing institutions responsible for economic and cultural development. The increasing extent of the economic dichotomy between a depressed Wallonia and a prosperous Flanders helped to fuel the political split which ripped the Belgian polity in the final decades of the twentieth century.

Universal suffrage shifted political leadership from the propertied and professional classes to those with closer ties to the once politically-excluded masses. Sectionalism arose with the new generation of politicians. The Flemings and the Walloons, like persons seeing reflections in a mirror from different angles, see different images of their country's history, heritage and present conditions and challenges, and fail to recognise that the images the other sees differ strikingly. Many Flemish feel that effete Walloons insist upon living in the past and many Walloons feel the brash Flemish do not appreciate the country's long unity and common heritage. To exacerbate this sectionalism many in both Flanders and Wallonia resent the increasing economic dominance of the Brussels region.

In the immediate post-war years the fact that Belgium preserved its monarchy and Baudouin helped restore its acceptance proved useful in the sectionally divisive troubled decades ahead. 'Belgium,' the Socialist Prime Minister Van Acker once said, 'needs the monarchy like it needs bread.' The role of the King would prove critical in the Flemish-Walloon electoral struggles and frustrations to come.

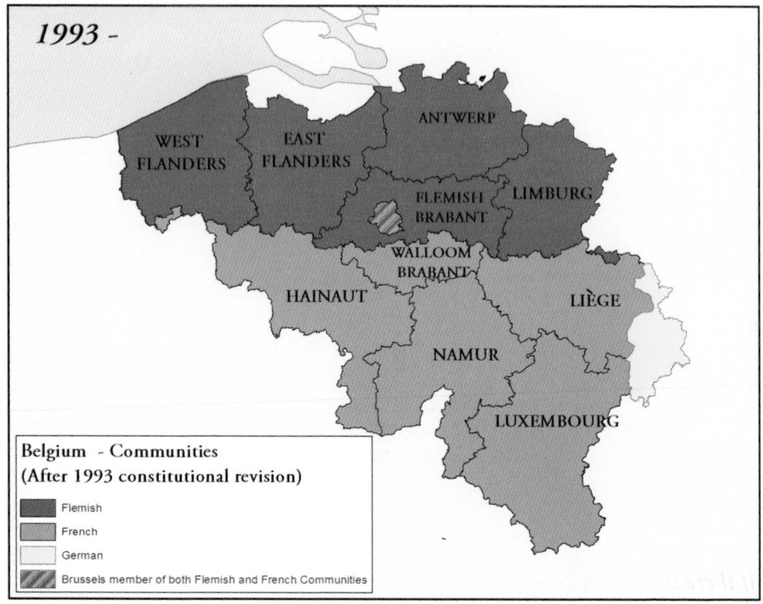

Map 18. The three Regions and three Communities of post-constitutional reform Belgium. The three regions are Wallonia, Flanders and Brussels/Capital; the three cultural communities are French, Flemish and German. There are ten provinces, Brabant having been divided into Flemish Brabant and Walloon Brabant. Based on a map from Witte, Els and Harry Van Velthoven, *Language and Politics*, Brussels, VUB Press, 2000.

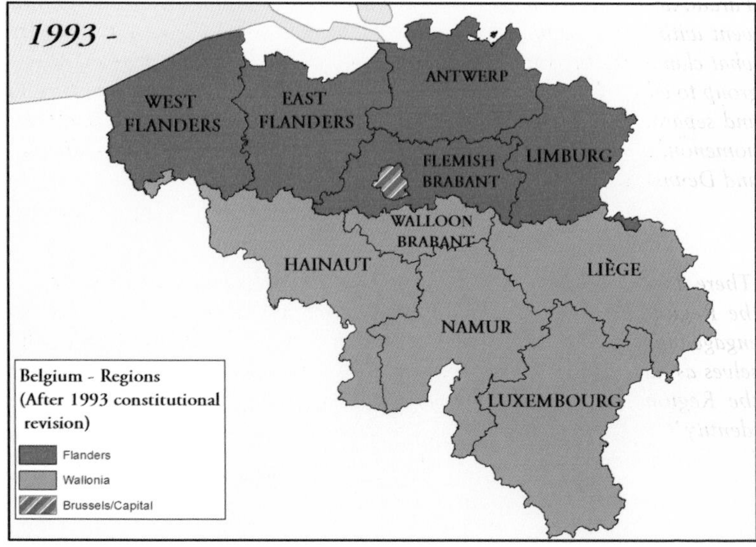

14

BELGIUM FEDERALISES

1968–1993

'If there is a microcosm of the diversified crises that have beset many industrialized states in the last decade, it is the tiny state of Belgium... A pluralistic, parliamentary democracy has experienced severe and persistent ethnolinguistic divisions that reflect a rupture of its two major cultures ... In short Belgium faces the mid-80's with a triad of complex interrelated conditions involving the constitutional devolution, economic/financial recovery, and reform...'[1]

Pierre-Henri Laurent (written in 1984)

'Paradoxically, but perhaps not surprisingly, this weakening of the nation-state went with a new fashion for cutting up the old territorial nation-states into what claimed to be (smaller) new ones, mostly based on the demand of some group to ethnic-linguistic monopoly. To being with, the rise of such autonomist and separatist movements, mainly after 1970, was primarily a Western phenomenon, observable in Britain, Spain, Canada, Belgium, even in Switzerland and Denmark...'[2]

Eric Hobsbawm

'There does not exist a single, self-evident national identity in Belgium ... as the Regions have gained a considerable amount of autonomy, they have engaged in nation-building projects of their own. The Regions consider themselves as nations in the making. This is especially the case in Flanders where the Regional Government exerts itself in promoting a Flemish national identity.'[3]

Maddens, Beerten and Billiet

Flemish Christian-Democrat prime ministers Martens and Dehaene lead federalisation of Belgium

From the 1960s to 1993, a long built-up combination of forces—namely one-person, one vote suffrage and nationalism—broke loose to bifurcate the Belgian polity and break down its unitary government. When a dam's headwaters build up beyond its capacity to withstand the increased pressure, the water pressure breaks down the dam. So when political pressures build up beyond the capacity of a system to constrain them, the pressures overwhelm the system. With many formerly national responsibilities devolved into two new sets of sub-national governments, three regions and three cultural communities, the allocation of responsibilities to the new sub-national governments abbreviated the national government's domestic functions. Likewise, participation in NATO and particularly the EU has limited the national government's role in international affairs, including security, trade, foreign, military and monetary affairs. The central government is essentially limited to justice, police, social affairs (including housing, pensions and utility regulation) and transport (including railways).

Language-driven pressures continued to grow in the late twentieth century, fostering the flourishing of sectionalist movements. Faster and more frequent travel, instant communication, globalisation and the presence of 'supra-governmental' organisations led many to become more conscious and more protective of their distinctiveness. Flemish-Walloon friction first split the party organisations along language-sectional lines, then forced the adoption of successive constitutional revisions federalising Belgian governance.

Flemish-Walloon tensions stem from long embedded grievances. Continuing Flemish frustration with long endured discrimination and anaemic anti-discrimination efforts provoked resentment and reaction. The economic decline of Wallonia contrasted with the growing economic growth of Flanders escalated the sectional friction. Party fragmentation undermined the ability of governments to develop policies supported by consensus. Despite numerous steps taken to alleviate sectional friction, tension increased.

By the late 1960s the Francophone propertied and professional elite's dominance had eroded. The clouds that had gathered ominously in the early twentieth century foreshadowed the storm that broke in the initial post-World War II decades and the deluge that followed in the twentieth century's final decades. Universal suffrage had opened the electorate up to workers, women and Flemish-speakers. In the changed political environment introduced with universal suffrage, the linguistic, socio-economic and clerical-secular divides increasingly interacted and reinforced one another.

King Baudouin, who died in 1993, reigned in interesting (read troubled) times. A series of coalition governments, mostly led by Christian Democrat prime ministers, attempted to cope with increasingly divisive political forces. The stridency of apparently irreconcilable demands and the complexity of issues, and experiments with innovative constitutional approaches that would alleviate, at least in part, the conflicting pressures, rendered the negotiations so frustrating that the process extended over decades and required four successive constitutional revisions in 1970, 1980, 1988 and 1993. A complex, cumbersome framework emerged with two distinctive overlapping sets of constituent parts: three regions and three communities, with each set serving the whole country. Since the Flemish community and region have a combined legislature and executive, the federal arrangement is asymmetrical. While confusing, the system reflects the ingenuity of Belgian leaders in negotiating a novel system designed to alleviate contending sectional concerns.

Flemish-Walloon tension splits major parties along linguistic lines

After the 1968 election, squabbles over dividing cabinet portfolios delayed for months the formation of a government. Finally the parties agreed that future cabinet portfolios, except for the prime minister who until 2011 was a Fleming and usually a Christian Democrat, should be evenly divided, a practice confirmed in the 1970 constitutional reform. The already existing split of the ministries of culture and education (one set each for Flanders and Wallonia) continued as a permanent arrangement. Henceforth Flemish-speakers and French-speakers equally divided senior appointments in the civil service, diplomatic corps and the military. The government also took the initial steps to create three regions: Flanders, Wallonia and Brussels.

Increasing economic, social and linguistic tensions escalated friction within the parties as well as between them. The stress drove each major party to divide along the language divide, splitting the Christian Democrats, the Liberals and the Socialists into three pairs of parties, each set of sister parties confronting its siblings across linguistic community borders. In 1968, just before the election in that year, the Christian Democrat Party split into the Christelijke Volkspartij (CVP) in Flanders and the Parti Social Chrétien (PSC) in Wallonia. In 1972 the Liberal Party also divided—into the Partij voor Vrijheid en Vooruitgang (PVV) in Flanders and the Parti de la Liberté et du Progrès (PLP) in Wallonia. Not until 1978 did the Socialists divide into the Parti Socialiste (PS) in Wallonia and the Socialistische Partij (SP) in Flanders.

It also led to an ideological division of the increasingly popular Flemish nationalist Volksunie (VU). Its radical wing formed the Vlaams Blok (VB), which promoted sectionalist causes including splitting the Belgian social security system (so that Flanders would not continue 'subsidising' Wallonia), providing amnesty for those Flemish nationalists convicted of World War II collaboration, ultimately gaining Flemish autonomy or independence, and advocating racist views consistent with those espoused in the 1930s by the Vlaamshe National Verbond (VNV). Its leader's stress on anti-foreign, anti-immigrant and neo-Nazi rhetoric helped the party increase its seats in the lower chamber of parliament from one seat in 1981 to twelve in 1991.

The language-driven split of the Christian Democrat, Liberal and Socialist parties, the rise of sectionalist ones and the advent of two linguistically divided 'green' parties (which first gained parliamentary seats in 1981) increased coalition fragility. In the twenty-five years from 1968 to 1993, sixteen coalitions rapidly succeeded one another, with the time required to negotiate a coalition occasionally extended to several months. Increasing sectional pressures contributed to the instability. Party fragmentation and the inherent fragility of multi-party coalitions increased the difficulty of coping with pressing political issues, especially ones requiring constitutional revisions, for which a two-thirds majority is needed. The incremental approach allowed political leadership at each stage the opportunity to appreciate the evolving pressures and innovative means of tackling not only the problems left unresolved earlier, but also new difficulties that subsequently emerging.

The 'Starter' 1970 constitutional revision

From 1970 to 1993 Belgium enacted four constitutional reforms: in 1970, 1980, 1988 and 1993. These transformed its unitary government into a federal one. The reforms took an incremental approach, which reflected the strengthening over twenty-three years of the separatist momentum. While in the initial 1970 constitutional reform the unitarists allowed only a minimum of devolution, the momentum of the changes and the stepped up efforts of the separatists and federalists later overpowered the unitarists, in a process that led to the more sweeping constitutional reforms of 1980, 1988 and 1993. Cumulatively these reforms created a complex federal structure composed of not just one set, as in other federal countries, but two sets of sub-national governments, with each set (with different borders and functions) covering the whole country. In the negotiations the Flemish insisted on creating new sub-national entities, rather than devolving more power to the already existing provinces. The Walloons insisted on creating not just one but two sets of new sub-national entities: three cultural communities and three regions.

Unlike federations formed in many countries, including the United States, Germany and Switzerland (formed by combining independent states), the Belgian federation resulted from the devolution of powers to newly formed constituent entities. While the movement for devolving more responsibilities has also gathered force in other European countries, including Spain, Italy, the United Kingdom and France (as well as independence for parts of the former Soviet Union, Yugoslavia and Czechoslovakia), no country that has remained united has devolved as much power to its constituent parts as has Belgium. Likewise, no other country has created two overlapping sets of federated entities, each of which serves the whole country. Marked differences in the views of those attempting to alleviate the sectional strife forced the prolonged step-by-step development of an innovative approach to federated government.

The 1968 elections, marked as they were by significant gains for the parties advocating more sectional autonomy, forced a few political leaders to recognise that they could no longer avoid constitutional devolution. 'Prime Minister Gaston Eyskens used every trick in the political book and relied on the support of opposition parties to push through constitutional reform in 1970.' Els Witte continues, 'The compromise called for the creation of two culture councils (Flemish and French, but not German) with limited decision-making powers. And ... three official regions',[4] but it included provisions preventing the creation of autonomous regional power centres. Compromise left every party achieving some of its demands, and impatient to do better in future rounds of negotiations. Each cultural community gained responsibilities in the fields of education and culture, and thus control of its half of the two ministries (education and culture) separated a few years earlier. While a Brussels region was envisaged, its cultural and welfare activities remained dependent on Wallonia and Flanders. While the 1970 reform took a first limited step toward a federal system, the temporising language that resulted from the many compromises negotiated to secure its passage left all sides unsatisfied. The consensus required to secure the two-thirds majority needed for passing the constitutional amendment left the text so ambiguous that it provided material for continued political disputes. This reform, however, did set in motion a process, whose progress depended repeatedly upon compromises regarding specifics. The major obstacle was how to deal with bilingual Brussels, a problem that challenged the parties' attempts to resolve the issue.

The 1980 constitutional revision

In 1977, the two Christian Democrat Parties scored major electoral gains, which allowed Leo Tindemans, a Flemish Christian Democrat (CVP), to form a broad coalition. The leaders of the parties comprising the coalition negotiated the 'Egmont compromise' envisioning a greater devolution of powers to the regions and communities, but in the October 1978 parliamentary session, according to Wilfried Martens, 'It was Leo Tindemans himself who opposed the Egmont compromise, not only as prime minister but also as leader of a substantial group of neo-unitarists within ... the CVP. Because of that resistance I couldn't guarantee any longer the support of my party to the constitutional reform ...'[5] This controversy was also the one that drove the Socialist Party to split between the Flemings and Walloons, and the Flemish VU's right wing to split off to form the more radical Vlaams Blok (VB). The failure of the compromise led to new elections in 1978 after which it took Martens three months to form a coalition of the two Christian Democrat parties, the two Socialist ones and the Brussels-based FDF (Front Démocratique des Francophones). The Belgian constitutional reform process had begun the unexplored path of superimposing a new level of governance rather than following the more conventional path of coping with linguistic-cultural-ethnic differences by using the existing provinces. Those pushing for more autonomy or independence for Flanders and Wallonia perceived that the new sub-national governments could look after their long-term interests better on a cross-provincial than a provincial basis. Not until 1980, when the Brussels-based FDF rather dropped from the coalition and the two Liberal parties joined, were the parties able to negotiate the second reform. It gave the cultural communities (including a new German one) responsibilities and provided each community with a council and an executive. The Flemish and Walloon Regions each gained a council and an executive, as well as and economic responsibilities. The ticklish Brussels Region issue continued in limbo regarding its institutions. Belgians were now governed by five layers of government: the nation, a region, a community, a province and a commune.

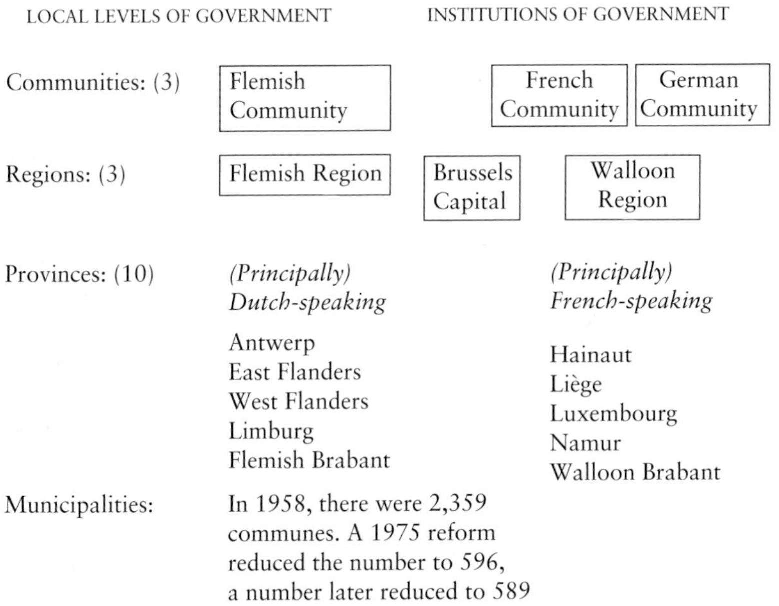

LOCAL LEVELS OF GOVERNMENT
INSTITUTIONS OF GOVERNMENT
Communities: (3)
Flemish Community
French Community
German Community
Regions: (3)
Flemish Region
Brussels Capital
Walloon Region
Provinces: (10)
(Principally) Dutch-speaking
Antwerp
East Flanders
West Flanders
Limburg
Flemish Brabant
(Principally) French-speaking
Hainaut
Liège
Luxembourg
Namur
Walloon Brabant
Municipalities:
In 1958, there were 2,359 communes. A 1975 reform reduced the number to 596, a number later reduced to 589

Levels of local governance: In addition to three Regions and three Communities, there are ten provinces (Brabant split into Flemish Brabant and Walloon Brabant in 1993).

The 1988 constitutional revision

After a brief interval in 1981, Martens returned as prime minister with a coalition of the two Christian Democrat parties and the two Liberal ones. Linguistic crises preoccupied the eight coalition governments he led. One coalition broke up over the refusal of the French-speaking burgomaster of the bilingual Voeren/Fourons commune (part of the Flemish-speaking province of Limburg but geographically separated from it) to speak Flemish when handling commune affairs.

Following the 1988 election only after a long delay (a record 148 days, not exceeded until 2007–08 and again in 2010–11) was a new government formed, again a coalition of the two Christian Democrat and two Liberal parties led by Martens. His cabinet secured passage of a third constitutional reform, which increased the role of the communities and gave the regions the responsibility for public works and transport. For the first time it gave the Brussels area its own regional governing body and powers, but it continued to reserve to the cultural communities the responsibility for education, welfare and related cultural affairs. The arrangement permitted Brussels to manage many of its own functions, while allowing the Walloon and Flemish communities to promote and protect their interests in the bilingual capital. The changes were so extensive that from 1988 sub-national government spent 70 per cent of the total Belgian public budget.

The 1993 constitutional revision declared Belgium a federation

After the 1991 election, a language-driven political crisis lasted through the summer and led to the resignation of Wilfried Martens, thus ending Martens' long-term tenure as prime minister. (he led eight cabinets from 1979 to 1992 with only a brief break in 1981). Jean-Luc Dehaene, long Martens' closest partner, finally was able to form a Christian Democrat-Socialist coalition that in 1993 negotiated a fourth constitutional reform. The 1993 constitution no longer opens with 'Belgium is divided into provinces' but with 'Belgium is a federal state that consists of communities and regions'. This revised text provides for the direct election of the regional and the community councils; previously national legislators had served in this additional role. At this same time, the province of Brabant split into two along Belgium's linguistic fault line: Flemish Brabant and Walloon Brabant. Dehaene's prowess in driving the fourth reform led many to call him 'the Plumber'. In 1994, his consensus-building talents in the EU and Belgium almost led to his selection to succeed Jacques Delors as EU Commission president, but British Prime Minister John Major, vetoed him, fearing he would prove an effective proponent for a stronger EU.

Cumulatively, these four reforms transformed Belgium from a unitary state into a federation with three communities and three regions.

The responsibilities of the regions now embrace matters related to territory, including town and country planning, agriculture and rural renovation, protection of the environment, economics and employment, energy, transport, housing and foreign trade. Communities, on the other hand, have cultural, social and health responsibilities such as education, sport, radio, museums, television, education, social assistance, health and family policy. Regions and communities may now conclude international treaties regarding their fields. The arduous protracted negotiations leading to these four reforms, plus the continually escalating sectional tensions, have distracted the government from such critical issues as the debt, structural unemployment and the criminal justice system.

Decades of strenuous efforts accommodating escalating sectional pressures produced a unique constitutional framework that strikes many as a Rube Goldberg-like contraption. Witte says 'The complexity of the new institutional framework clearly showed that Belgium's federalism was unique ... An extremely complex political growth process made sure that the regional institutions eroded the unitary state. An institutional maze was created and was a source of bafflement to all, bar the political insiders.'[6]

Did Belgium really need to insert two new sets of governments, regions and communities between the national government and the provinces in order to achieve the concurrence of the warring factions? One may question whether such a complex arrangement was necessary. But those who work within a system of unrelenting sectional partisan conflict, as well as the job-preservation realities of politicians and bureaucrats, may appreciate the pragmatism, patience and ingenuity that led to the incremental development of the Belgian system. As far-reaching as the cumulative impact of these constitutional revisions were, sectionalists have continued to press their demands for increased autonomy, and the separatists for independence.

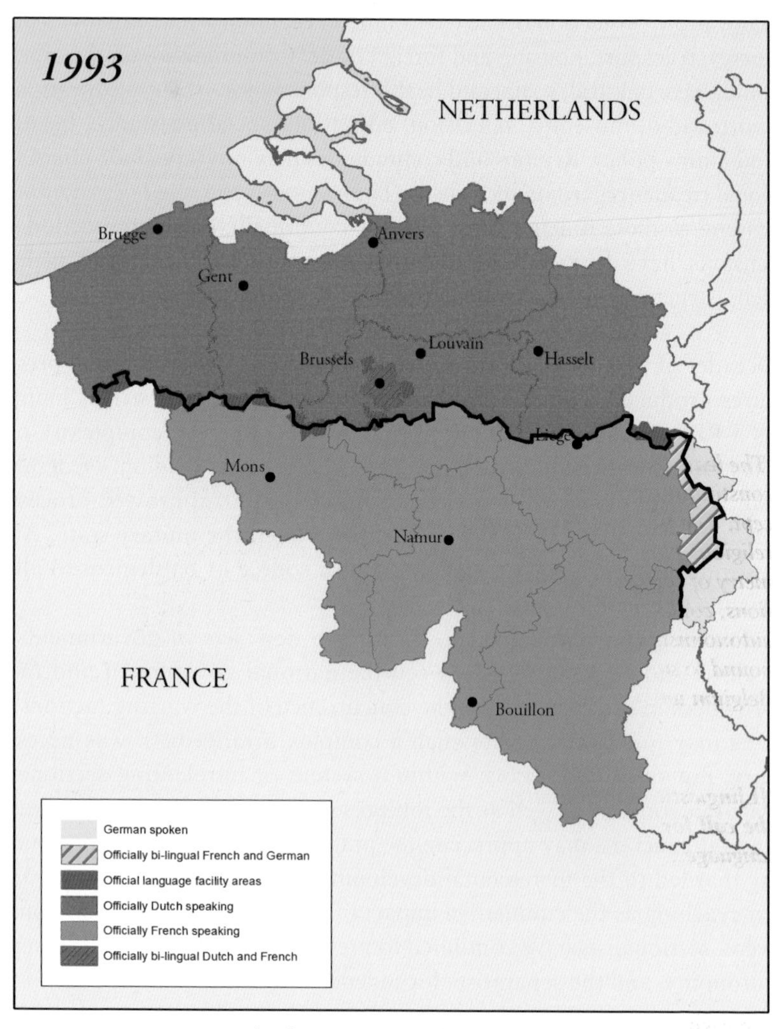

Map 19. The linguistic patchwork of Belgium

15

INCREASINGLY ISOLATED FLANDERS AND WALLONIA COLLIDE

1993–

'The least that could be said about Belgian federalism was that the successive constitutional reforms of 1988 and 1993 produced an extremely original concept. The parts that made up the whole differed greatly on economic, social, religious-philosophic, linguistic and cultural issues. The complexity and asymmetry of the institutions, especially when it came to Brussels' political institutions, could easily boggle the mind. The tension between the unionists and the autonomists turned Belgium into such a unique brand of federalism, and was bound to surprise everyone with more original solutions in the future. In short, Belgium will never pass for the prototype of a federal state.'[1]

Els Witte

'[L]inguistic nationalism had a built in bias towards secession. And conversely, the call for independent state territory seemed increasingly inseperable from language...'[2]

E.J. Hobsbawm

Flemish Liberal Verhofstadt and Flemish Christian Democrat prime ministers cope with separatist challenges

1993 was a transformation year for Belgium. The country not only passed the fourth constitutional reform, which completed the conversion of Belgium into a federation, it also witnessed the death of King

Baudouin and the accession of his brother Albert II, the coming into effect of the Treaty on European Union (TEU) and the establishment of the European Single Market, which energised the lobbying activity at the European Union headquarters and the Brussels' hospitality and related industries. A few highlights of the decades that followed demonstrate the continuing saga of Belgium's divided polity and enhance the perspective for considering Belgium's prospects.

Despite the efforts to defuse the strident sectional tensions, they persisted. Increasing economic disparities between Flanders and Wallonia aggravated the dissension. Different attitudes to religion and philosophical outlooks on life in the two parts of the country affected political alignments. Contrasting approaches to the welfare state exacerbated Flemish-Walloon sectional stresses and challenged the dynamics of Belgium's partisan politics. In the years that followed 1993 a number of crises, from corruption to food contamination and paedophilia, shook the confidence of Belgians in their governance. The increasing impact of the EU upon daily lives, marked by the common currency and by the increasing inflow of refugees and other foreigners which accompanied the EU-facilitated integration of Europe, aroused apprehension among many regarding the threat to national autonomy from the growing impact of supra-national institutions.

A coalition led by the Flemish Christian Democrat (CVP) Jean-Luc Dehaene governed Belgium from 1992 to 1999. Following the CVP's almost unprecedented defeat in 1999, a coalition led by the Flemish Liberal (VLD) Guy Verhofstadt governed until its defeat in 2008. Challenged by the election results, including the rising strength of the separatist Flemish Vlams Blok (VB) and after the declining appeal of socialism in prosperous Flanders and of Catholicism in Wallonia, most mainstream parties again redirected their strategies and renamed their organisations. Following months of protracted deliberations attempting to form a government, an essentially caretaker Christian Democrat-led coalition headed by Yves Leterme staggered on until it was succeeded by a short-lived Herman van Rompuy-led coalition, which ended when the new prime minister was selected for the newly created post of EU presidency. Leterme then returned as prime minister until his party's defeat in the 2010 election, but he carried on leading a caretaker government until December 2011.

Universal suffrage had advanced the cause of representative governance and thereby enabled the assertiveness of those previously politically disenfranchised, hence undermining the long-time elite-dominated political framework facilitating governance. The language-driven cultural chasm between Flanders and Wallonia seriously threatened efforts to sustain even a compromised united Belgian polity.

A strengthened European Community

It may appear ironic that a country that has so long championed European unification has endured so much disunification pressure. But the more Europe integrates, the fewer the evident adverse economic or security consequences there would be for dividing Belgium. From 1985 on an emboldened European Community took a number of steps that propelled it to be a supra-national organisation with many of the characteristics of a multi-national state. The Schengen Agreement, negotiated in 1965 and implemented in 1990, created what is now a twenty-six country area without internal border controls. The Single European Act, which was signed in 1986 and led to the Single Market in 1992, expedited the free movement of goods, services, workers and capital throughout the member states. The Treaty on European Union, negotiated in 1992 in Maastricht, which folded the European Community into the European Union, organised three pillars: the first carrying on the work of the European Community; a second dealing with 'Common Foreign and Security Policy'; and a third handling justice and home affairs. The Treaty of Amsterdam, signed in 1997 and implemented in 1999, called for the expansion of EU membership, gave it a social policy role, laid the groundwork for a common defence policy, strengthened the role of the European Parliament and planned a common currency. The Treaty of Nice, which was signed in 2001 and came into effect in 2003, reformed the EU governing institutions. Six countries founded the EC, three joined in the 1970s and three more in the 1980s, bringing its membership to twelve. Three more joined in the 1990s, ten more in 2004, and two more in 2007, bringing the total EU members to twenty-seven (twenty-eight in 2013). In 1999, the euro became operational electronically; euro bills and coins became legal tender in 2002. By 2010 seventeen countries had joined the Eurozone, and six smaller countries used the euro. While some believed it was premature to introduce the euro without a stronger political base to support it, such a base would have been a long time, coming, if it ever did. The expectation was that its introduction would expedite the development of such a stronger base. In fact the fiscal crisis beginning in 2008, which hit Greece, Ireland, Portugal, Spain and Italy hard, has led to debate over the role of the EU and the European Central Bank in regulating member country fiscal policies and practices—and creating a central treasury capable of issuing bonds and buying those of the member states.

The EU's development has surpassed expectations. While remaining an essentially inter-governmental organisation, it has acquired significant attributes of statehood, including an executive, parliament, supreme court, civil service, single market and common currency and even a flag and an anthem. While the budget remains minuscule (about 1 per cent of the total EU GDP), EU legislation now accounts for a major share of new national laws. Since the inter-governmental institutional arrangements sufficient for six original member countries and a few functions no longer appeared adequate, the EU organised a drafting convention to recommend a constitutional treaty with the former French president Valéry Giscard d'Estaing as chair and Belgium's Jean-Luc Dehaene as one of the vice-chairs. In 2003 this body proposed a lengthy document whose provisions included giving the EU a legal personality, committing it to developing a common defence policy, incorporating a Charter of Fundamental Rights, adopting a double majority voting system in the Council, creating a European Council presidency, reducing the number of commissioners and extending the powers of the EU Parliament. The European Council, comprising the heads of government, approved the document with amendments. But since a major change in the EU governance requires ratification by all EU member states, the French and Dutch referenda rejecting the proposed constitutional treaty temporarily stymied EU reform.

The heads of the member governments then modified the proposed constitutional treaty in an abbreviated version at a European Council meeting in Lisbon. Although Ireland initially defeated its ratification in a referendum, this vote was subsequently reversed. The Treaty was finally adopted in 2009 and came into effect in January 2010. It is safe to predict that the member states will continue to enact new treaties modifying the EU's role and organisation and add new states. Though most Europeans will continue to fear growth of super-government, the governments will continue to take steps toward an 'ever closer union'. And while Belgian leaders will continue to press for the further development of the EU, its separatists will continue to advocate their cause for the disintegration of Belgium.

Succession, scandals and strains

King Baudouin's death in August 1993 deprived Belgium of a king who had overcome the disrespect for the crown that the 'Royal Question' had engendered. His conscientious refusal to sign legislation permitting abortion, a stand that reopened the question of the prerogatives of a constitutional monarch, only briefly dented his public standing. Typical Belgian ingenuity allowed him to abdicate for a day. As the breach deepened between the Flemish and the Walloons, some called him 'the only Belgian'. Since Baudouin and his Spanish queen, Doña Fabiola de Mora y Aragón, had no children, and his brother Albert had said he would defer to his oldest son, Prince Philippe was widely considered the heir apparent. In fact, a popular 1980s Belgian 'coffee-table' book carried a full page photograph of Philippe with a caption describing him as the 'heir apparent', but a Belgian heir presumptive does not automatically succeed upon the death of a king. Instead of the 'The King is dead, God save the King' tradition, the government exercises the prerogatives of the monarch until the new one has taken the oath and reserves the right to determine the next sovereign. When Baudouin died, the cabinet, after hours of protracted discussion while many wondered what was delaying any announcement regarding the monarchical transition, asked Baudouin's brother Albert rather than his nephew Philippe to accept the throne, stressing the maturity required in times ahead.

Albert's evident relaxed affability has gained him popular support. The public celebrated Philippe's 1999 marriage to Mathilde d'Udekem d'Acoz and the 2001 birth of a daughter, Elisabeth, put her, by the terms of the revised constitution, next in line after her father as heir to the Belgian throne. Somewhat ironically, since the Walloons were the ones most opposed to the return of Leopold III after World War II, there is a growing disenchantment in Flanders with the monarchy, which some see as too pro-Francophone and hostile to Flemish separatist aspirations. The press criticised Albert for attacking a Flemish think-tank calling for an independent Flanders.

Respect for Belgian politicians has never been high. Several scandals in the 1990s further undermined public confidence in government. The murder in 1991 of the Socialist André Cools, president of the Walloon Region, led many to speculate that political motives lay behind the assassination. The arrest of several top Socialists for soliciting bribes in connection with defence procurements in the Agusta-Dassault case shocked the country; in the case, the three Guys (Guy Spitaels, Guy Coeme and Guy Mathot) and Willy Claes stood trial for corruption. Claes, a former Belgian foreign minister, resigned as NATO secretary general in 1995 and was later convicted. Spitaels was forced out as chair of the Walloon Assembly.

Government delay in handling the dioxin threat further reduced the government's credibility. Even after the government knew that poisonous chemicals had entered the feed supply for cattle and chickens, months passed before meat and dairy products were removed from grocery shelves, a lapse that led the European Commission to bring legal action against Belgium.

Mysterious disappearances of girls raised questions about the competence and corruptibility of the police and judiciary. During the search for the abductors, tension mounted throughout the country. Placards mounted in stores and other public places named the missing young women; the practice of placing placards continues. Among those finally arrested was Marc Dutroux, charged in 1996 with raping and imprisoning six girls and murdering two. The justice system was embarrassed when later investigation revealed that when police first searched the house where Dutroux had imprisoned the girls, cries coming from victims locked in the basement did not lead to action. A massive 'White March' in 1996 united Belgians throughout the country in expressing outrage, sympathy for the victims and anger over the incompetence of the police and the judiciary. The Dutroux trial did not get underway until February 2004; in June the court found him guilty and sentenced him to life imprisonment.

Anecdotal evidence illustrates the continuing extent of the Flemish-Walloon tension. When at a Flemish Orchestra concert given in Brussels the conductor began introducing each piece with a few comments in Dutch, so many in the audience shouted 'en Français' that he stopped and explained that 'he was just a conductor.' One hears a few Flemish-speakers saying to Walloons who speak French in Flanders, 'We speak your language, why won't you speak ours?' English-speakers speaking French in Flanders have received the retort 'You speak English, then speak English, not French!' While only a minority expresses such sectional hostility so stridently, it is a very vocal minority. *La Libre Belgique*, a Belgian journal, provided an indication of Belgian loyalties in a 2007 survey which noted that while 70 per cent of Walloons identified themselves primarily as Belgian, and only 24 per cent primarily as Walloon, only 50 per cent of the Flemish indicated that they thought of themselves primarily as Belgian, compared to 34 per cent Flemish.

The fact that the Flemish get their news and political commentary almost exclusively from Flemish TV, radio and journals, and the Walloons almost exclusively from theirs, exacerbates the conflicting interests of French-speaking and Dutch-speaking Belgians. The country's leading politicians seldom address audiences outside their language community, which escalates the distrust between the regions. The sensitivity of the Walloon-Flanders issue was illustrated in December 2006 when a French-speaking Belgian radio station aired what appeared to be a newscast reporting that Flanders had declared independence, splitting Belgium into two, and the evacuation of the royal family (the broadcast may be compared with Orson Welles' 'War of the Worlds' 1930s radio programme that described the landing of aliens in New Jersey and panicked many Americans). Many Belgians initially believed the hoax despite advance announcements and a sidebar that provided a caution. Many were not amused. Prime Minister Guy Verhofstadt called the head of the station to express his concern. The incident played on the continuing tensions.

The political enigma of the expanding, mainly Francophone Brussels enclave totally surrounded by Dutch-speaking Flanders continues to frustrate the efforts of politicians to alleviate the issues arising from the outward growth of the metropolitan area. Not only Belgians but also foreigners, attracted by the growth of the EU and NATO and the increasing number of multinational corporations and non-government offices established in this international community, continue to migrate into the Brussels region and its outskirts.

The disparate Belgian economy

In 2007 Belgium had 10.4 million people, which is more than any of the Nordic countries. Its GDP was $371 billion and its GDP per head $35,660 (ranking seventeenth and sixteenth respectively among nations). Its average annual growth (1995–2005) in real GDP was 2.1 per cent, which was helped by over $23 billion in foreign investment (ranked eighth largest among nations). The major sources of this GDP are chemicals, transport equipment, machinery, food, drink and tobacco—with agriculture accounting for less than 2 per cent. These statistics, however, disguise a significant dichotomy between Flanders where most investment and growth have focused and Wallonia which has not prospered, and where much of the country's 1995–2005 unemployment of 8 per cent was focused.

The exigencies of globalisation led several prominent Belgian companies to merge with or sell out to foreign-led multinational corporations. Générale de Banque/General Bank, along with a smaller bank, was absorbed into Dutch-Belgian Fortis, which later collapsed and was absorbed by BNP Paribas, a leading French financial conglomerate. Banque Bruxelles Lambert became part of Dutch multinational ING. SABENA, one of Europe's oldest airlines, went bankrupt along with the Swiss national airline, with which it had negotiated a management takeover; the resurrected Belgian national airline, which merged with Virgin Atlantic, has also gone bankrupt and merged into Lufthansa. Belgium's two largest energy suppliers have been taken over by foreign-owned multi-nationals, one French and the other British. The global recession forced many other companies to close down or to reduce the number of employees despite the difficulty of doing so in a welfare state. On the other hand, a few Belgian companies have expanded globally. A notable example is InBev, which in 2004 combined Interbrew of Belgium with AmBev of Brazil to become one of the world's two largest beer brewers with brands including Stella-Artois and Beck's, and in 2008 concluded negotiations to purchase Anheuser–Busch. The combined Leuven-headquartered company, Anheuser-Busch InBev, is the world's largest, exceeding even SAB-Miller of London.

Economic disparity north and south of the linguistic border has escalated. Flanders prospers, helped by foreign investment, its location between three large European economies, and its four ports: Ghent, Oostende, Zeebrugge and Antwerp, the second largest port in Europe and fourth largest in the world. In contrast, Wallonia has not recovered from the earlier decline in its mining and steel industries. Even before the 2000–01 global slowdown unemployment in Wallonia was 12 per cent compared with 5 per cent in Flanders. In 2007 it was 6 per cent in Flanders and 16 per cent in Wallonia. The rising unemployment in Wallonia has increased budget strains, especially because when the EU planned the euro, it stipulated that to participate in the common currency a government's expenditure must not exceed its revenue by more than 3 per cent of GNP. Some made the EU a scapegoat for steps

Belgium took to reduce its deficit, including reducing economic development and increasing museum and other fees. The recession beginning in 2008 further depressed the economy and escalated the Flemish-Walloon strains—a fact that reflected in inter-party tensions.

Since Belgian federalisation split the responsibility of promoting investment and tourism between Flanders and Wallonia regions, the country has had a dichotomous approach to promoting its international image and development; it was an unusual display of inter-regional co-operation when in March 2008 the Belgian prime minister and the three regional premiers launched a media and television advertising campaign focusing on the country's creative edge. Announcing the campaign, the government noted that the UNCTAD World Investment Report lists Belgium as fourth in the world, ahead of even China, in inward investment and the fifth most popular country for regional or global headquarters of banks and financial institutions.

Sectionalism changes party names and strategies

The depressed Wallonia economy, the greater alienation of Walloons from the Church, and the influx of North Africans into Antwerp and the Brussels region has escalated the extent to which economic, religious and ethnic issues as well as language issues divide the sister parties. The consequent splitting, along language lines, of the Christian Democrat, Liberal and Socialist parties into sister parties magnified the difficulty of forming and maintaining coalition governments. The fact that newspapers, radio and TV—and party literature—serve single language audiences imposes a public affairs myopia on most Belgians, limiting them to a Walloon or Flemish perspective. It follows that single-language parties do not even bother to campaign across the linguistic frontier. Only one of Belgium's eleven electoral constituencies is bilingual: the controversial bilingual Brussels-Halle-Vilvoorde (BHV) that extends from the city into the once almost exclusively Flemish suburbs which now have an ever increasing number of non-Dutch speaking residents. Despite years of efforts to unravel the issue, it has become so inflammatory that in 2010 it brought down the Leterme-led government.

Once considerable consistency existed in voting patterns between most elections, but swings in allegiance have become more frequent. Modern voters are less likely to remain committed to the party their parents and grandparents supported. No wonder parties have been so challenged to change their strategies and their names. The increasing disparity in the ideologies of the expanding number of parties, coupled with their increasing competitive, contentious spirit, has made it more difficult than ever to overcome the increasing divergence of their objectives in making the compromises required to form coalitions.

The five national elections—in 1995, 1999, 2003, 2007 and 2010—that followed the 1993 constitutional reform affected the balance of power among the major parties. Following the 1995 election, the Christian Democrat and Socialist parties continued their coalition under Dehaene. The dioxin scare and paedophile scandals that broke just before the 1999 election brought more losses to the coalition parties, and gains for the two Green parties, the Flemish VU and, more ominously, the xenophobic Vlaams Blok (VB). After the election, the Liberal, Socialist and Green parties formed a 'rainbow' coalition led by the Flemish Liberal Guy Verhofstadt. This marked the first time since 1958 that the Flemish Christian Democrat Party (CVP) was not a coalition partner, and the first time since 1978 that a Flemish Christian Democrat did not serve as prime minister.

Continued sectional pressures led the Verhofstadt-headed government to introduce a further constitutional reform, which included granting the regions control over the provinces and communes, giving the regions and communities the competence to negotiate agreements with developing countries and increasing financing for education. The passage of these changes, which required a two-thirds majority, came only after the Walloon Social Christians abstained, allowing the proposals to squeak through. A major sectional issue that threatened Verhofstadt's coalition from the beginning of his prime ministership and remained unresolved when he left office in 2008—(he remained in a caretaker role after his defeat until 2008) was the pressure to divide the electoral district which embraced Brussels and several 'facility' suburban communes in the Brussels-Hal-Vilvoorde constituency.

The skill Verhofstadt demonstrated in promoting consensus in the EU as well as in juggling the competing Belgian sectional interests, led President Chirac to back him for the EU Commission presidency in 2004. Tony Blair, however, having first pledged support for Verhofstadt, reversed his position, thus becoming the second British prime minister (following Major's veto of Dehaene) to scuttle the EU Commission presidential candidacy of a Belgian prime minister.

After the 1999 election, several Belgian parties once again revised their strategies and changed their names to attract more voters—steps that escalated and reflected the differences in political values which separated what were once sister parties, and further confused the Belgian party political scene. In Wallonia, the Social Christian PSC disclaimed its Catholic roots by renaming itself the Centre Democrat Humanists (CdH), thus hoping to enhance its appeal to the growing number of secular Walloons. A small faction broke away and called itself the Francophone Christian Democrats. The Walloon Liberal PRL and the Brussels-based FDF joined to become the Mouvement Réformateur (MR). The Flemish mainstream parties, challenged by the rising strength of Flemish sectionalism, stressed their Flemish credentials. Already in the mid-1990s, the Flemish Liberal PVV had changed its name to Flemish Liberal Democrat (VLD) and just before the 2007 elections it again altered its name to OpenVLD. In 2001, the Flemish Christian Democrat Party stressed its Flemishness by renaming itself Christian Democrat and Flemish (CD&V). The Flemish sectional VU broke in two: the more moderate faction (Spirit) allied with the Socialists in the 2003 election and the other faction, Nieuw-Vlaamse Alliantie (N-VA), allied with the CD&V. The Flemish Socialists softened their left-wing image, which was no longer as attractive in prosperous Flanders, by renaming itself Socialistische Partij Anders (Different Socialist Party—SP.A). Myriad changes of party name have meant that there are no longer two parties carrying the name Christian, only one Liberal Party continues to call itself Liberal, and one of the Socialist parties proclaims it is different. Critically, the once sister parties have grown further apart; each of the three major Walloon parties is less church-supportive and more welfare oriented than its northern counterparts. The Belgian political scene baffles not only foreigners but also many Belgians, who find its politics too complex, its politicians too politically self-serving and its government too corruption prone.

In the 2003 elections, the two Socialist and two Liberal parties together won ninety-seven seats—three short of a two-thirds majority required for constitutional amendments—mostly at the expense of the Christian Democrats, which continued to lose support in part because of concern regarding reports of clerical child abuse and cover-ups. The radical, separatist Flemish VB, whose leader Filip Dewinter describes himself as a 'right-wing nationalist' and by others as a 'fascist demagogue', gained eighteen seats (up from one in 1981), winning a plurality of votes in Antwerp (with 30.5 per cent of the vote) and Mechelen (25.5 per cent). During the 1990s when Belgium received more than 200,000 mainly Balkan and Middle Eastern asylum seeking refugees, the party had extended its inflammatory rhetoric to all foreigners to gain support from those demanding action on immigrant issues.

Following the 2003 election, the mainstream parties formed a *cordon sanitaire* barring any coalition with the radical separatist VB. Following the 2003 election, Verhofstadt formed a coalition of two Liberal and two Socialist parties, without the Green parties this time, but only with extensive negotiation over the distribution of cabinet portfolios and policy differences. These included such vexing issues as health care funding (the Socialists wanted more), taxation (the Liberals desired tax cuts) and whether the 'anti-democratic' Flemish separatist VB and the similar Walloon-based Front National should continue to receive public subsidies as the other parties do (the Francophone parties wanted them withdrawn). In November 2004 the Belgian appeals court upheld a lower court decision that the VB was 'racist' and thus no longer eligible to receive public subsidies. The party immediately disbanded, formed a new party, the Vlaams Belang (Flemish Interest), and issued a less provocative declaration of objectives, intended to retain its hardcore followers while hoping to gain support for their 'martyred' cause.

The 2007 and 2010 elections produce instability

In the 2007 national elections the Flemish Christian Democrats (CD & V) and the Walloon Socialists (PS) gained, mainly at the expense of the Flemish Liberals (Open VLD). The VB lost one seat. Despite several months of protracted and unsuccessful horse-trading, this time the deadlock proved more obdurate. The country endured the longest period in its 177-year history without a government, surpassing the previous record set in 1988 when Wilfried Marten's eighth coalition finally took office after 143 days delay. The Flemish political leaders insisted on constitutional changes, which they felt reflected the demographic and electoral shifts over the past century, granting them more autonomy. They also stressed their lack of tolerance for continuing subsidies for Wallonia, for which the corruption-prone Walloon administrations have provided inadequate accounting. The Walloon political leaders pressed their case for maintaining a strong, or at least viable, federal government and undiminished subsidies.

Particularly striking was the dispute on the future of the bilingual Brussels-Hal-Vilvoorde (BHV) constituency, the only Belgian national electoral district that, by combining the Brussels capital region with a part of the Brabant-Flemish province, transcends provincial and linguistic boundaries. Even though the Supreme Court has declared this exception must be eliminated, the parties have not been able to agree on how to resolve the issue. This dispute represents the latest incarnation of the long simmering agitation over the continuing demographic transformation of Brussels from a Flemish city to a mainly French-speaking metropolitan enclave surrounded by Flanders, within which 96 per cent generally speak French, only 28 per cent Flemish, and 35 per cent speak English either as their first language or—if they are from, for instance, Japan or Sweden—as their preferred second one. Many Belgians, especially those in Flanders and Brussels, speak two or three of these languages. While the Flemish parties demand that the Hal and Vilvoorde areas become part of the Flemish Brabant electoral constituency, the Francophone ones insist that these by now mainly French-speaking suburban areas must be incorporated into the Brussels metropolitan region. The Francophone parties have resorted to filibusters and other tactics to stop the Flemish majority's manoeuvres that they consider inconsistent with Belgian traditions of cross-lingual consensus.

While the parties quarrelled, the Verhofstadt-led coalition cabinet remained in a caretaker capacity. Some international publications began to question the continued viability of Belgium. The coalition-forming negotiations were handicapped by the poor public image of Yves Leterme (the former Flemish Minister-Premier and leader of the Flemish Christian Democrat Party winning the largest delegation in the lower house of parliament), whom the King asked to organise a cabinet. Making derogatory comments during the election about the Walloons; calling Belgium an 'accident of history'; and echoing the cliché that Belgium amounted to nothing more than a 'King, the national football team, and certain brands of beer' led many to call him a buffoon and bigot. Twice he informed the King that he was unable to form a cabinet because of his inability to secure an agreement on the critical issues required for forming a coalition. The stand-off resembled a game of 'chicken' in which two drivers speed toward each other on a single lane road with the 'chicken' the one who first swerves to avoid a collision.

The deadlock was resolved only after a 'committee of wise men', with difficulty, determined a few matters that the parties could agree to implement at once: transferring powers concerning the economy, housing, some family services and agriculture to the regions, funding of the federal government, and strengthening the Brussels region. More controversial issues, including splitting the Brussels-Halle-Vilvoorde (BHV) constituency and transferring employment, health and more family services to the regions were postponed, to be dealt with, it was hoped, by July. After a six-month impasse, in desperation the parties agreed to a temporary caretaker government led by Verhofstadt as prime minister and Leterme as vice prime minister, with the hope that a Leterme-led coalition would take office after three months. In June the Flemish Christian Democrat Party led by Leterme took office, forming a five-party coalition: the Flemish Christian Democrat, the Francophone Centre Democrat Humanist (CdH), the Flemish Liberal Open (VLD), the Francophone Liberal (MR) and the Francophone Socialist (PS), but not the Flemish Socialist Different (SP.A). Failing to resolve the postponed issue, Leterme resigned in July, only a few months later, but lacking a viable alternative the King asked him to continue with the hope that this would allow the government to struggle on at least until the scheduled mid-2009 regional and EU elections.

The Leterme-led coalition limped on until the 2008 world financial crisis hit Europe. In the efforts to cope with the insolvency of Fortis it took steps to arrange its sale to the French-based financial conglomerate BNP Paribas, but in the process the government was accused of trying to influence an appeals court decision and was forced to resign. King Albert, following the advice of former Prime Minister Wilfried Martens, whom he had asked to broker a new coalition, asked a very reluctant Herman van Rompuy, speaker of the lower chamber of parliament and a Flemish Christian Democrat leader, to form a government. As confirmed by Parliament, the van Rompuy-led five-party coalition (the Flemish Catholic CD&V, the former Walloon Catholic (CdH), the Flemish Liberals VLD, the Francophone MR and the Walloon Socialists, but again not the Flemish Socialist SP.A) retained most members of the cabinet it replaced, except for Leterme and the more radical Flemish ones. When van Rompuy, after several months, was selected for the newly created post of EU President, Leterme was once again asked to head the government. But the government collapsed in April over the long standing row over the Brussels-Halle-Vilvoorde electoral district.

In the June 2010 elections the separatist New Flemish Alliance (N-VA), led by Bart de Wever, won more seats in the lower chamber than any other party. No longer in a cartel with the Flemish Christian

Democrats (as it had been in 2007), it increased the number of seats from 19 to 27. At its victory celebration the cheering crowd sang the Flemish (not the Belgian) anthem. The more radical separatist Vlaams Belang (VB), however, lost seats (from 17 to 12), perhaps an indication that its popularity is past its peak. The Walloon Socialists (PS) led by Elio Di Rupo won 26 seats (a loss of two), relegating them to second place; their Flemish counterparts (the SP.A) won only 13 seats (down two). The Flemish Liberals (Open VLD) and their sister party the Walloon MR lost significantly (from 18 to 13 and from 23 to 18 respectively). The Open VLD lost in part because the public resented the fact that it had called the vote of non-confidence that had led to the calling of an election a year earlier than scheduled. The Flemish Christian Democrats (CD & V) and Centre Democrat Humanists (CdH) suffered even heavier losses (from 23 to 17 and from 12 to 9 respectively). CD &V and the CdH lost in part because of increasing secularism and growing concern over what was perceived as a cover-up by the Catholic hierarchy of clerical abuse of children. After the elections the government raided the offices of the archdiocese for incriminating documents, while the bishops, who were in conclave, were held *incommunicado*. The Vatican immediately voiced its vigorous disapproval of the unprecedented action.

Since the avowed goal of the de Wever-led N-VA to split the country differs dramatically from the Socialist objectives, negotiations to form a coalition following the 2010 elections proved to be even more frustrating than earlier ones. For months a Leterme-led caretaker administration carried on, even taking Belgium's turn chairing the EU Council from 1 July, as King Albert II attempted to find a *formateur* who could succeed in forming a government. Continuing frustration in the efforts to form a coalition government following the June 2010 elections led to a longer caretaker interregnum than ever before in Belgian history: 542 days. The elongated saga wore out the patience of almost everyone, from the king to the public—who reacted with a sense of desperation mixed with sarcasm and humour.

In 2010, Belgium celebrated the 180th anniversary of its independence and the thirtieth anniversary of the significant 1980 constitutional reform. The divide that the Franks originated in the first millennium of its recorded history has emerged as the dominant divisive political issue challenging Belgium in its third. In the coming decades how will Belgium cope with the linguistic divide threatening to tear its polity apart?

Many sceptics, in Belgium and elsewhere, doubt that the parties can continue to muddle on merely by accommodating the more pressing, conflicting interests. A few Belgians, including most separatists predicting the break up of Belgium. So do many foreigners, whose reading is generally limited to articles stressing the schismatic strains but not the steps taken to alleviate them. Most Belgians, though, believe their country will go on muddling through. Constitutional reforms will continue to curtail the central government's role, reducing it to little more than defence, foreign affairs and the economy, functions that it shares with the EU and NATO. The coming few decades will be as eventful as the last few decades have been.

A crisis facilitates making the impossible possible. Many months of prodding by King Albert II, successive efforts of '*formateurs*' to resolve the impasse and numerous demonstrations made no headway until July when the Flemish Christian Democrats (CD&V) broke ranks with the Flemish separatist New Flemish Alliance (N-VA) with which the disagreements were too basic. Strenuous bargaining on the key issues among the remaining parties led to ingenious compromises regarding key issues, including the future of nuclear energy, dividing of the Brussels-Halle-Vilvoorde electoral constituency (with French-speakers in the suburban area allowed to vote elsewhere) and a constitutional amendment transferring more power from the federal government to the regions. In November, the departure of the interim prime minister, Leterme, for an OECD post and the downgrading by Standard and Poor of the Belgian credit rating from AA+ to AA and the corollary threat of being engulfed in the euro fiscal crisis forced a final resolution of the 18 months deadlock.

So, after 541 days of an interim caretaker administration, following the indecisive 13 June 2010 election, Elio Di Rupo, a French-speaking Socialist (SP) succeeded in forming a six-party coalition comprising two Socialist parties (the Flemish SP.A and Walloon PS), the two Liberal parties (the Flemish Open VLD and Francophone MR), and what were once the two Christian Democratic parties (the Flemish CD&V and Francophone CdH)—but not the Flemish separatist N-VA. Di Rupo, leader of the party with the second most seats in the 2010-elected parliament, was the first Socialist and the first Walloon Francophone to head the government since 1974—in a country where the Flemish are a significant majority.

Given the intensity of the continuing geographical–partisan schism, onlookers anticipated that the elections of May 2014 would be as traumatic as they had been in recent years, the results to be as inconclusive, and efforts to form a coalition government as frustrating. Party leaders would be called upon to be imaginative and flexible as they sought to form a government which could secure parliamentary support and deal with the myriad pressing issues. Playing a key role in this effort would be the new King. Upon the abdication of 79 year-old Albert II on 21 July 2013, the national Independence Day, his son 53 year-old Philippe was sworn in as the seventh monarch since Leopold I was installed in 1831.

As anticipated and feared by many the federal elections to the Chamber of Representatives held on 25 May 2014—along with those for the regional legislatures and the Belgian MEPs for the European Parliament—were frustratingly divisive and inclusive. In the federal election the N-VA (the separatist New Flemish Alliance) scored an even more impressive victory than it did in the 2010 federal elections, gaining six more seats to bring its total in the new Chamber to thirty-three. Its gains came primarily from the more radical anti-immigrant, pro-secessionist Vlaams Belang, which lost nine seats, reducing their Chamber representation to three and signalling their decline as a populist force. The Walloon Socialist Party (PS) continued to hold the second largest number of seats (twenty-six), three fewer than in 2010. The Flemish Socialists (SP.A) continued with thirteen seats. Of the descendants of the Christian Democrats, the Flemish CD&V gained one seat, bringing their total to 18; the Walloon CdH held its own at nine. Of the Liberal parties, the Flemish Open VLD gained one seat, giving them eighteen in total; the Walloon MR gained two, bringing their total to twenty. The Greens added one seat, bringing their total to six, making their delegation the eighth largest in the Chamber of Representatives.

The campaign stressed socio-economic reforms, jobs, tax reforms, and pension issues—and in the case of the N-VA, secession. One week before the election the former prime minister Jean-Luc Dehaene died suddenly, and one day before the balloting there was a shooting at the Belgian Jewish Museum in Brussels, with three people reported dead.

Following the ingrained custom of nominating the leader of the party with the plurality of members elected to the Chamber of Representatives as 'informateur', King Philippe initially charged the N-VA leader Bart De Wever with the task of exploring possibilities for forming a cabinet. As in 2010 his efforts to form a coalition including his party failed and the post-2010 coalition government, without the N-VA, emerged only after many months of strenuous negotiations. The post-2014 efforts to form a coalition have required comparable patience and persistence.

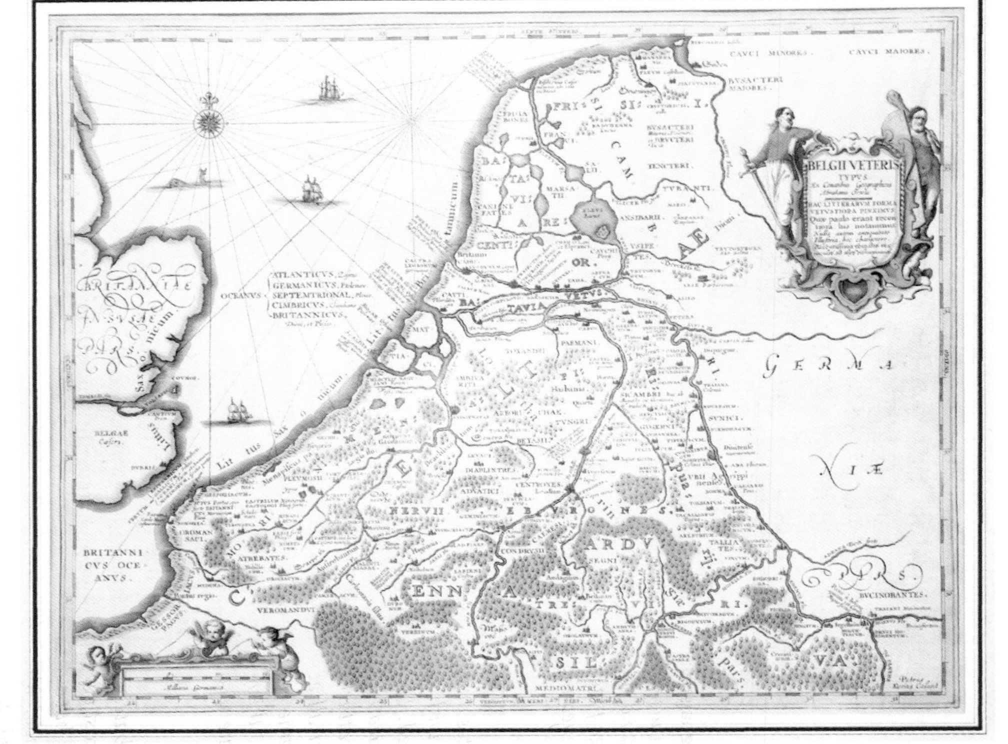

Map 20. 'Belgii Veteris'—Abraham Ortelius (1567). It depicts the land long called Belgium, as well as the Netherlands and the Low Countries..

Retrospect and Prospects

KEEPING A DIVIDED LAND UNITED

Language provides '*access to a vast array of knowledge and belief, assets that empower us, when we think, when we listen, when we speak, read, and write, to stand on the shoulders of so much ancestral thought and feeling. Our language places us in a cultural continuum, linking us to the past, and showing our meanings also to future fellow–speakers.*'[1]

Nicholas Ostler

'*States and regimes had every reason to reinforce, if they could, state patriotism with the sentiments and symbols of "imagined community". As it happened, the time when the democratisation of politics made it essential to "educate our masters", "to make Italians", to turn "peasants into Frenchmen" and attach all to nation and flag, was also the time when popular nationalist, or at all events, xenophobic sentiments and those of national superiority... became easier to mobilize* ... [and] *underlined the differences between "us" and "them". And there is no more effective way of bonding together the disparate sections of restless peoples than to unite them against the outsider.*'[2]

E. J. Hobsbawm

'*Debates over national identity are a pervasive characteristic of our time. Almost everywhere people have questioned, reconsidered, and redefined what they have in common and what distinguishes them from other people: Who are we? Modernization, economic development, and globalization have led people to rethink their identities and to redefine them in narrower, more intimate, communal terms. Sub-national cultural and regional identities are taking precedence over broader national identities. People identify with those who are most like themselves and with whom they share a perceived common ethnicity, religion, traditions, and myth of common descent and common history* ... [In many] *countries it takes the extreme form of communal movements demanding political recognition, autonomy, or independence. These have included movements on behalf of Quebecois, Scots, Flemings, Catalonians, Basques, Lombards, Corsicans, Kurds, Kosovars, Berbers, Chiapans, Chechens, Palestinians, Tibetans, Muslim Mindanaoans, Christian Sudanese, Abkhazians, Tamils, Acehans, East Timorese, and others.*'[3]

Samuel Huntington

Why and how has Belgium split in recent decades?

Why and how did the language issue, which had remained politically benign for so many centuries, erupt in the twentieth century to divide the Belgian polity between Dutch-speaking Flanders and French-speaking Wallonia? How could Belgium—with so long a collective identity, shared heritage, unified rule and a sufficient sense of common community to secure its independence more than 180 years ago—have its unity so threatened? The evolution of democracy from a minute to universal suffrage—driven by the rise of labour, the spread of literacy and the growing impact of expanded government—led the once excluded labourers and Flemish-speakers to assert their right to participate more directly in their governance. The post-war rise of linguistic-, ethnic- and culturally-driven 'national' consciousness and pride—along with pervading globalism—drove sectional schism. These events have transformed Belgium from a country long governed by an exclusive, unilingual, propertied elite into a more electorally inclusive and language-divided polity. Consideration of Belgium's present challenges provokes consideration of four questions: How long has there been a Belgium? Is there still a Belgium? Will there be a Belgium for long? Does the sovereign 'nation-state' have a future?

Has Belgium existed long?

Has Belgium existed for long? Opinions differ. How people view issues depends on their values and attitudes, which reflect and derive from what they have been carefully taught by their families and societal leaders about their religion, their culture and their history—and what is expressed in their language. The contrast in Flemish and Walloon social, economic and political perspectives and values drives the sectional schism.

Jules Destree's famed 1912 'There are no Belgians' letter to the King stressed the entrenched differences between Flanders and Wallonia, denied the existence of a shared Belgian identity and contended that the land was an artificial creation brought about by an accident of history. The journalist Paul Belien has recently repeated the familiar separatist dogma: 'Belgium was an artificial state...the result of an international ... compromise constructed ... where no similar state had ever existed and where people had no common identity that would enable them to acquire a national consciousness and, hence, become a genuine nation.'[4] As already noted, Leterme, the recent prime minister, voiced similar opinions in the 2007 election campaign.

In contrast, Henri Pirenne, in *Histoire de Belgique* (1900), makes the case that almost two millennia of shared identity and more than 500 years with uniting governmental institutions supported the country-wide spirit of the members of the first Belgian congress who were 'devoted to the same cause, and ... wanted to be and were only Belgians.'[5] Pirenne glosses over the fact it was an exclusive French-speaking propertied and professional elite who maintained this common community; nevertheless, history supports the reality that there has long been a Belgium. The land has long carried the name and identity given it by Caesar. The Burgundian dukes united most of the land in the fifteenth century. In contrast, Italy and Germany did not have unified governments until the nineteenth century. In addition, all of Belgium shares a remarkable artistic heritage.

To dismiss Belgium's creation as an accident of history stemming from an imposed great power mandate ignores the fact that most of the major powers opposed the 1830 revolt that its centuries-long struggle for self-government had fostered. Despite opposition by the major European powers, Belgians rebelled, developed a constitution, and recruited a king, acts that facilitated the leading European powers, and the Netherlands' final recognition of its independence. Every country has evolved as the product of a concatenation of critical events (or 'accidents'). Fortuitous circumstances, along with 'manifest destiny,' supported the events that forged the birth and shape of France, Britain, Germany, Italy, the United States and other well-established nation-states. No one calls these countries 'accidents of history' or considers their histories to have begun only with the founding of their national governments.

Over twenty centuries, many factors strengthened the Belgian extended community. Not only did Low Country rulers strengthen the institutions of central governance; its leaders also supported or imposed religious conformity (as Philip II attempted), promoted language hegemony (as William I of the united Netherlands tried with 'proper' Dutch and nineteenth century Belgian rulers with French) and wrote a common history (as did Justus Lipsius and Henri Pirenne). Rivers, canals, roads and railways provided transport networks strengthening communication and commercial ties. Architecture, painting, literature and other aspects of its cultural heritage enhanced a shared sense of pride. Continued foreign interference, invasions, the loss of land and other humiliations imposed by the Dutch and French fuelled the Belgian sense of community. These commonalties have long abetted the efforts of rulers to develop the shared identity and community spirit that paved the way for the founding of an independent Belgium. The propertied and professional—and Francophone (even those from the Flemish-speaking towns of Antwerp, Ghent, Bruges, Brussels and Louvain)—elite—dominated the early decades of the Belgian nation-state. The French spoken by the governmentally dominant elite divided them socially as well as politically from those who spoke either one of the scorned Dutch dialects spoken by the Flemish or the disdained Walloon patois version of French. Like most people, this elite viewed public affairs from the perspective of their values and vested interests.

The Francophone elite's efforts to suffocate, or at least ignore, the use of Flemish failed, in part because Dutch was the prevailing language of the immediate neighbour, an advantage that the Flemish (unlike the Bretons and the Basques) had. Belgium's neighbours were more successful in achieving a linguistic cultural hegemony. When the United Kingdom formed in 1707, its peoples thought of themselves as English, Scottish, Welsh or Irish, but its ruling class extended the use of English and developed an overlying, complementary British identity. The prevalence of a standard French represents a triumph of the Paris-based dialect of *langue d'oil* over not only the various patois of *langue d'oc* once found in southern France and the variety of *langue d'oil* dialects in northern France but also other tongues; as recently as 1900, only about half of the French spoke standard French as a first language, the rest spoke a Celtic, German, Flemish or a non-French Romanic tongue. Well into the nineteenth century, Europe remained a mosaic of small communities, each speaking its own patois or dialect. In their evolution modern states have endeavoured, with mixed success, to superimpose a national tongue throughout the country and along with it a sense of national community.

In Belgium, the Francophone propertied elite long remained dominant. For centuries, Low Country rulers encountered only limited, sporadic resistance to the conduct of business in French. The French-speaking propertied, privileged and powerful dominated the governance of the court, the church and commerce, and overlooked the grievances of the economically and politically disadvantaged, dialect-speaking working classes. The country's Francophone propertied elite so dominated its public affairs that the language-driven class divide did not affect its governance. In contrast to other countries, such as the United Kingdom, the United States and France, whose national language now generally dominates even those parts where another tongue once prevailed, the long-time Francophone hegemony over the southern Low Countries never significantly permeated the Flemish working class.

Europe's industrial and political revolutions began a transformation of the economic, social and political dynamics of Belgium. The shift from an agriculture-based to an industry-based economy spurred the growth of a professional and entrepreneurial middle class, and in time an extension of the right to vote from a minute fraction to universal suffrage, a dramatic increase in the number of schools and consequently in working class literacy, the emergence of a Flemish literature and the rise of labour and Flemish movements. Together these changes nurtured a language-based sectional nationalism that mutated the political dynamics of Belgium. Even in the late nineteenth century not only did most of those in the north speak a different language from the political, economic and social elite, but also in the south most continued to speak a Walloon dialect of French. The government did not succeed, as did those in many other countries, in significantly reducing the language disparity, perhaps in part because French and Dutch are not just different languages but belong to different language groups, and France and the Netherlands are next door.

Forceful rulers, despite the linguistic, economic and social divides, forged the common institutions and collective community enabling development of a united Belgian polity. For centuries, this unilingual elite exerted political, economic and social hegemony over the land. This domination, as in other lands, bred a sense of superiority that manifested itself in strong class barriers, striking distinctions in dress, housing, literacy, education and speech and a conviction that what was good for their interests was best for the country.

By the twentieth century an expanded suffrage, increased literacy and Flemish literature combined to nurture a Flemish self-consciousness, erode the Francophone propertied elitist hegemony and arouse a

Walloon reaction. Jules Destrée's 1912 declaration that there were no Belgians warned the country's leaders against complacency regarding the long-shared sense of Belgian-ness. Nevertheless, there has long been a Belgium, albeit one long dominated by the Francophone elite. A rising Flemish consciousness, however, began eroding this hegemony in the early decades of the twentieth century, and undermined it in the last decades.

Does Belgium still exist?

Is there (still) a Belgium? Many ask the question that Tony Judt did in his essay 'Is there a Belgium?'[6] While the question arouses debate, one should not equate the stridency of a few separatist voices with the moderation of far more numerous voices that reject such stridency. While before the nineteenth century the language divide generated little political unrest, the Age of Revolutions drove the concerns of the previously politically disadvantaged for more participation in the governing process. The rise of linguistic consciousness in the latter part of the twentieth century fostered antipathy between Flanders and Wallonia that extends to disparities in economic viability and religious-philosophical values.

Over the centuries, the focus of southern Low Country affluence moved from Wallonia under the Romans to the county of Flanders by the twelfth century, to the duchy of Brabant in the fourteenth century. The development of mines and mills in Wallonia in the nineteenth century spurred the emergence of a prosperous Walloon economy, but the second half of the twentieth century witnessed its decline. Flanders, in contrast, has attracted more foreign investment and industries and developed as the more economically and politically dominant part of the country.

Religious and philosophical differences between the regions are just as striking as the language ones. Catholics prevailed in Flanders and the freethinkers were the majority in Wallonia. The Catholic education network dominated Flanders while public and private school systems competed in Wallonia. In health care too, Catholic Flanders contrasted with more secular Wallonia. This difference affects and reflects the stronger support for the Christian Democrats in Flanders and the Socialists in Wallonia, and the contrasting positions these parties take on the 'welfare state'.

An increasingly self-confident Flanders has strengthened its ties with the Netherlands in literature, media, arts and education, and standing side by side with its neighbour, supported the Dutch language on the international stage. Francophone Belgium has a cultural affinity with France, strengthened by the fact that such Belgian born-and-raised artists as the author Georges Simenon and the singer Jacques Brel spent most of their careers in France. The result has been that Flanders and Wallonia have developed into two different cultural worlds with their own ways of considering political issues. Sectionalism has undermined Belgium's collective identity and contributed to the apparent diffidence of many Belgians regarding their history and heritage.

Cumulatively these differences have profoundly reoriented the parties. Not only have the Christian Democrats, Liberals and Socialists split along linguistic lines into twin sets of parties, but each one of these sister parties has dramatically redeveloped its platform and its strategy, and renamed itself, thus significantly increasing its ideological distance from its traditional sister party. The Flemish Socialist Party emphasises that it is different. What was once the Walloon Catholic Party has named itself not 'Christian' but 'Humanist'. The Flemish Christian Democrats and Liberals, reacting to aggressive Flemish separatism, have added the word Flemish to their name. The Walloon Liberals, when they merged with the Brussels-based FDF, named themselves Mouvement Réformateur (MR). These changes reflect changing election strategies and different political approaches to public policy and politics, manifested in the contrasting views on education, social security policies and more devolution. Migration into the Brussels metropolitan area continues to undermine the use of Dutch in the city; many shop windows carry signs in two languages: French and English, but not Dutch. The sectional differences extend to populist attitudes. Many Walloons perceive the Flemish as arrogant and pushy, many Flemish view the Walloons as effete and lazy. While once there was one dominant, albeit elitist-driven, national mindset, now contrasting sectional perspectives compete for the allegiance of Belgians. Politicians no longer work to develop the cross-language support which has in the past helped support nationwide Belgian politics.

Globalisation and the growth of the supra-national EU and NATO have helped the sectional cause. Rivers and canals, roads and railways once nurtured southern Low Countries interdependence and prosperity, and common government institutions fostered a Belgian community.

Today air transport, limited access highways, high-speed railways and instant communication have sped the emergence of an international community—whose hallmarks are the multinational corporations, limited Europe-wide supra-governance and an incipient European sense of collective identity. With commercial as well as military threats abated, separatists question the need to continue a Belgian state.

Through most of the nineteenth century Belgium's power elite shared the French language (with the upper class speaking French in Flanders as well as Wallonia), the Catholic religion (even if divided between the conservatives and the anti-clerical factions over the extent of clerical control of education), a sense of community (they were not Dutch, French or German), economic interdependence and an appreciation of their common cultural heritage. The shared values of this politically dominant class fostered nationhood. By the early twentieth century, however, convergent political forces were eroding this hegemony. Newly enfranchised voters supported the Workers Party, especially in the south and the Flemish movement in the north. The divisive policies and practices of German occupations, differing reactions to the Royal Question and the trials of collaborators exacerbated regional stress. Shared perceptions that long strengthened the Belgian sense of identity have been overtaken by preoccupation with conflicting Flemish and Walloon interests, and perceptions of their history.

The shifting focus of partisan conflict reflects this changing environment. For most of the nineteenth century, the major issue over which the Liberals fought with the generally dominant Catholic Party was the extent of clerical control of education. By the early twentieth century, the decline in the influence of the Catholic Church and the rise of the Socialist Party reflected and affected the increasing importance of socio-economic interests in politics. By the late twentieth century, language-driven sectional issues dominated the political agenda, dividing first the parties and then the governance of the country.

Interrelated language and culture differences have driven sectional pressures splitting the Belgian polity, as reflected in the mounting differences between the sister Christian Democrat, Liberal and Socialist parties. Each of the main Flemish parties is less sympathetic to the welfare state and more sympathetic to separatism than the Walloon parties. While many believe the country is already too divided, many discontented Flemish people continue to press for more devolution or outright independence—and many Walloons would be happy to see them go. Meanwhile, the language split so frustrates politics that the government does not devote adequate attention to such vital issues such as unemployment, pensions, debt and criminal justice.

Yes, the Belgium polity is fractured, but there remains a Belgian sense of community. While its sense of extended community has weakened, it continues to exist. While those mesmerised by Flemish or Walloon loyalties discount the extent of Belgian national consciousness, this perception overlooks the fact that people have multiple, not single, community allegiances. Most English, Welsh and Scots also think of themselves as British. Prussians as well as Bavarians recognise themselves as Germans. Californians and New Yorkers, and even Texans, consider themselves Americans. While at home people stress their local identity, abroad the national identity is often more evident and expressed.

What do Belgians still have in common? Besides a monarch and a few remaining national institutions, including the foreign service, armed forces, postal service, railways (which the government has proposed splitting into two) and social security (a major point of contention), they share almost six centuries with a common government, an illustrious artistic heritage and a conviction that they are not German, Dutch or French. And significantly, they share Brussels, the mainly French-speaking enclave within Flanders that is the national capital, the seat of the Flemish region and community and the seat of NATO and the EU. Separatists may press for dividing Belgium, but many more Belgians prefer to preserve a united Belgium. Whatever Belgian sense of extended community remains may be fragile and fractured, but not (at least not yet) dismembered. Is there still a Belgium? Does one see a cup half full or half empty?

Will Belgium exist for long?

Does a sufficient sense of Belgian extended community remain to sustain a federal Belgium? Given how critically divided the Belgian sense of collective identity and community is, what is the outlook for the country remaining united? The accelerating difficulty of forming a coalition cabinet capable of addressing the key issues dividing the country provokes concerns regarding Belgium's prospects for continuing to contain separatist pressures. Those who predict the tearing apart of Belgium include not only separatists but also many who myopically project recent trends and others who judge separatism support by the high volume of strident populism. Globalisation has added to the ferment, letting demagogic separatists exploit the emotions of those who feel their lifestyles and security threatened.

Political opportunism, populist demagoguery and journalist rhetoric lead many to forecast the breakup of Belgium. Several factors may be cited for this pessimism. Els Witte points out what may be the basic one: 'Culture may have created the widest gap of all. The creation of cultural autonomy during the 1960s already produced starkly contrasting results. Flanders reinforced its cooperation with the Netherlands in the area of literature, media, the arts and education. Francophone Belgium has always been drawn to France. The result was that Flanders and Wallonia became two different worlds with their own cultures.'[7]

The animosity between Wallonia and Flanders appears to be growing even stronger. Those on both sides of the linguistic divide are limited to a unilingual presentation of views through news media and community communication, a phenomenon that continues to polarise perspectives. The continued pressure for further devolution leads many to forecast that Belgium is on a 'slippery slope' that can only end in a breakup. Continuing comments in the press predicting the future of Belgium have a psychological impact leading many to believe that dissolution is inevitable. Many politicians appear to relish the opportunity to exploit separatist rhetoric as a means of gaining political traction.

On the other hand, a less myopic perspective presents a more positive scenario. While in politics emotion often trumps reason several factors lead an 'outsider' student of Belgian politics to be hopeful regarding the prospects for this long divided, long united country remaining united—if only loosely. First, constitutional revisions have alleviated many of the concerns of the moderates advocating sectional autonomy. One may ask whether it was necessary to override the provinces with a new intermediate level of governance, and with not just one set but two overlapping sets of these new intermediate jurisdictions. Having created the regions and communities, was it necessary to retain the provinces (apart from the pressure for preserving political and civil service posts, which was the political price for securing the legislative support to pass the necessary laws)? Are three regions, three communities, ten provinces, and more than 500 municipalities needed for a country with less than 11 million people? But this is decades later second-guessing, mainly by armchair watchers.

Second, demagogues generally self-destruct (although there are enough exceptions to provoke concern). In time as they, in their effort to extend their appeal, escalate their demands and stridency, their pandering becomes more obvious and obnoxious and their extremism loses creditability. Memories of earlier injustices often recede. New arrangements for governing become time-tested and accepted. Mainstream parties expropriate the less demagogic appeals. While the separatists speak loudly of splitting Flanders and Wallonia into two countries, they are outnumbered not only by those less receptive, if not angered, by the continued sectional stridency but also by many autonomists who, while striving for more power for the constituent regions and communities, work to preserve the unity of the country. As the regions and communities gain more power, the radicals may lose traction. New political issues may rise to crowd the old from the top of the political agenda.

Third, those pressing for dividing Belgium into separate nation-states cannot expect other states of Europe to facilitate the breakup of their neighbour. There are many more nationalities than there are nation-states; countries have a vested interest in discouraging, indeed suppressing, separatist forces in their own countries. In Europe only former republics within the old strong-armed communist federations, and the two parts of the former soviet satellite Czechoslovakia, have become independent. To allow a long-united country such as Belgium to divide would increase separatist pressures in many long-established countries as well as many more lands that more recently secured their independence and whose inherited colonial borders embrace a host of minorities. Spain and Italy are not the only countries concerned with rich regions seeking autonomy or independence; the United Kingdom, France and Hungary are not the only ones concerned with dissident regions; but breaking up a country at the political seat of the EU would threaten not only the stability of other European governments but also the EU government itself. While the presence of NATO, the EU and a host of other supra-national organisations has prompted separatist movements to dream of independence without the inconvenience of losing military and economic security, member countries are hardly likely to support the split of a fellow member, especially if they have dissident minority sections, such as Scotland and Catalonia, which have long pressed for and secured more autonomy, and some of whose political leaders continue to press for independence.

Fourth, Belgium has, to use a cliché, long 'punched above its weight' in European affairs (as illustrated by the fact that two Belgian prime ministers secured strong backing for the EU Commission presidency and a third was selected for the newly created post of EU President). Dividing the country would severely undermine its credibility and its influence on the international scene.

Fifth, history notes that granting more autonomy or status to parts of a country to mitigate sectionalism does not resolve divisive minority tensions, as countries from Britain to Nigeria have experienced. Other parts want similar consideration, and the newly created parts often have their own minority groups which demand attention. The more culturally diverse an area, the less likelihood that a single elite will dominate its political affairs. Carving out one section from a polity often leaves the remaining parts of the larger polity less culturally diverse, and thus potentially less appreciative of minorities. While some separatists believe that a total split of Flanders from Wallonia could occur without severe economic and political consequences, to unravel Belgium's commercial life would be not only expensive but also traumatic. While section-based minorities in many lands assert their distinctive cultural identity and demand more autonomy or independence, Belgium is the only one where it is the most populous and prosperous part that more stridently presses the separatist case. Many issues would complicate a split of Belgium, ones that would embitter a divorce. One would be allocating the enormous debt. Among the others would be determining the responsibilities for pensions and absorbing the overblown public payroll.

More critically, dividing Belgium would force a Solomon-like decision regarding Brussels, the once Flemish-speaking but now mainly French-speaking capital, which both the Flemish and the Walloons claim as their own. Neither Flanders, whose government headquarters were deliberately placed in downtown Brussels, nor Wallonia is prepared to give up Brussels or any part of it. Divorce leads to fights over common possessions, including a favoured child or a cosmopolitan metropolis. Some suggest giving Brussels to the EU as a capital (like Washington), but whatever would be included in such a district—the 'European Quarter', all of the Brussels region, or something in between—difficult issues would remain. How many Bruxellois would accept consignment to a city-without-a-country? Even resolving the impossible Brussels muddle would not address the difficulty of the bilingual communes along the language border. Brussels is a major source of the tension dividing Belgium, it may also prove to be the principal factor keeping it together, just because neither parent will give up the child or allow it to be cut in half. Having repeatedly failed to resolve even their long festering dispute regarding the Brussels-Halle-Vilvoorde bilingual electoral district, even when a court judgment has directed that it be resolved, how can Belgians be expected to tackle the far more complex and impassioned conundrum of the Brussels enclave, which constitutes the crucial core of a tangled web of critical issues that must be negotiated in any effort to divide Belgium into two nation-states? Continuing to share Brussels will prove less formidable than splitting the metropolis or allocating it to Flanders or Wallonia.

The resourcefulness and creativity of Belgian leaders in facing past challenges sustains the prospects for keeping the country united. Belgium's future depends not only on how creatively its future leaders define the responsibilities of its constituent parts, but also on how well they re-energise a sense of extended community supporting its national institutions. Leaders of this long-divided, long-united land have had centuries of experience in bridging its language and other divides with compromises and consensuses. Its twenty-first century leaders may be as capable of devising means to accommodate Belgium's diversity of interests.

The energy, patience and ingenuity of earlier Belgian leaders in developing and maintaining the country's unity provides optimism regarding future efforts to muddle through, if only to retain a weak casing holding its autonomous parts, promoting cooperation among the parts and representing their interests at the EU, NATO and other international organisations. Most Belgians—Walloons, Flemings and Bruxellois—will be disappointed if their leaders cannot contain the separatist threat sufficiently to preserve a united polity that can accommodate diversity. If Belgium, with its long shared collective identity, common institutions of government and a tradition of resolving conflicts with compromise and consensus, cannot remain united, what can be expected of other countries—ones that have a shorter history, a less developed sense of collective identity, and internal borders which separate even more linguistically, ethnically and/or religiously distinctive communities with little or no common history, no shared culture and limited transport and communication networks? The example of Belgian innovative efforts to hold together a multi-lingual/cultural country may provide other nations with relentless sectional movements the promise of reconciling diversity with unity.

Belgium has a long history and renowned heritage that have helped maintain its unity. While the language-driven schism has fractured the country, its parts are not severed. Its leaders face the challenge of keeping the language-divided country united, a challenge that will probably require the concession of even more powers to its regions and communities. As a corollary it will demand revival its 'Belgian-ness', an appreciation of what all Belgians share. Cultivating an enhanced national sense of pride should not pose an insurmountable challenge for although Belgians are modest, they have a rich common history and heritage to be immodest about. Revitalising a common sense of community would provide centripetal pressures counterbalancing the centrifugal sectional ones. For more than six centuries, the country's leaders have weathered conflicts threatening its survival and negotiated compromises supporting a shared identity and common institutions. Belgian leaders, as Pierre-Henri Laurent said in assessing Belgian politics in 1984 in an article 'Divided Belgium Walks a Tightrope', the Belgians have 'repeatedly demonstrated ingenuity in negotiating compromises to what once appeared to be irresolvable conflicts. Their success in muddling through provides an example to many other countries trying to cope with a linguistic-cultural divide.'[8] Such imagination and innovation constitute a vital skill, one that will be required to meet the challenge of keeping a language-divided nation united. Continuing to find solutions will be stressful, requiring difficult negotiations, but breaking up the country would be far more challenging.

As Belgium continues to devolve functions to its sub-national parts and share an increasing number of functions with the EU and NATO, the Belgian national government will more closely resemble a confederation than a federation. A federation, according to the constitutional expert K. C. Wheare, divides powers between general and regional authorities so that each in its own sphere is co-ordinate with the others, while a 'confederation' is 'a form of association between governments whereby they set up a common organisation to regulate matters of common concern but retain to themselves, to a greater or lesser degree, some control over this common organisation.'[9] Wheare's definition in some particulars already appears to describe the EU. While many prognosticators forecast the end of Belgium, a better bet would be that it will remain a federation or confederation.

Does the sovereign 'nation-state' have a future?

A more relevant question may be: can nationalism adjust to changing global and local challenges by developing a more complementary, not competitive, role with supra-national and sub-national governments? Belgium may provide a portent.

Since emerging from imperial rule more than a thousand years ago Belgium has experienced critical transitions in its governance. The first was a collection of feudal principalities, whose autonomy varied dramatically from time to time and principality to principality. In the second, foreign rulers—Burgundian, Spanish and Austrian Habsburg, French and Dutch—unified the land and centralised its administration, governing Belgium as a subject, subordinate government. In the third, independent Belgium continued the nurturing of a cohesive sense of community and developing a unitary nation-state, which monopolised governmental control over the country's diplomatic, security, monetary and domestic affairs. In its emerging fourth stage, the Belgian general government increasingly shares power with its recently created federated parts, the regions and communities, and with the EU and NATO. The gradually increased sharing of power with these supra-national organisations may invite some to compare the role of the present Belgian national government with that of the nineteenth and early twentieth century third-world protectorate governments—and with the Belgian governments under Spanish and Austrian rule. Except, of course, notably that Belgium possesses more autonomy and shares with its fellow member governments control of the EU and NATO.

Belgium has long been a part of a Europe-wide process that transformed a feudal jigsaw puzzle of principalities into a series of sovereign nation-states, which have defended their right to govern without international or internal interference. The era of the unbridled nation-state may, however, be in terminal decline. International organisations such as the EU and NATO have emerged in the same half-century as the collapse of the last of the traditional empires: the British, French and Russian. Unlike these colonial-capital-centric empires, however, the new supra-national organisations are polycentric; their sovereign member governments determine their policies and oversee their administration. However limited the role of many of these international organisations, though, their emergence signals recognition that the sovereign nation-state no longer can maintain the fiction of unfettered independence. National governments, even the most powerful ones, share power with one or more supra-national institutions. Just as feudalism was fading long before its collapse and monarchs lost their role as 'head of government' long before it was popularly recognised, so our descendants may consider the concept of 'sovereignty' as the relic of a bygone age.

Belgium and other countries, including that long-time paragon of centralised governance France, have significantly not only shared power with supra-national organisations, but also extended power to sub-national administrations, thus further differentiating the newly-emerging stage of governance from the centralised nation-state model. The emerging stage may introduce more sharing of power—from the supra-national to the national to the sub-national and municipal institutions. Increasing globalisation and popular assertiveness fuel the change. Politics is the pragmatic application of values to contemporary issues. The rise of modern representative governance, of which the advent of universal suffrage has been the vital contributor, has aroused the heretofore politically disadvantaged to assert the distinctive identity and spirit of their communities.

Where the language and related culture have been significantly different, national governments have often been challenged by separatist movements. The political unleashing of those once denied access to the ballot box has aroused popular assertiveness at the local as well as the national level. This is especially true of communities with a distinctive tongue, ethnic literature and religion, and consequently a different history, heritage and mythology. The rise of modern democracy, with its gradual extension of the right to vote, has not only increased popular access to national decision-making but also led to a desire for meaningful local self-government.

Many national governments face the challenge of maintaining a united government, if only in a more decentralised form. Jerry Z. Muller points out that 'Increased urbanisation, literacy, and political mobilisation; differences in the fertility rates and economic performance of various ethnic groups; and immigration will challenge the internal structure of states as well as their borders. Whether politically correct or not, ethnonationalism will continue to shape the world in the twenty-first century ... Since ethnonationalism is a direct consequence of modernisation, it is likely to gain ground in societies undergoing such a process. It is hardly surprising, therefore, that it remains among the most vital—and most disruptive—forces in many parts of the contemporary world.'[10]

Belgium's preservation of its unity by decentralising its unitary state provides a case study of how a divided country may meet the challenge of increasingly assertive diversity. The seventeenth century concept of sovereignty, facilitated by the Treaty of Westphalia (1648), is no longer applicable to the international political scene. Until the twentieth century powerful countries successfully expanded their territory and centralised their authority. The hundreds of principalities in Europe in the sixteenth century contracted to only a few dozen states by the beginning of the twentieth century. Over the same period national governments exponentially expanded their budgets, functions and work force, extending their direct impact upon everyone.

Such growth, however, was checked by the momentous events of the twentieth century, which notably included two World Wars, an expanding suffrage, instant communication, rapid transport and accompanying societal changes. Globalisation and the rise of international organisations, ironically, have increased local perception of the exceptionalism of their communities. The rise in education, literacy and the suffrage spurred political activism and strengthened the political assertiveness of local communities, especially ones with a distinctive tongue and culture. The end of World War I saw the dismemberment of the Austro-Hungarian and Ottoman empires, and the late decades of the twentieth century saw the breakup of the Soviet Union, Yugoslavia and Czechoslovakia. Several countries, including the United Kingdom, France and Spain, have devolved power to constituent parts. Meanwhile, supra-national organisations have emerged. The EU has led the way in Europe; others are following, however slowly and fitfully, on other continents.

Language and culture intertwine and interact upon one another. Culture manifests itself in language; language expresses and interprets culture. Together they define political values, drive political rhetoric and artistic achievement and nurture communities. How have these changes affected the nation-state? Stressing national conformity at the expense of local diversity, nation-states have long expanded and centralised political power. They began early to develop their resources, bureaucracies and military forces. They also developed a sense of national community by promoting a common (or at least an elite) tongue, a pervasive (or at least a dominant) religion, a common monetary system, an integrated internal transport system of waterways, roads, railways and highways, an internally self-reliant economy and a mythology that glorifies a common history, heritage and fear of military and economic threats to the country's welfare. These efforts strengthened the nation-state's efforts to enhance its independence in international relations, its ultimate power in internal affairs and the primary source of identity and allegiance of its people.

In a globalising world, even powerful countries delude themselves in clinging to outdated shibboleths of sovereignty. To be relevant internationally, even the most powerful nations cooperate within a framework of international organisations. However, while steps to develop international organisations have proven difficult, even more arduous have been the efforts to improve, or in many cases just sustain or even resuscitate, local governance. The case for subsidarity (leaving to the lower level of governance what it can do as well as, or better than, the higher), which national governments champion in an international context, applies equally at the local level—for reasons of effectiveness as well as for avoiding a democratic deficit at the level nearest and most accessible to most people. Recognition of the need for more effective local security, roads, water, health and human services, has accelerated the demand for locally responsive and responsible governments.

This leads to demands for more potent and accountable local governance, allowing local governments to adapt to local conditions and priorities and strengthen the seamless web of the process of delivering public services. Citizens are more likely to appreciate their national government when it recognises the diversity of its local communities and provides local residents with the means to participate effectively in public affairs. Accommodating competing imperatives of localism, nationalism and internationalism will continue to challenge public leadership. The more opportunities citizens have to participate politically in their governance, the less likely they are to become antipathetic, or apathetic towards their governments. Why are those countries that are most aggressive internationally when it comes to their national powers the least sympathetic regarding the role of their local governments?

Belgium provides a model of the ingenuity and patience required to keep a divided country united. The case of Belgium illustrates the impact of representative governance, and accompanying local assertiveness, upon the political dynamics of a modern government, especially ones with a multilingual, multicultural heritage. To retain its unity, the Belgian government decentralised its governance. In an increasingly interrelated world, democracy, nationalism, internationalism and localism are interactive, competing yet complementary forces. Effective governance requires the accommodation of these continuing pressures affecting local, national and international politics and polities.

APPENDICES

Reviewing the history of Belgium, from Caesar to the present, demonstrates that its governance has experienced critical transitions: from tribal, to imperial, to feudal, to emerging state, to proto-nation-state, to modern nation-state. Tribes governed most of Europe until the Caesar-led continental extension of Roman rule; the Roman, Merovingian, and Carolingian empires, with a small cadre, ruled in their far-flung domains; the Feudalism began in the tenth century when counts and dukes across Europe asserted their autonomy; by the fourteenth century many forceful rulers, including the Burgundian dukes, created states by extending their domains and centralizing their governing institutions.

By the seventeenth century the Renaissance and printing, the Reformation and Counter-Reformation, the Enlightenment and nascent nationalism and critical wars and their treaties introducing the concept of sovereignty had begun nurturing national identities, monarchical and princely power and proto-nation-states—which ranged from established to embryonic. A few established countries, such as England and France, significantly expanded their realms, revenues, military forces and civil bureaucracies. Regions whose neighbouring states shared linguistic-cultural heritages enhanced their collective consciousness, which phenomena later facilitated the unification of Germany and Italy. Long-subordinated polities with a common political heritage, such as Belgium, increased their yearning for national independence.

Modern nation-states had begun emerging by the nineteenth century. Political and industrial revolutions, economic and urban growth, more inclusive and educated electorates, advances in transport and communication, 'new men' displacing the landed aristocracy as the power elite and surging nationalism hastened this change. States forged nation-states by promoting an 'official' nation-wide vernacular and schools to spread its use, a common folklore and festivities celebrating its heroes, its commerce and financial institutions to support its growth, its economy and networks of water, rail and motorways binding it together and sprawling bureaucracies and expanding omnipresent services. Modern nation-states pervasively shape lives and loyalties, while continuing their efforts to strengthen national identity and unity.

Rapidly eroding, though, is the illusive reality of sovereignty, which legitimises the monopoly of force exerted by the nation-state and its predominance in internal and international affairs. Environmental, economic, technological and socio-humanitarian issues drive the evolution of supra-national institutions, such as the UN, the EU and other regional organisations. Collaterally, local communities, with their instinctive aversion to centralised power, are demanding greater devolution to sub-national governments. These parallel phenomena shrink the role of national governments in managing their foreign and domestic affairs. Consequently today's national governments are integrating, albeit slowly, into just one of the layers of community governments, from local to global, governing us. Eroding the omnipotence of the modern nation-state continues to metamorphose governance—expediting the fading of the modern nation-state era.

Reducing the powers of the Belgian federal government will mitigate the pivotal issue driving the Walloon-Flemish separatism, which is polarising the country's politics and paralysing its policy-making. Minimising the role of the federal government will help divided Belgium to remain united.

APPENDIX 1

CHRONOLOGY FROM THE ROMAN CONQUEST (58–51 BCE) TO 2012

BELGICA

1. *The Romans conquer, name and colonise Belgica*

58–51 BCE	Julius Caesar subjugated the tribes in northern Gaul uniting the land he called Belgica.
22 BCE	Emperor Augustus splits *Provincia Belgica* into three provinces.

2. *The Franks create a linguistic frontier*

406	Germanic tribes surge across the Rhine, subjecting Belgica.
466	Clovis extends his Tournai-based Merovingian kingdom to include most of modern France.
511	Clovis dies; his sons later expand the realm.
560s	The Frankish realm split into the kingdoms of Neustria and Austrasia.
630s	The *rois fainéants* (do-nothing kings) era begins; 'mayors of the palace' become the effective rulers.
751	Pepin III declares himself 'King of the Franks', thus ending the *rois fainéants* era.
768	Charlemagne succeeds Pepin III and extends his empire to include much of modern Western Europe.
800	Charlemagne crowns himself Holy Roman Emperor.
814	Louis the Pious succeeds his father as emperor.
843	The Treaty of Verdun between Charlemagne's grandsons divides his empire into three parts.

870	The Treaty of Mersen splits the 'middle kingdom' between East Francia and West Francia; the Low Countries are divided between them.

3. *Flanders and Lotharingia develop commerce, cities and civic conflict*

862	Baldwin the Iron Arm elopes with the daughter of the West Francia king and becomes the first Count of Flanders.
900	Regnier the Long-Necked defeats and kills the German Emperor's son; Regnier rules Lotharingia.
980	The emperor appoints Notger Prince-Bishop of Liège.
1099	In the first Crusade, Godfrey of Bouillon leads forces that capture Jerusalem. He becomes its king.
1214	In the battle of Bouvines, the French king defeats an English-Low Country alliance and imprisons the Flemish count.
1288	Jean I of Brabant wins the battle of Worringen and gains control of Limburg.
1302	Flemish commoners defeat the French cavalry at the Battle of the Golden Spurs.
1312	Charter of Cortenburg granted to Brabant.
1340	In the sea battle of Sluys the French fleet destroys the English one.
1346	In the battle of Crécy, Edward III of England and his longbows defeat the French king.
1356	First 'Joyous Entry' into Brabant sets forth rights for the 'estates'.
1382	In the battle of Beverhout, Philip van Artevelde defeats the Flemish count; the French defeat the Flemish under van Artevelde at West Rozebeke.

BURGUNDY

4. *Burgundian dukes unite the southern Low Countries*

1384	Philip the Bold, Duke of Burgundy (who had married Margaret, the Flemish heiress in 1369) becomes Count of Flanders upon the death of Louis of Male.

1404	John the Fearless succeeds his father Philip the Bold as Duke of Burgundy.
1419	Philip the Good succeeds John the Fearless as Duke of Burgundy. He acquires Namur in 1429, Brabant in 1430, Hainaut in 1433 and Luxembourg in 1443.
1415	The battle of Agincourt.
1467	Charles the Bold succeeds Philip the Good as duke. He attempts to unite his geographically separated domains by conquering the intervening lands.
1477	Charles the Bold is defeated and killed at the battle of Nancy in 1477.

5. *Charles V unites all the Low Countries*

1477	Mary of Burgundy, the heiress of Charles the Bold, marries Maximilian of Austria, thus making the duchy of Burgundy a Habsburg possession.
1504	Philip the Handsome, at sixteen, becomes Low Country ruler. After he dies in 1506, his sister Margaret of Austria serves as regent until Charles V is declared 'of age.'
1515	Charles V becomes ruler of the Low Countries; in 1516, King of Spain; and in 1519 emperor. Margaret of Austria is regent from 1518 to 1530; his sister Mary of Hungary serves as regent from 1531 to 1555.
1548–49	Charles V, having added several principalities north of the Rhine to his Habsburg possessions, unites all seventeen Low Country principalities into the Burgundian circle.
1555	Charles V abdicates as ruler of the Low Countries. His son Philip II succeeds him.

6. *The Beggars' Revolt against Spain divides the Low Countries*

1559	Philip II returns to Spain.
1567	Philip II appoints the Duke of Alba to head the Spanish forces in the Low Countries. In 1568 his efforts to suppress the Counter-Reformation lead to the arrest and beheading of Counts Egmont and Horne in the Grand Place of Brussels. Armed conflict begins shortly thereafter.

1576	The 'Spanish Fury' erupts. The rebel leaders agreed to the Pacification of Ghent creating a union of the seventeen provinces.
1579	Some southern provinces form the Union of Arras; northern ones organise the Union of Utrecht.
1584	William the Silent, leader of the revolt, is assassinated.

SOUTHERN LOW COUNTRIES

7. *The Spanish Habsburgs rule an impoverished land*

1598	Archdukes Albert and Isabelle marry and become 'joint sovereigns'. Philip III succeeds as Spanish king.
1609	A twelve-year truce begins.
1621	Philip IV becomes the Spanish king in 1621, the last year of the truce.
1648	The Treaties of Westphalia end the Eighty Years War in the Low Countries and the Thirty Years War.
1665	Charles II succeeds Philip IV as King of Spain.
1667–1713	The wars of Louis XIV deprive the Low Countries of most of French-speaking (Walloon) Flanders.
1700–1713	The War of Spanish Succession, set off by the death of Charles II of Spain.

8. *The Austrian Habsburgs react to the Enlightenment*

1713	The War of Spanish Succession ends with the Treaty of Utrecht, which awards the Spanish Low Countries to Austria but confirms the French acquisition of most of Walloon Flanders.
1740	Marie-Theresa succeeds Charles VI as Empress. Despite the efforts to guarantee her succession, the War of Austrian Succession breaks out.
1748	The War of Austrian Succession ends with the Peace of Aix-la-Chapelle, which restores the Austrian Low Countries to Austria.
1780	Joseph II succeeds Marie-Theresa as emperor. His efforts to introduce reforms provoke resistance.

9. *Two revolts, French occupation and union with the Dutch*

1789	The Brabant revolt leads to creation of the short-lived United Belgian States. Liège also revolts.
1794	France's revolutionary forces, supported by Belgium and Liège insurgents, defeat Austria at Fleurus. French troops occupy the Austrian Low Countries.
1795	France annexes the southern Low Countries.
1799	Napoleon becomes First Consul.
1809	Napoleon proclaims himself emperor.
1814	Napoleon surrenders.
1815	Napoleon escapes from Elba, marches towards Brussels and is defeated at Waterloo. The Congress of Vienna makes Belgium part of the Kingdom of the Netherlands, with William I as King.

BELGIUM

10. *A Francophone elite wins Belgium its independence*

1830	The Belgian revolution begins.
1831	Leopold I installed as King.
1839	The Kingdom of the Netherlands signs a treaty that recognises Belgian independence.
1846	The Liberals break from the Union coalition to form a party separate from the Catholics.
1850–52	The Liberals challenge the Catholic control of education.

11. *Labour and Flemish movements begin to develop*

1865	Leopold II succeeds his father as King.
1879–84	The first School War.
1885	The Belgian Workers' Party is founded. It later becomes the Socialist Party.
1889	Leopold II recognised at Congress of Berlin as ruler of the Congo.
1893–94	Universal plural-voting male suffrage is introduced.
1898	Equality Law recognises Dutch language for the first time as an official Belgian language.

1908	The Congo, which had been King Leopold's personal property, becomes a Belgian colony.
1909	Albert I, a nephew of Leopold II, becomes the third Belgian king.

12. *Two German invasions and a depression speed change*

1914	World War I begins with German invasion of Belgium. Belgium is occupied, except for the southwest corner, until the war ends in 1918.
1919	Treaty of Versailles signed.
1920	Universal single-vote male suffrage adopted.
1922	Belgium enters into Economic Union with Luxembourg.
1934	Albert I dies in climbing accident, Leopold III becomes king. His wife Astrid dies in a road accident in 1935.
1936	Belgium renounces military pact with France.
1940	Germany invades Belgium. Leopold III surrenders. German forces occupy Belgium.
1942	Government-in-exile commits to Allies.
1944	Belgium liberated, Prince Charles, brother of Leopold III, becomes regent while the King remains in exile.

FLANDERS AND WALLONIA

13. *The Francophone, propertied and dominant elite erodes*

1949	Belgium joins NATO. Women gain the vote.
1951	Baudouin crowned following the abdication of his father.
1952	Another school crisis erupts, not settled until 1958.
1957	Treaty of Rome signed; Belgium becomes an original member of European Economic Community, the predecessor of the European Union (EU).
1960	The Belgian Congo gains independence. The economic union of Benelux, negotiated in 1958, comes into effect.
1960	Workers stage mass strike protesting at 'Unity' Law.

14. *Belgium federalises*

1968	Language riots precipitate split of both the Catholic University of Louvain and the Free University of Brussels into French and Dutch-speaking universities. The controversy leads to the split along language lines of the Catholic, Liberal and Socialist parties.
1970	The first constitutional reform begins the process of federalising Belgium.
1980	A four-party coalition led by CVP Martens passes the second constitutional reform, providing the Flanders and Walloon regions and communities with a council and an executive.
1987	Martens' sixth coalition government falls over issue of the mayor of the bilingual Fourons/Voeren, because its burgomaster refuses to speak Dutch.
1988	Martens' eighth coalition government succeeds in passing the third constitutional reform, which increases the role of the communities and gives the regions public works and transport powers.
1993	A four party coalition led by CVP Dehaene passes the fourth constitutional reform, which completes the federalisation of Belgium.

15. *Increasingly isolated Flanders and Wallonia collide*

1993	Baudouin dies; Albert II succeeds his brother as King.
1996	Kidnappings, rapes and murders lead to investigations and proposals for reform. Concern prompts a 'White March' of concerned parents and their supporters.
1997	Inadequate response to 'mad cow' disease further erodes public confidence in government.
1999	The euro became operational electronically; euro bills and coins became the sole legal tender in 2002. The two Liberal parties (VLD and MR), the CdH and CD&V, and the Green parties form a Verhofstadt-led coalition; a fifth constitutional revision is enacted. The *Vlaams Blok* gains in the elections. The leading parties revise their strategies and change their names.

2003 In national elections the two Liberal parties (VLD and MR) and the CdH and CD&V continue their Verhofstadt-led coalition without the Green ones.

2007 In national elections in June, Flemish Christian Democrats (CD&V) achieve a plurality. It takes six months of negotiations to form a caretaker coalition government.

2008 In March a five-party coalition with CD&V Leterme as prime minister takes over and continues negotiations about transferring more powers from national to regional governments.

In July Leterme resigns, but the king asks him to continue efforts to resolve constitutional crisis. In December Leterme resigns again; king accepts resignation. Van Rompuy forms a five-party coalition government.

2010 Van Rompuy selected to be fill the newly-created post of EU president; Leterme returns as Belgian prime minister.

Government collapses over Brussels-Halle-Vilvoorde issue; election called for June.

Flemish separatist N-VA Party wins plurality of seats (twenty-seven) in lower house of parliament in general election; Walloon Socialists do well; Christian Democrats and Liberals do poorly; coalition formation difficult; Leterne-led caretaker government continues into 2011.

2011 A six-party coalition headed by Elio Di Rupo, a Walloon Socialist, forms government after a record-breaking 542 days of a caretaker administration since June 2010 elections.

APPENDIX 2

SOUTHERN LOW COUNTRY RULERS FROM BALDWIN THE IRON ARM (864) TO THE BELGIAN REVOLUTION (1830)

A) From 9th century to 1477/1482

Flanders (and Artois), Counts of	*Hainaut, Counts of*	*Leuven, Count of*	*Namur, Counts/ Margraves of*	*Luxembourg, Counts/ Dukes of*	*Liege, Prince-Bishop of*
BALDWIN the Iron Arm 864–879 = Judith, daughter of Charles the Bald					
BALDWIN II, 879–918	REGNIER the Long-necked 877–915 also Duke of Lotharingia and grandson of Lothair I, Emperor		BERANGER 910–922 = Symphoriane (daughter of Regnier the Long-Necked)		
ARNULF I, the Elder 918–965	REGNIER II 916–940				
BALDWIN III 958–962	REGNIER III 932–971		ROBERT I 932–981	SIGFRID d'Ardennes 963–998	NOTGER 972–1008
ARNULF II, the Younger 965–988	REGNIER IV 998–1013	LAMBERT OF LOUVAIN 973–1015 (son of Regnier III of Hainaut)	ALBERT I 981–1011	HENRY I 998–1026 (also Duke of Bavaria)	BALDERICK 1008–1018
BALDWIN IV, the Bearded 988–1035	REGNIER V 1013–1040	HENRY I the Elder 1015–1038	ROBERT II 1013–1018	HENRY II 1026–1047 (also duke of Bavaria)	WALBODO 1021–1025
BALDWIN V, of Lille 1035–1067	HERMAN of Valenci-ennes 1041–1051 (=Richilde)	LAMBERT II 1040–1063	ALBERT II 1021–1063	GILBERT 1047–1059	DURAND 1025–1027 REGINARD 1025–1037
					NITHARD 1037–1042 WAZO 1042–1048

*BALDWIN VI, of Mons 1067–1070	*BALDWIN I of Mons = RICHILDE 1051–1070	HENRY II 1063–1079	ALBERT III 1063–1102	CONRAD I 1059–1086	THEODUIN 1048–1075
*ARNULF III, the Unfortunate 1070–1071	*ARNULF 1070–1071	HENRY III the younger 1079–1095		HENRY III 1086–1096	HENRY de Verdun 1075–1091
ROBERT I, the Frisian 1071–1093	BALDWIN II (brother of Arnulf) 1071–1098	*Brabant, dukes of*	GODFREY 1102–1139	WILLIAM 1096–1131	OTBERT 1091–1119
					FREDERIK of Namur 1119–1121
ROBERT II, of Jerusalem 1093–1111 BALDWIN VII 1111–1119	BALDWIN III 1098–1120	GODFREY the Bearded 1095–1128 first Duke of Brabant 1106–1128; deposed		CONRAD II 1131–1136	ADALBERT of Leuven 1121–1128
CHARLES the Good 1119–1127 (grandson of Robert I)	BALDWIN IV 1120–1171	WALFRAM II of Luxembourg 1128–1139			ALEXANDER of Julich 1128–1134
					ADALBERT of Chiny 1134–1145
WILLIAM CLITO 1127–1128 (great-grandson of Baldwin V		GODFREY II 1139–1142	*HENRY the Blind 1139–1196	*HENRY IV the Blind 1136–1198 (grandson of Conrad I)	HENRY of Leez 1145–1164
THIERRY d' Alsace 1128–1168 (grandson of Robert I, the Frisian)		GODFREY III 1142–1190			ALEXANDER of Oeren 1165–1167
PHILIP d' Alsace 1168–1191 MARGARET I d' Alsace 1191–1194					RUDOLPH of Zahringon 1167–1191

Flanders (and Artois), Counts of	*Hainaut, Counts of*	*Leuven, Counts of*	*Namur, Counts/ Margraves of*	*Luxembourg, Counts/ Dukes of*	*Liège, Prince-Bishop of*
*BALDWIN VIII 1191–1194	*BALDWIN V 1175–1195	HENRY I 1190–1235	*BALDWIN seized county 1188–1195		ALBERT de Leuven 1191–1192 (murdered)
					SIMON of Limburg 1193–1195
*BALDWIN IX 1194–1205	*BALDWIN VI 1195–1205		PHILIP I 1195–1212	ERMESINDE 1196–1247	ALBERT of Cuyck 1194–1200
*JOANNA 1205–1244	*JOANNA 1205–1244	HENRY II 1235–1248	YOLANDA 1212–1216 = Peter, Emperor of Constaninople		HUGH of Pierrepont 1200–1229
			PHILIP II 1219–1226		JOHN of Eppes 1229–1238
			MARGARET 1226–1237		WILLIAM of Savoy 1238–1239
					ROBERT of Thourotte 1240–1246
*MARGARET I 1244–1278	*MARGARET I 1244–1278	HENRY III 1248–1261	BALDWIN II 1237–1263 sold Namur to Guy de Dampierre	HENRY V 1247–1281	HENRY de Guelders 1247–1274
					JOHN of Eddigton 1274–1281
*GUY de Dampierre 1278–1305	JOHN d' Avesnes 1299–1304 (Margaret's grandson) from 1299 Holland and Hainaut united under one ruler	HENRY IV 1261–1267	*GUY de Dampierre 1263–1298	HENRY VI 1281–1288	JOHN of Flanders 1282–1291
					vacant 1291–1296

					HUGH of Chalons 1296–1301
					ADOLPH of Waldeck 1301–1302
ROBERT III 1305–1322	WILLIAM I 1304–1337	JOHN I the Victorious 1267–1294 added Limburg 1289		HENRY VII 1288–1310 Emperor 1308–1313	THIBAUT of Bar 1303–1312
		JOHN II 1294–1312			
			JOHN de Dampierre 1298–1330	JOHN the Blind 1310–1346	
LOUIS I of Nevers 1322–1346	WILLIAM II 1337–45			(also King of Bohemia)	ADOLPH de la Marck 1313–1344
LOUIS II de Male 1346–1384	MARGARET (abdicated for son) 1345–1354/6	JOHN III 1312–1355	JOHN II 1330–1335 GUY II 1335–1336	CHARLES (IV) 1346–1353 abdicated; also emperor	ENGELBERT de la Marck 1345–1364
			PHILIP III 1336–1337	*WENCELAS I 1353–1383 (first 'Duke' of Luxembourg)	
Burgundy, Duke of	WILLIAM III (deposed) 1354/6–1358	JOANNA 1355–1404 = *WENCESLAUS	WILLIAM I 1337–1391		JOHN of Arkel 1364–1378
PHILIP the Bold=MARGARET III 1363/84–1404	ALBERT regent 1358–1389, 1389–1404	MARGARET regent 1404–1406			ARNOLD of Horne 1378–1389
JOHN the Fearless 1404–1419	WILLIAM IV 1404–1417	ANTHONY 1406–1415 (brother of Philip the Good)	WILLIAM II 1391–1418	WENCESLAS II 1383–1419 (also Emperor) pawned duchy to niece, Elisabeth de Goerlitz	JOHN of Bavaria 1389–1418 never crowned, abdicated to marry Elizabeth of Gorlitz

Flanders (and Artois), Counts of	*Hainaut, Counts of*	*Leuven, Counts of*	*Namur, Counts/ Margraves of*	*Luxembourg, Counts/ Dukes of*	*Liège, Prince-Bishop of*
		JOHN IV 1415–1427			JOHN of Wallenrode 1418–1419
*PHILIP the Good 1419–1467	JACQUELINE 1417–1433 abdicated in favour of PHILIP the Good, Duke of Burgundy	PHILIP of St Pol 1427–1430 brother of John IV succeeded by his nephew PHILIP the Good, Duke of Burgundy	JOHN III 1418–1429 sold Namur PHILIP the Good, Duke of Burgundy	SIGISMOND 1419–1437 also Emperor, King of Hungary	JOHN of Heinsberg 1419–1456 (resigned)
	PHILIP the Good 1433–1467	PHILIP the Good 1430–1467	PHILIP the Good 1429–1476	ALBERT of AUSTRIA 1437–1439	
				WILLIAM of SAXONY 1439–1443	
	CHARLES the Bold 1467–1477	CHARLES the Bold 1467–1477	CHARLES the Bold 1467–1477	ELISABETH of Goerlitz niece of Wenceslas II acting duchess 1409–1443 ceded duchy to Philip the Good, Duke of Burgundy 1443–1467	
CHARLES the Bold 1467–1477				CHARLES the Bold 1467–1477	LOUIS de Bourbon 1456–1482

Dates depicted are years of rule.
= marriage.
*ruler of more than one principality. (Note ruler of two or more principalities may be, for example, Baldwin I of one principality, and Baldwin II of another).

B) Southern Low Country rulers from 1477/1482 to 1830

BURGUNDY, Dukes of	*LIEGE, Prince-Bishops of*
	vacant 1482–1484
MARY of Burgundy (daughter of Charles the Bold) 1477–1482 = MAXIMILIAN of Austria (Emperor 1493–1519)	JOHN of Horne 1484–1505
	EVERHARD de la Marck 1505–1538
PHILIP the Fair 1482–1506 King of Castille in wife's right 1504–1506	CORNELIUS of Bergen op Zoom 1538–1545
CHARLES V 1506–1555 (King of Spain 1516,-1556; Emperor 1519–1558; abdicated)	GEORGE of Austria 1544–1557
SPANISH HABSBURGS	ROBERT of Bergen op Zoom 1557–1565
PHILIP II, King of Spain 1555–1598	GERARD van Groesbeek 1564–1580
ISABELLA and ALBERT 1598–1621	ERNEST of Bavaria 1581–1612 FERDINAND of Bavaria 1612–1650
PHILIP IV, King of Spain 1621–1665	MAXIMILIAN-HENRY of Bavaria 1650–1688
CHARLES II, King of Spain 1665–1700	JEAN-LOUIS d'ELDEREN 1688–1694
War of Spanish Succession 1700–1713	JOSEPH-CLEMENT of Bavaria 1694–1723
AUSTRIAN HABSBURGS	GEORGE-LOUIS of Berges 1724–1743
CHARLES VI, Emperor 1713–1740	JOHN-THEODORE of Bavaria 1744–1763
MARIA-THERESA, Empress 1740–1780	CHARLES d'Outremont 1763–1771
JOSEPH II, Emperor 1780–1790	FRANZ CARL von Velbruck 1772–1784
LEOPOLD II, Emperor 1790–1792	CAESAR CONSTANT van Hoensbroek 1784–1792
FRANCIS II, Emperor 1792–1797	FRANÇOIS de Mean 1792–1794
	French Annexation 1794

FRANCE

DIRECTORY 1797–1804
NAPOLEON 1804–1814

KINGDOM OF THE NETHERLANDS
(which until the Belgian revolution included Belgium)
WILLIAM I 1815–1830

Sources: Paul Arblaster, *A History of the Low Countries*, New York and Basingstoke, Palgrave Macmillan, 2006, 250–260 and Pierre Houart, *Deux Mille Ans d'Histoire Princière de la Belgique Romaine* à *Albert II*, Braine-l'Alleud, J.-M. Collet, 1997. (The sources do not always agree with regard to early dates).

APPENDIX 3

KINGS, PRIME MINISTERS AND CABINET COALITIONS FROM 1830 TO 2012

A. 1830–1944 — Parties comprising coalition—* indicates prime ministers

King	*Prime Minister*	*Year took office*	*Unionist*	*Catholic*	*Liberal*	*Worker/Socialist*
E.L. Surlet de Chokier (Regent) 1831						
	L. De Potter	1830				
	S. Van de Weyer	1831				
	J. Lebeau	1831				
Leopold 1831–65	F. A. de Muelenaere	1831	Unionist *			
	J. A. Goblet	1832	Unionist *			
	B. T. de Theux	1834	Unionist *			
	J. Lebeau	1840			Liberal*	
	J. B. Nothomb	1841	Unionist *			
	S. Van de Weyer	1845	Unionist *			
	B. T. de Theux	1846		Catholic *		
	Ch. Rogier	1847			Liberal *	
	H. De Brouckère	1852	Unionist *			
	P. De Decker	1855	Unionist *			
	W. Frère-Orban	1857			Liberal *	
Leopold II 1865–1909	J. d'Anethan	1870		Catholic *		
	J. Malou	1871		Catholic *		
	W. Frère-Orban	1878			Liberal *	
	J. Malou	1884		Catholic *		
	A. Beernaert	1884		Catholic *		
	J. de Burlet	1894		Catholic *		
	P. J. de Smet de Naeyer	1896		Catholic *		
	E. Vandenpeereboom	1899		Catholic *		

	P. J. de Smet de Naeyer	1899	Catholic *		
	J. de Trooz	1907	Catholic *		
Albert I 1909–1934	F. Schollaert	1908	Catholic *		
	Ch. de Broqueville	1911	Catholic *		
	Ch. de Broqueville	1914 (Le Havre exile)	Catholic *	Liberal	Workers
	L. Delacroix I	1918	Catholic *	Liberal	Workers
	L. Delacroix II	1919	Catholic *	Liberal	Workers
	H. Carton de Wiart	1920	Catholic *	Liberal	Workers
	G. Theunis I	1921	Catholic *	Liberal	
	A. Van der Vyvere	1925	Catholic *		
	P. Poullet	1925	Catholic *	Workers	
	H. Jaspar I	1926	Catholic *	Liberal	Workers
	H. Jaspar II	1927	Catholic *	Liberal	
	J. Renkin	1925	Catholic *	Liberal	
	Ch. de Broqueville	1932	Catholic *	Liberal	
Leopold III 1934–51 (prisoner 1940–45,in exile 1945–50)					
	G. Theunis II	1934	Catholic *	Liberal	
	P. van Zeeland I	1935	Catholic *	Liberal	Workers
	P. van Zeeland II	1936	Catholic *	Liberal	Workers
	P-E. Janson	1937	Catholic	Liberal *	Workers
	P-H. Spaak	1938	Catholic	Liberal	Workers*
	H. Pierlot I	1939	Catholic *		Workers
	H. Pierlot II	1939	Catholic *	Liberal	
	H. Pierlot III	1939	Catholic *	Liberal	Workers
	H. Pierlot IV	1940 (London exile)	Catholic *	Liberal	Workers

B. 1944–2012

King	*Prime Minister*	*Year took office*	*Catholic CVP/PSC/ CVP&V/ CdH*	*Liberal PVV/PLP/ PRL/ VLD/MR*	*Socialist (B)SP PS(B) SP.A*	*Green Agalev Green Ecolo*	*Other sectional/ separatist VU FDF RW UDB*	*Communist*
Charles—Prince Regent 1944–50								
	H. Pierlot	1944	Catholic*	Liberal	Socialist			Communist
	A. van Acker I	1945	Catholic	Liberal	Socialist*			Communist
	A. van Acker II	1945		Liberal	Socialist*		VDB	Communist
	P.-H. Spaak I	1946			Socialist*			Communist
	A. van Acker III	1946		Liberal	Socialist*			Communist
	C. Huysmans	1946		Liberal	Socialist*			
	P-H. Spaak II	1947	Catholic		Socialist*			
	G. Eyskens I	1949	Catholic*	Liberal				
	J. Duvieusart	1950	Catholic*					
	J. Pholien	1950	Catholic*					
Baudouin 1951–93								
	J. van Houtte	1952	Catholic*					
	A. van Acker IV	1954		Liberal	Socialist*			
	G. Eyskens II	1958	Catholic*					
	G. Eyskens III	1958	Catholic*	Liberal				
	Th. Lefèvre	1961	Catholic*		Socialist			

P. Harmel	1965	Catholic*		Socialist		
P. Van Boeynants	1966	Catholic*	Liberal			
G. Eyskens IV	1968	CVP* PSC		Socialist		
A. Cools	1968	CVP PSC		Socialist*		
G. Eyskens V	1972	CVP* PSC		Socialist		
E. Leburton	1973	CVP PSC	PVV PLP	Socialist*		
L. Tindemans I	1974	CVP* PSC	PVV PLP (PRLW)			RW
L. Tindemans II	1977	CVP* PSC		Socialist		VU FDF
P. Van Boeynants	1978	CVP PSC*		Socialist		VU FDF
W. Martens I	1979	CVP* PSC		SP PS		FDF
W. Martens II	1980	CVP* PSC		SP PS		
W. Martens III	1980	CVP* PSC	PVV/PRL	SP PS		
W. Martens IV	1980	CVP* PSC		SP PS		
M. Eyskens	1981	CVP* PSC		SP PS		
W. Martens V	1981	CVP* PSC	PVV/PRL			
W. Martens VI	1985	CVP* PSC	PVV/PRL			
W. Martens VII	1987	CVP* PSC	PVV/PRL			
W. Martens VIII	1988	CVP* PSC		SP PS		VU
J-L. Dehaene I	1992	CVP* PSC		SP PS		
Albert II 1993–2003						
J-L. Dehaene II	1995	CVP* PSC		SP PS		
G. Verhofstadt I	1999		VLD* PLP	SP PS	Agelev Ecolo	
G. Verhofstadt II	2003		VLD* PLP	SP PS		

G. Verhofstadt	2007	CD&V	Open VLD*	
(caretaker)		CdH	MR	
Y. Leterme I	2008	CD&V*	Open VLD	PS
		CdH	MR	
H. van Rompuy	2008	CD&V*	Open VLD	PS
		CdH	MR	
Y. Leterme II	2010	CD&V	Open VLD	PS
		DdH	MR	
E. di Rupo	2011	CD&V	Open VLD	PS* SP
		DdH	MR	

Source for years 1830–1995: Witte, Craeybeckx, and Meynen, *Politieke Geschiedens van belgie van 1830 tot Heden*, 1997, Bijlage 2.

APPENDIX 4

GUIDE TO CHANGES IN PARTY NAMES 1965 TO 2009

Catholic/Christian Democrat

Dutch-speaking	CVP > CD&V	Christelijke Volkspartij (CVP) changed its name to Christen-Democratisch & Vlaams (CD&V) in 2001
French-speaking	PSC > CdH and CDF	Parti Social Chrétien (PSC) changed its name to Centre Démocrate Humaniste (CdH) after the 1999 elections; dissidents split off to form Chrétiens Démocrates Francophones (CDF)

Liberals

Dutch-speaking	PVV > VLD > Open VLD	Partij voor Vrijheid en Vooruitgang (PVV) changed name in mid-1990s to Vlaamse Liberalen Democraten. In 2007 it amended its name to Open VLD.
French-speaking	PLP > PRL > MR	Parti des Réformes et la Liberté en Wallonie (PRL), once the Parti de la Liberté et du Progrès (PLP), changed its name to Mouvement Réformateur

		(MR) before the 2003 elections and allied with the Brussels-based FDF.
Brussels French-speaking	FDF > MR	Front Démocratique des Bruxellois Francophones (FDF) aligned in 1995 and 1999 with the Walloon Liberals before forming an alliance with the PRL before the 2003 elections.

Belgian Workers/Socialist

Dutch-speaking	SP > SP.A	Socialistische Partij (SP) changed its name in 2001 to Socialistische Partij. Anders (SP.A) and after 2003 Social Progreesief Alternatief (SP.A)
French-speaking	PS	Parti Socialiste (PS)

Green

Dutch-speaking	Agalev > Groen!	*Angelev* after its poor performance in the 2003 elections changed its name to Groen!
French-speaking	Ecolo	

Separatist/Sectional

Dutch-speaking separatist VU > N-VA	Volksunie(VU) split into the left-wing Spirit, which allied with SP.A before the 2003 elections, and the right wing Nieuw-Vlaamse Alliatie (N-VA), which allied with the CD&V after the 2003 elections, but fielded its own list in 2010.
Dutch-speaking radical separatist VB> VB	Vlaams Block (VB) in 2004, after court denied party access to funds, case changed its name to Vlaams Belang (VB), Flemish Interest
French-speaking RW	Rassemblement Wallon (RW)
French-speaking radical FN	Front National (FN)

Communist

Dutch-speaking	FPB	Kommuistische Partij Belgie (KPB)
French-speaking	PCB	Parti Communist Belge (PCB)

APPENDIX 5

PERSON AND PLACE NAME VARIATIONS

Writing about persons and places in a multilingual country, especially when writing in another language, presents dilemmas. For example, while English-speakers call the first Count of Flanders Baldwin (the Iron Arm), in Dutch he is called Boudewijn and in French Baudouin. Yet English speakers call a twentieth century Belgian king Baudouin. I have followed current English-speaking usage.

In some cases the same place name has been used for different areas at different times. The name Burgundy, for example, has been applied over history to many different polities occupying differing land areas. While what is now Belgium was once incorporated in the Duchy of Burgundy, the name 'Burgundy' now applies only to an eastern region of France. While the term 'Flanders' once referred to the feudal county that extended well into modern-day northwest France but did not include Limburg or Brabant, today the term embraces all of Dutch-speaking Belgium, including northern Brabant and Limburg but not Arras, now in northwest France. Brabant once referred to the duchy that governed the present-day Belgian provinces of Flemish Brabant, Walloon Brabant, Limburg and Antwerp, the Region of Brussels, and the Dutch provinces of Limburg and North Brabant.

The land called 'the Low Countries' has expanded and contracted through history and has been called many names, including 'Belgica', 'Belgium', 'Burgundy' (in the late medieval era), 'the Netherlands' for many centuries, and 'Benelux' (in the twentieth). After the war that divided what is now the Netherlands from what is now Belgium the latter was often called the Spanish Netherlands (or the 'Catholic' or

'Royal' Netherlands or 'Belgium regium') to distinguish it from the Dutch Republic. To avoid confusion I use the term 'the southern Low Countries' to describe the land that Caesar conquered and that remained a Spanish-Habsburg possession following the war that divided the Low Countries.

City names present a special problem. The following are a few examples of cities that have different names in French, Dutch, and German and English.

Flemish region			Walloon region			Brussels Capital region		
Dutch	French	English	Dutch	French	German	Dutch	French	English
Antwerpen	Anvers	Antwerp	Bergen	Mons		Brussel	Bruxelles	Brussels
Brugge	Bruges	Bruges	Doornik	Tournai				
Gent	Gand	Ghent	Luik	Liège	Lüttich			
Ieper	Ypres							
Kortrijk	Courtrai		Namen	Namur				
Leuven	Louvain		Nijvel	Nivelles				
Mechelen	Malines							
Tongeren	Tongres							

NOTES

FROM BELGICA TO BELGIUM

1. Tony Judt, *Postwar*, London, Pimlico, p. 708.
2. Eric Hobsbawm, *The Age of Extremes*, London, Abacus, 1995, p. 147.

1. BELGICA: THE ROMANS CONQUER, NAME AND COLONISE BELGICA: 57BCE–406CE

1. Julius Caesar (John Warrinton trans.), *The Gallic Wars*, New York, Heritage Press, 1995, p. 3.
2. Adrian Goldsworthy, *Caesar, Life of a Colossus*, New Haven, CT and London, Yale University Press, 2006, p. 238.
3. Caesar, *The Gallic Wars*, p. 45.
4. Charles A. Kupchan, *The End of the American Era*, New York, Vintage Press, 2002, p. 126.

2. THE FRANKS CREATE A LINGUISTIC FRONTIER: 406–861

1. Adrien de Meeus, *History of the Belgians*, New York, Praeger, 1962, p. 32.
2. Friedrich Heer, *Charlemagne and His World*, New York, Macmillan, 1975, p. 9.
3. Rosamond McKitterick, *Charlemagne, The Formation of a European Identity*, Cambridge University Press, 2008, p. 215.
4. Edward Gibbon, *The Decline and Fall of the Roman Empire*, vol. 2, New York, Heritage Press, 1946, p. 1181.
5. Fustel de Coulanges as quoted in Christopher Dawson, *Religion and the Rise of Western Culture*, New York, Sheed and Ward, 1950, p. 84.
6. Alessandro Barbero, *Charlemagne, Father of a Continent*, Los Angeles, University of California Press, 2004, pp. 156–216.

7. Marc Bloch, *Feudal Society*, Chicago, IL, University of Chicago Press and London, Routledge & Kegan Paul, 1961, p. 194.
8. Roger Collins, *Charlemagne*, London, Macmillan, 1998, p. 102.
9. André Maurois, *A History of France*, New York, Farrar, Straus, and Cudahy, 1956, p. 33.
10. Peter Sawyer, 'The Age of the Vikings, and Before' in Peter Sawyer (ed.), *The Oxford Illustrated History of the Vikings*, New York, NY, Oxford University Press, 1997, p. 13.

3. FLANDERS AND LOTHARINGIA DEVELOP COMMERCE, CITIES AND CIVIC CONFLICT: 861–1384

1. Raoul C. Van Caenegem, 'The Age of Principalities' in Herman Balthazar et al., *The Drama of the Low Countries*, Antwerp, Mercator, 1996, p. 41.
2. King John II of France wrote these words in 1360 after his cession of almost a third of French territory to the English.
3. Robert Payne, *The Dream and the Tomb—A History of the Crusades*, New York, Stein and Day, 1984, p. 31.
4. Jacques Le Goff, *The Birth of Europe*, Oxford, Blackwell, 2005, p. 113.
5. Henri Pirenne, *Medieval Cities, Their Origins and the Revival of Trade*, Princeton University Press, 1925, p. 25.
6. Richard Vaughn, *Valois Burgundy*, London, Longman, 1975, p. 12.
7. Caenegem, 'The Age of Principalities' p. 41.
8. David Nicholas, *Medieval Flanders*, London, Longman, 1992, p. 16.
9. Ibid., p. 192; Henri Pirenne, *Histoire de Belgique des* origines à *nos jours*, Brussels, La Renaissance du Livre, 1972, vol. 1, pp. 418–19.

4. BURGUNDIAN DUKES UNITE THE SOUTHERN LOW COUNTRIES: 1384–1477

1. Richard Vaughn, *Valois Burgundy*, London, Longman, 1975, pp. 3–5.
2. Emile Cammaerts, *Belgium from the Roman Invasion to the Present Day*, London, T. F. Unwin, 1921, p. 130.
3. James Bryce, *The Holy Roman Empire*, London, Macmillan, 1906, p. 529.
4. Desmond Seward, *The Hundred Years War*, London, Constable and Robinson, 2003, p. 144.
5. Juliet Barker, *Agincourt, the King, the Campaign, the Battle*, London, Little, Brown, 2005, pp. 15–16.
6. Seward, *The Hundred Years War*, pp. 195; 202.
7. Robin Neillands, *The Hundred Years War*, London, Routledge, 1990, p. 230.
8. John Hale, *The Civilization of Europe in the Renaissance*, New York, Maxwell Macmillan, 1993, p. 82.

9. W. P. Blockmans, 'The Formation of Political Union', in J. C. H. Blom and E. Lamberts (eds), *History of the Low Countries*, New York, Berghahn, 1999, p. 89.
10. Francis Hackett, *Francis the First*, New York, The Literary Guild, 1934, p. 14.
11. H. A. L. Fisher, *A History of Europe*, London, Edward Arnold, 1930, p. 463.

5. CHARLES V UNITES ALL THE LOW COUNTRIES: 1477–1555

1. William Maltby, *The Reign of Charles V*, New York, Palgrave, 2002, p. 1.
2. Denys Hay, 'Introduction' in *The New Cambridge Modern History*, Volume I *The Renaissance 1493–1520*, Cambridge University Press, 1961, p. 1.
3. W. P. Blockmans, 'The Formation of Political Union' in J. C. H. Blom and E. Lamberts (eds), *History of the Low Countries*, New York, Berghahn, 1999, p. 131.
4. H. Koenigsberger 'The Empire of Charles V in Europe' in G.R. Potter (ed.), *The New Cambridge Modern History—Volume II The Reformation 1520–1559*, Cambridge University Press, 1958, p. 318.

6. THE BEGGARS' REVOLT AGAINST SPAIN DIVIDES THE LOW COUNTRIES: 1555–1599

1. Pieter Geyl, *The Revolt of The Netherlands 1555–1609*, London, Ernest Benn, 1958, p. 69.
2. John Lothrop Motley, *The Rise of the Dutch Republic*, London, Bickers & Son, 1864, p. 61.
3. Diarmaid MacCulloch, *The Reformation*, London, Penguin, 2004, p. 367.
4. Ibid., p. 369.
5. Geyl, *Revolt of The Netherlands 1555–1609*, pp. 92–3.
6. Emile Cammaerts, *Belgium from the Roman Invasion to the Present Day*, 1921, p. 184.
7. Blockmans, 'The Formation of a Political Union' in J. C. H. Blom and E. Lamberts (ed.), in *History of the Low Countries*, New York, Berghahn, 1999, p. 133.
8. Ibid.
9. Peter H. Wilson, *The Thirty Years War, Europe's Tragedy*, Cambridge MA, Belknap Press of Harvard University Press, 2009, p. 108.
10. Fisher, *A History of Europe*, p. 594.
11. Geyl, *Revolt of The Netherlands 1555–1609*, pp. 183–84.
12. Henry Kamen, *Philip of Spain*, New Haven, CT, Yale University Press, 1977, p. 320.

THE SOUTHERN LOW COUNTRIES

1. Tim Blanning, *Pursuit of Glory, Europe 1648–1815*, London, Penguin, 2007, p. xxiv.

7. THE SPANISH HABSBURGS RULE AN IMPOVERISHED LAND: 1599–1713

1. Emile Cammaerts, *Belgium from the Roman Invasion to the Present Day*, London, Longman, 1975, pp. 205–6.
2. John A. Lynn, *The Wars of Louis XIV*, London, Longman, 1999, pp. 6, 17.
3. Karen Armstrong, *The Battle for God*, New York, Ballantine Books, 2000, p. 22.
4. Diarmaid MacColloch, *The Reformation*, London, Penguin, 2004, p. 377.
5. Pieter Geyl, *The Netherlands in the Seventeenth Century, Part One 1609–1648*, London, Ernest Benn, 1961, p. 161.
6. Russell Shorto, *The Island in the Center of the World*, New York, Doubleday, 2004, pp. 224–25.
7. Ibid., pp. 40, 45–6; Thomas J. Condon, *New York Beginnings*, New York, New York University Press, 1968, pp. 90–93; Henry J. Bayer, *The Belgians, First Settlers in New York and the Middle States*, New York, Devon-Adnir, 1925, p. 40.
8. Philippe Erlanger, *Louis XIV*, London, Weidenfeld & Nicholson, 1970, p. 105.
9. John A. Lynn, *The Wars of Louis XIV*, p. 161.
10. Adrien de Meeus, *History of the Belgians*, New York, Praeger, 1962, pp. 220–21.

8. THE AUSTRIAN HABSBURGS REACT TO THE ENLIGHTENMENT: 1713–1794

1. E. H. Kossman, *The Low Countries*, London, Oxford, 1999, p. 47.
2. Andrew Wheatcroft, *The Habsburgs Embodying Empire*, London, Penguin, 1995, p. 132.
3. Kossmann, *The Low Countries*, pp. 47–8.
4. R. J. W. Evans, 'The Most Dynamic Ruler', *New York Review of Books*, 24 June 2010, p. 56.
5. James Bryce, *The Holy Roman Empire*, London Macmillan, 1906, p. 531.
6. Tim Blanning, *The Pursuit of Glory, Europe 1648–1815*, London, Penguin, 1948, 2007, p. 282.
7. A. J. P. Taylor, *The Habsburg Monarchy*, Harmondsworth, Penguin, 1964, p. 22.

9. TWO REVOLTS, FRENCH OCCUPATION AND UNION WITH THE DUTCH: 1789–1830

1. Eric Hobsbawm, *The Age of Revolution*, London, Abacus, 1977, p. 13.
2. Paul Johnson, *The Birth of the Modern*, New York, Harpers Perennial, 1991, p. 904.

3. E. H. Kossman, *The Low Countries 1780–1940*, Oxford University Press, 1978, p. 80.
4. Adam Zamoyski, *The Rites of Peace, The Fall of Napoleon and The Congress of Vienna*, New York, HarperCollins, 2007, p. 140.
5. Tim Blanning, *The Pursuit of Glory, Europe 1648–1815*, 2007, p. 351.
6. Els Witte 'The dawn of a new nation (1830–1848)' in Els Witte, Jan Craeybeckx and Alain Meynen, *The Political History of Belgium from 1830 onwards*, Antwerp, Standaard Uitgeverij/VUB Press, 2000, p. 17.

10. A FRANCOPHONE ELITE WINS BELGIUM ITS INDEPENDENCE: 1830–65

1. As quoted by De Schryver in Arend Lijphart (ed.), *Conflict and Coexistence in Belgium: The Dynamics of a Culturally Divided Society*, Berkeley, CA, University of California, IIS, 1981, p. 14.
2. Henri Pirenne, *Histoire de Belgiques des origines à nos jours*, Brussels 1972.
3. de Meeus, *History of the Belgians*, New York, Praeger, 1962, pp. 286–7.
4. Peter Paret, *Clausewitz and the State*, New York, Oxford University Press, 1976, p. 396.
5. Neal Ascherson, *The King Incorporated, Leopold II and the Congo*, London, Granta, 1999, p. 18.
6. Xavier Mabille, *Histoire Politique de la Belgique*, Brussels, Crisp, 1992, pp. 147–9.
7. Ascherson, *The King Incorporated*, p. 82.
8. Jean Sigmann, *1848: The Romantic and Democratic Revolutions in Europe*, New York, Harper & Row, 1973, p. 96.
9. Els Witte, 'The Triumph of Liberalism' in E. Witte, J. Craeybeckx and A. Meynen, *The Political History of Belgium from 1830 onwards*, Antwerp, Standaard Uitgeverij/VUB Press 2000, pp. 49–50.

11. LABOUR AND FLEMISH MOVEMENTS BEGIN TO DEVELOP: 1865–1914

1. E.H. Kossman, *The Low Countries*, London, Oxford University Press, 1999, p. 375.
2. Els Witte, 'The Expansion of Democracy' in E. Witte, J. Craeybeckx and A. Meynen, *The Political History of Belgium from 1830 onwards*, Antwerp, Standaard Uitgeverij/VUB Press, 2000, p. 73.
3. A. J. P. Taylor, *The Habsburg Monarchy, 1809–1918*, Harmondsworth, Penguin Books, 1964, pp. 34, 187.
4. Carl Strickwerde, *A House Divided: Catholics, Socialists, and Flemish Nationalists in Nineteenth Century Belgium*, London, Rowman & Littlefield, 1997, pp. 71, 401.
5. Witte, 'The Expansion of Democracy', pp. 85–86.
6. Robert B. Edgerton, *The Troubled Heart of Africa*, New York, NY, St. Martin's Press, 2002, pp. 162–3.

7. Jean-Luc Vellut (scientific adviser), *Memory of the Congo, The Colonial Era*, Tervuren, Musée Royal de l'Afrique Centrale, 2005, p. 11.
8. Alexander Murphy, 'Landscape for whom?' in Catherine Labio (ed.), *Belgian Memories*, New Haven, CT, Yale University Press, 2002, p. 176.
9. Ascherson, *The King Incorporated, Leopold II and the Congo*, London, Granta, 1999 p. 300.
10. Witte, 'The Expansion of Democracy', p. 73.
11. Destrée 'Open Letter to the King, Concerning the Separation of Flanders and Wallonia' in Theo Hermans and Louis Vos and Lode Wils (eds), *The Flemish Movement, A Documentary History 1780–1990*, London, Athlone, 1992, p. 206.

12. TWO GERMAN INVASIONS AND A DEPRESSION SPEED CHANGE: 1914–1945

1. Larry Zuckerman, *The Rape of Belgium, the Untold Story of World War I*, New York, New York University Press, 2004, p. 1.
2. Jan Craeybeckx, 'From the Great War to the Great Depression' in Els Witte, Jan Craeybeckx and Alain Meynen, *The Political History of Belgium from 1830 onwards*, Antwerp, Standaard Uitgeverij/VUB Press, 2000 p. 105.
3. Roger Keyes, *Outrageous Fortune*, London, Secker & Warburg, 1984, p. 308.
4. Winston Groom, *A Storm in Flanders*, New York, Atlantic Monthly, 2002, p. 35.
5. Ibid., p. 77.
6. Zuckerman, *The Rape of Belgium*, p. 95.
7. E.H. Kossman, *The Low Countries*, 1780–1940, Oxford, Oxford University Press, 1999, p. 639.
8. Martin Conway, *Collaboration in Belgium: Léon Degrelle and the Rexist Movement*, New Haven, CT, Yale University Press, 1993, p. 3.
9. Theo Aronson, *The Coburgs of Belgium*, London, Cassell, 1969, pp. 230, 232.
10. Robert Jackson, *Dunkirk, The British Evacuation, 1940*, London, Casswell, 2002, pp. 16–17.
11. Hugh Sebag-Montefiore, *Dunkirk, Fight to the Last Man*, Cambridge, MA, Harvard University Press, 2006, p. 321.

13. THE FRANCOPHONE, PROPERTIED AND DOMINANT ELITE ERODES: 1945–68

1. Els Witte, 'Restoration and Renewal after World War II' in E. Witte, J. Craeybeckx and A. Meynen, *The Political History of Belgium from 1830 onwards*, 2000, p. 165.

2. Alain Meynen, 'Economic and Social Policy since the 1950's' in E. Witte, J. Craybeckx and Meynen, *The Political History of Belgium from 1830 Onwards*, 2000, p. 205.

14. BELGIUM FEDERALISES: 1968–1993

1. Pierre-Henri Laurent, 'Divided Belgium Walks a Tightrope', *Current History* 83, April 1984, p. 189.
2. Eric Hobsbawm, *The Age of Extremes, 1914–1991*, London, Penguin, 1995, p 425.
3. Maddens, Beerten and Billiet, 'The National Consciousness of the Flemings and the Walloons: An Empirical Investigation' in Kas Deprez and Louis Vos (eds), *Nationalism in Belgium, Shifting Identities*, London, Macmillan, 1990, p. 99.
4. Els Witte, 'Increasing Tensions between the Communities and the creation of a federalized Belgium' in E. Witte, J. Craeybeckx, and A. Meynen, *The Political History of Belgium from 1830 onwards*, Antwerp, Standaard Uitgeverij/VUB Press, 2000, p. 251.
5. Wilfried Martens in a letter to the author, 14 June 2006.
6. Els Witte, 'The Post-war and Contemporary Political System' in Witte, Craeybeckx and Meynen, p. 295.

15. INCREASINGLY ISOLATED FLANDERS AND WALLONIA COLLIDE: 1993–

1. Els Witte, 'The Post-war and Contemporary Political System' in E. Witte, J. Craeybeckx and Meynen, *The Political History of Belgium from 1830 onwards*, Antwerp, Standaard Uitgeverij/VUB Press 2000, p. 297.
2. Eric Hobsbawm, *The Age of Empire*, 1875–1914, London, Abacus, 1991, p. 158.

RETROSPECT AND PROSPECTS: KEEPING A DIVIDED LAND UNITED

1. Nicholas Ostler, *Empires of the World A Language History of the World*, London, Harpers Perennial, 2005, p. xix.
2. Eric Hobsbawm, *Nations and Nationalism since 1780*, Cambridge University Press, 1990, p. 91.
3. Samuel Huntington, *Who are we?*, New York, Simon & Schuster, 2004, pp. 12–13.
4. Paul Belien, *A Throne in Brussels, Britain, the Saxe-Coburgs, and the Belgianization of Europe*, Exeter, Imprint Academia, 2005, pp. vi-vii.
5. Henri Pirenne, *Histoire de Belgique des origines à nos jours*, Brussels, La Renaissance du Livre, 1972.
6. Tony Judt, 'Is there a Belgium?' in Benno Bernard et al., *How can one* not *be interested in Belgian History, War, Language and Consensus in Belgium*

since 1830, Dublin/Ghent, Trinity College Dublin/Academia Press, 2005, p. 13.

7. Els Witte, 'The Post-war and Contemporary political system', in E. Witte, J. Craeybeckx and A. Meynen, *The Political History of Belgium from 1830 Onwards*, Antwerp, Standaard Uitgeverij/VUB Press, p. 295.
8. Pierre-Henri Laurent, 'Divided Belgium walks a tightrope' *Current History* 83, April 1984, p. 189.
9. K. C. Wheare, *Modern Constitutions*, London, Oxford University Press, 1962, p. 33.
10. Jerry Z. Muller, 'Us and Them—The Enduring Power of Ethnic Nationalism', *Foreign Affairs*, vol. 87, no. 2, Apr./May 2008, pp. 20, 33.

SELECTED SOURCES

Books

Alverez, Manuel Fernandez, *Charles V, Elected Emperor and Hereditary Ruler*, London, Thames & Hudson, 1975 (Published in Spanish as *Carlos V, Un hombre para Europa*, Madrid, 1976; *Carlos V: El César y el Hombre*, Madrid, 1999).

Anderson, Benedict, *Imagined Communities*, New York, Verso, 1991.

Arblaster, Paul, *A History of the Low Countries*, New York, Palgrave Macmillan, 2006.

Armstrong, C. A. J., *England, France and Burgundy in the Fifteenth Century*, London, Hambleton Press, 1983.

Armstrong, Edward, *The Emperor Charles V*, London, Macmillan, 1902.

Armstrong, Karen, *The Battle for God*, New York, Ballatine Books, 2000.

Aronson, Theo, *The Coburgs of Belgium*, London, Cassell, 1969.

Ascherson, Neal, *The King Incorporated, Leopold the Second and the Congo*, London, Granta, 1999; London, George Allen & Unwin, 1963 (published in the United States as *The King Incorporated, Leopold II in the Age of Trusts*, Garden City, NY, Doubleday, 1964).

Ashley, Maurice, *The Golden Century—Europe 1598–1715*, New York, Frederick A. Praeger, 1969.

Bagrow, Leo and R. A. Skelton, *History of Cartography*, London, C. A. Watts, 1964.

Baie, Eugene, *Le Siècle des Geux* (two vols.), Brussels, Nouvelle Societe d'Editions, 1937–8.

Balthazar, Herman et al, *The Drama of the Low Countries*, Antwerp, Fonds Mercator, 1996 (published simultaneously by the same publisher in Dutch as *de Gouden Delta* and in French as *le Delta d'Or des Plats Pays*).

Barbero, Alessandro, *Charlemagne: Father of a Continent*, Los Angeles, University of California Press, 2004.

Barker, Juliet, *Agincourt: The King, the Campaign, the Battle*, London, Little, Brown, 2005.

Barraclough, Geoffrey (ed.), *The Times Atlas of World History*, Maplewood, NJ, Hammond, 1979.

Barteleous, Jean, *Nos Premiers Ministres*, Brussels, J.-M. Collet, 1983.

Bates, David, *William the Conqueror*, Brussels, Tempus, 2002.

Bauer, Ludwig, *Leopold the Unloved*, Boston, MA, Little, Brown, 1935.

Bayer, Henry J., *The Belgians—First Settlers in New York and in the Middle States*, New York, Devon-Adnir, 1925.

Beales, Derek, *Joseph II* (two vols.), Cambridge, Cambridge University Press, 1987 and 2010.

Belien, Paul, *A Throne in Brussels, Britain, the Saxe-Coburgs and the Belgianisation of Europe*, Exeter, Imprint Academic, 2005.

Bernard, Benno, *Belgian History, War, Language and Consensus in Belgium since 1830*, Dublin and Ghent, Trinity College, Trinity Academic Press, 2005.

Binding, Paul, *Imagined Corners—Exploring the World's First Atlas*, London, Headline 2003.

Bitsch, Marie-Thérèse, *Histoire de la Belgique, de l'antiquité à nos jours*, Brussels, Editions Complexe, 2004.

Blaeu, Joan, *Toonneel des Steden van's Konings Nederlanden*, 1649.

Blanning, Tim, *The Pursuit of Glory, Europe 1648–1815*, London, Penguin, 2007.

Bloch, Marc, *Feudal Society* (two vols.), Chicago, University of Chicago Press and London, Routledge & Kegan Paul, 1961 (published in French as *La Société Féodale*).

Blockmans, Wim, *Emperor Charles V*, London, Arnold, 2002.

Blom, J. C. H. and E. Lamberts (ed.), *History of the Low Countries*, New York, Berghahn, 1999 (published in Dutch as *Geschiedenis van de Nederlanden*, Amsterdam, Agon, 1994).

Blyth, Derek, Alistair MacLean and Rory Watson, *The Belgian House of Representatives, from Revolution to Federalism*, Brussels, 2008.

Bock, Walter de, *Les plus belles années d'une génération, l'ordre nouveau en Belgique*, Brussels, Vie Ouvrière, 1982.

Bodenehr, G., *Force d'Europe*, Augsburg, 1720–25.

Boffa, Sergio, *Warfare in Medieval Brabant*, Woodbridge, Suffolk, England, Boydell Press, 2004.

Boorstin, Daniel J., *The Discoverers*, New York, Vintage, 1983.

Borchgrave d'Altena, Count Joseph de (ed.), *Castles of Belgium*, Brussels, Desoer, 1967 (published in French as *Les Châteaux de Belgique*).

Bral, Guido Jan, *De Kathedrall Sint Michel and Sint Goedele*, Tielt, Lannoo, 2000.

Braun, Georg and Frans Hogenberg, *Civitates Orbis Terrarum*, Cologne, 1572.

Braunfels, Wolfgang, *Die Welt der Karolinger und ihre Kunst*, Munich, George D. W. Callweg, 1968.

Brodsky, Alexandre Fanny, *A Fragile Identity—Survival in Nazi-occupied Belgium*, London, Ratcliffe Press, 1998.

Bronne, Carlo, *Beloeil et la Maison de Ligne*, Beloeil, Editions Gamma, 1979.

Bryce, James (Viscount), *The Holy Roman Empire*, London, Macmillan, 1906.

Bryssinck, René, Marina Boudart and Michel Boudart (eds), *Modern Belgium*, Brussels, Modern Belgium Association, 1990.

Buyle, Marjan et al., *Architecture Gothique en Belgique*, Brussels, Racine, 1997.

Caesar, Julius (John Warrington, trans.), *The Gallic Wars*, New York, Heritage Press, 1955.

Calleo, David P., *Rethinking Europe's Future*, Princeton University Press (A Century Foundation book), 2003.

Calmette, Joseph, *The Golden Age of Burgundy*, New York, W. W. Norton, 1963 (published in French as *Les Grands Ducs de Bourgogne*, Paris, Albin Michel, 1949).

Cammaerts, Emile, *Belgium from the Roman Invasion to the Present Day*, London, T. F. Unwin, 1921.

Campbell, Thomas P., *Tapestry in the Renaissance, Art and Magnificence*, New York, NY, Metropolitan Museum of Art, 2002.

Carson, Patricia, *The Fair Face of Flanders*, Ghent, E. Story Scientia, 1978 (republished in four languages, Tielt, Lannoo, 2001: in English as *The Fair Face of Flanders*, in Dutch as *Het fraaie gelaat van Vlaanderen*, in French as *Miroir de la Flandre*; and in German as *Zauber und Schieeksal Flanderas*).

Cartwright, Frederick F. (with Michael D. Biddis), *Disease and History*, New York, Dorset Press, 1972.

Catrou and Rouille, *Roman History with Notes*, London, Boyyenham, 1737.

Christyn, Jan Baptiste, *Histoire générale des Pais-Bas* (four vols.), Brussels, François Foppen, 1720.

Claus, Hugo, *The Sorrow of Belgium*, London, Viking, 1990 (published in Dutch as *Het Vendriet van Belgie*).

Cleven, Jean, Johan Decavale and Frieda van Tyghen, 'Belgium: Architecture' in *Grove Dictionary of Art*, New York, Grove's Dictionaries, 1999.

Clough, Shepard B., *A History of the Flemish Movement in Belgium*, New York, Octagon, 1968.

Collins, Roger, *Charlemagne*, London, Macmillan, 1998.

Commynes, Philippe de, *Chronique ...*, Paris, Galloit du Pre, 1524.

Condon, Thomas J., *New York Beginnings*, New York, New York University Press, 1968.

Conrad, Joseph, *The Heart of Darkness*, New York, NY, Penguin Books, 1999.

Conscience, Hendrik, *The Lion of Flanders*, London, Lambert, 1855 (published in Dutch as *Leeuw van Vlaanderen*, Antwerp, J. E. Buschmaan, 1848 and in French as *Le Lion de Flandres*, Paris, Levy frères, 1871).

Conway, Martin, *Collaboration in Belgium: Léon Degrelle and the Rexist Movement*, New Haven, CT, Yale University Press, 1993 (published in Dutch as *Collaboratie in Belgie*, Groot-Bijgaarden, Globe, 1994 and in French as *Degrelle, les années de collaboration*, Brussels, Labor, 2005).

Cook, Dr Frederick A., *Through the First Antarctic Night*, Pittsburgh, PA, and Frederick A. Cook Society, Hurleyville, NY, Polar, 1998.

Coomans, Thomas, *L'abbaye de Villers-en-Brabant*, Brussels, Racine, 2000.

Coster, Charles de, *The Legend of the Glorious Adventures of Tyln Ulenspiegel in the Land of Flanders & Elsewhere*, London, Journeyman, 1867.

Crane, Nicholas, *Mercator: The Man Who Mapped the Planet*, London, Weidenfeld & Nicolson, 2002.

Davies, Norman, *Europe*, Oxford University Press, 1996.

Davis, James C., *Pursuit of Power*, New York, Harper Torchbooks, 1970.

Dawson, Christopher, *Religion and the Rise of Western Culture*, New York, Sheed and Ward, 1950.

Declier, Hugo and Claude De Broyer (eds), *The Belgica Expedition Centennial*, Brussels, VUB Brussels University Press, 2001.

Delehouzee, Laurent et al., *Architecture Romane en Belgique*, Brussels, Racine, 2000.

Delhaize, Jules, *La Domination Française en Belgique* (six vols.), Brussels, J. Lebegue, Libraires-Editeurs, 1908–1912.

Delmarcel, Guy, *Flemish Tapestry*, New York, Harry Abrams, 2000 (published in Dutch as *Vlaamse wandtapijter*).

Deprez, Kas and Louis Vos (ed.), *Nationalism in Belgium, Shifting Identities, 1780–1995*, London, Macmillan, 1990 (also published in 1998 as *Nationalisme in Belgie, Identiteiten in beweging 1780–2000*, Antwerp, Uitgeverij Houtekiet).

De Witte, Ludo, *The Assassination of Lumumba*, New York, Verso, 2001.

Dickson, P. G. M., *Finance and Government under Maria Theresa* (two vols.), Clarendon Press/Oxford University Press, 1987.

D'Hondt, J., *Les Origins de la Flandre et de l'Artois*, Arras, Centre d'Etudes Régionales du Pas-de-Calais, 1944.

Dollinger, P. (D.S. Ault and S.H. Steinberg trans. and eds), *The German Hansa*, Stanford, CA, Stanford University Press, 1970.

Dorchy, Henry, *Histoire des Belges*, Brussels, A. De Boeck, 1982.

Duby, Georges, *Atlas Historique*, Paris, Larousse, 1978.

Duke, Alastair, *Reformation and Revolt in the Low Countries*, London and New York, Hambledon and London, 2003.

Dumont, G,-H., *Léopold II, Roi des Belges*, Brussels, Dessart, 1994.

———, *Histoire de la Belgique*, Brussels, Le Cri, 1999.

Dumoulin, Michel, *La Belgique et les débuts de la construction européene (1945–1957)*, Louvain-la-Neuve, Ciaco, 1988.

Dunn, Susan, *Sister Revolutions—French Lightning, American Light*, New York, Faber & Faber, 1999.

Duvieusart, Jean, *La question royale, Crise et dénouement: juin, juillet, août 1950*, Brussels, Crisp, 1975.

Dwyer, Philip, *Napoleon, The Path to Power*, New Haven, CT and London, Yale University Press, 2008.

Economist, *Pocket World in Figures 2008 Edition*, London, The Economist in association with Profile Book, 2007.

Ellis, Peter Berresford, *The Celtic Empire, The First Millennium of Celtic History c.1000 BC-51AD*, Durham, NC, Carolina Academic Press, 1990.

Erlanger, Philippe, *Louis XIV*, London, Weidenfeld & Nicholson, 1970 (first published in Paris by Librairie Arthème Fayard, 1965.

Essen, Léon van der, *Deux mille ans d'histoire*, Brussels, Editions Universitaires, 1946.

Etemad, Brouda, *La Possession du monde: Poids et mesures de la colonisation (XVIIIe-XXe siècles)* Brussels, Editions Complex, 2000.

Filipczak, Zirka Z., *Picturing Art In Antwerp*, 1550–1700, Princeton University Press, 1987.

Fisher, H. A. L., *A History of Europe*, London, Edward Arnold, 1936.

Fitzmaurice, John, *The Politics of Belgium*, London, Hurst, 1983.

Fletcher, Richard, *The Barbarian Conversion*, New York, Henry Holt, 1997.

Foppens, Jean Fran, *Historia episcopatus Antvepiensis*, Brussels, apud Franciscom Foppens, 1717.

Fralon, Jose-Alain, *Bodewijn, De man die geen koning wilde zige*, Antwerp, Standaard, 2001.

Froissart, Jean (D. Pollute, trans.), *Chronique...*, Paris, Antoine, c.1550.

Galbert of Bruges, *The Murder of Charles the Good*, New York, NY, Columbia University Press, 1960.

Ganshoff, F.L., *La Flandre sous les premiers comtes*, Brussels, La Renaissance du Livre, 1943.

Genicot, Léopold, *Histoire de la Wallonie*, Toulouse, Privat, 1973.

George, Stephen and Ian Bache, *Politics in the European Union*, Oxford, Oxford University Press, 2001.

Gerson, H. and E. H. Ter Kuile, *Art and Architecture in Belgium 1600–1800*, Baltimore, Penguin, 1960.

Gestel, Cornelius van, *Historia Sacra et Profana Archiepiscopates Machinensis*, Hagae Comitum, apud Christianum van Lom, 1725.

Gevaert, Marc, *Van Boudewijn tot Boudewijn—10 Eeuen Vlanderen*, Rooselare, Globe, 2002.

Geyl, Pieter, *The Revolt of the Netherlands, 1555–1609*, London, Ernest Benn, 1958.

———, *The Netherlands in the Seventeenth Century Part One 1609–1648*, London, Ernest Benn, 1961.

———, *The Netherlands in the Seventeenth Century Part Two 1648–1715*, London, Ernest Benn, 1964.

Gibbon, Edward, *The Decline and Fall of the Roman Empire*, (3 Vol), New York, Heritage Press, 1946 (first published in 6 vols., London, A. Strahan and T. Cadell, 1780).

Giedion, Sigfried, *Space, Time, and Architecture*, Cambridge, MA, Harvard University Press, 1967.

Gijsels, Hugo, *Le Flams Blok*, Brussels, Luc Pire, 1993.

Goldsworthy, Adrian, *Caesar, Life of a Colossus*, New Haven, CT and London, Yale University Press, 2006.
Goltzius, Hubert, *Lebendige Bilder Gar Nach Aller Keysern*, Antwerp, Coppendius, 1557.
Groom, Winston, *A Storm in Flanders*, New York, Atlantic Monthly, 2002.
Grotius, Hugo, *Annales et Histoire de Rebus Belgicis*, Amsterdam, Joannes Blaeu, 1657.
Guicciardini, Ludovico, *Tout le Pais-Bas*, Antwerp, Guillaume Silvius, 1567.
Hackett, Francis, *Francis the First*, New York, The Literary Guild, 1934.
Hale, John, *The Civilization of Europe in the Renaissance*, New York, Maxwell Macmillan, 1993.
Halkin, Léon-E., *La Réforme en Belgique sous Charles Quint*, Brussels, La Renaissance du livre, 1957.
Harvard, Robertt, *The War of Wars, The Epic Struggle between Britain and France 1789–1815*, London, Constable, 2006.
Hasquin, Hervé, *Historiographie et politique en Belgique*, Brussels, Editions de l'Université de Bruxelles, Institut Jules Destrée, 1996.
———, (direction scientifique), *La Belgique autrichienne, 1713–1794, Les Pays-Bas meridionaux sous les Habsbourg d'Autriche*, Brussels, Crédit Communal, 1987.
———, *La Wallonie, son histoire*, Brussels, Luc Pire, 1999.
Heer, Friedrich, *Charlemagne and His World*, New York, Macmillan, 1975.
Henne, Alexandre and Alphonse Wauters, *Histoire de la Ville de Bruxelles* (3 vols), Brussels, Librairie Encyclopédique de Perichon, 1845.
Herm, Gerhard, *The Celts*, New York, St. Martin's Press, 1977
Hermans, Theo, Louis Vos and Lode Wils (eds), *The Flemish Movement, A Documentary History 1780–1990*, London, Athlone, 1992.
Hibbert, Christopher, *Wellington*, Reading, MA, Perseus, 1997.
Histoire Générale des Pais-Bas, Brussels, chez François Foppen, 1720.
Historical Atlas of the World, Rand McNally, Skokie, Illinois, 1997.
Hobsbawm, Eric, *The Age of Empire 1875–1914* (first published by Weidenfield and Nicholson 1987), London, Abacus, 1994.
———, *The Age of Extremes 1914–1991* (first published by Michael Joseph 1994), London, Abacus, 1995.
——— *Nations and Nationalism Since 1780: Programme, Myth, and Reality*, Cambridge University Press, 1990.
———, *The Age of Revolution 1789–1848* (first published by Weidenfield and Nicholson 1962), London, Abacus, 1977.
———, *The Age of Capital 1848–1875* (first published by Weidenfield and Nicholson 1975), London, Abacus, 1997.
Hochschild, Adam, *King Leopold's Ghost, a Story of Greed, Terror, and Heroism in Colonial Africa*, New York, NY, Houghton Mifflin, 1998.
———, *To End All Wars*, New York, Houghton Mifflin Harcourt, 2011.
Hofschroer, Peter, *1815, The Waterloo Campaign*, London, Greenhill, 1998.
Hollande, Francisco de, *De la Pintura Antigua*, Madrid, J. Rates, 1548.

Holme, Bryan, *Medieval Pageant*, London, Thames and Hudson, 1987.

Holt, Elizabeth, *Literary Sources of Art History*, Princeton University Press, 1947.

Horne, John and Alan Kramer, *German Atrocities, 1914: A History of Denial*, New Haven, CT, Yale University Press, 2001.

Houart, Pierre, *Deux Mille Ans d'Histoire Princière de la Belgique Romaine a Albert II*, Braine-l'Alleud, J.-M. Collet, 1997.

Huggett, Frank Edward, *Modern Belgium*, New York, Frederick A. Praeger, 1969.

Hughes, Robert and Piero Bianconi, *The Complete Paintings of Brueghel*, Bologna, Capitol, 1979.

Huizinga, J., *The Waning of the Middle Ages*, London, Edward Arnold, 1976.

———, *Paul Henri Spaak de l'émeute à l'OTAN*, Brussels, Legain, 1998.

Humes, Samuel IV, *Local Governance and National Power, A Worldwide Comparison of Tradition and Change in Local Govenment*, London, Harvester Wheatsheaf, 1991.

Hunter, George Leland, *Tapestries, Their Origin, History, and Renaissance*, London and New York, John Lane, 1912.

Huntington, Samuel P., *Who are We?*, New York, Simon & Schuster, 2004.

Huyse, Luc, *De gewapende vrede, politiek in Belgie tussen 1945 en 1980*, Leuven, KRITAR, 1980.

———, 'Lode Outrine', in Jean-Luc Dehaene, *Machtsgroepen in de Samenleving*, Leuven, Davidsfonds, 1973.

Israel, Jonathan, *The Dutch Republic, Its Rise, Its Greatness, and Fall 1477–1806*, Oxford, Clarendon Press, 1995.

Jackson, Robert, *Dunkirk, The British Evacuation, 1940*, London, Cassell, 2002.

Janssens, Valéry, *Le Franc belge, un siècle et demi—histoire monétaire*, Brussels, Services Inter-enterprises, 1976.

Johnson, Paul, *Elizabeth I*, New York, Holt, Rinehart and Winston, 1974.

———, *The Birth of the Modern*, New York, Harpers, 1991.

———, *Napoleon*, London, Lipper/Viking, 2002.

Jordan, William Chester, *Europe in the High Middle Age*, New York, Viking/Penguin, 2003.

Judt, Tony, *Postwar: A History of Europe since 1945*, London, Pimlico, 2004.

Kamen, Henry, *Philip of Spain*, New Haven, CT, Yale University Press, 1977.

Kardux, Joke and Eduard van de Bilt, *Newcomers in an Old City, The American Pilgrims in Leiden 1609–1620*, Leiden, Uitgeverij Burgersdijkrmans, 2001.

Keen, Mayrice (ed.), *Medieval Warfare, A History*, Oxford University Press, 1999.

Kennedy, Joseph P. and James M. Landis, *The Surrender of King Leopold*, New York, 1950.

Kestergat, Jean, *Quand le Zaire s'appel Congo, l'aventure coloniale belge*, Brussels, Legrain, 1985.

Keyes, Roger, *Outrageous Fortune*, London, Secker & Warburg, 1984.

Koll, Johannes (ed.), *Belgien: Geschichte Politik, Kultur, Wirtschaft*, Munster, Aschendorff Verlag, 2007.

Kossmann, E. H., *The Low Countries, 1780–1940*, Oxford, Oxford University Press, 1999.

Kupchan, Charles A., *The End of the American Era*, New York, NY, Vintage Press, 2002.

Labio, Catherine (ed.), *Belgian Memories*, New Haven, CT, Yale University Press, 2002.

Lagrou, Pieter, *The Legacy of Nazi Occupation, Patriotic Memory and National Recovery in Western Europe, 1945–1965*, Cambridge University Press, 2000.

Lang, Paul Henry, *Music in Western Civilization*, New York, W. W. Norton, 1997.

Le Goff, Jacques, *The Birth of Europe*, Oxford, Blackwell, 2005.

Leopold III, *Kroon getoige over de grote gebeurtenissen tijdens mijn koningschap*, Tielt, Lannoo 2001 (published in French as *Pour l'Histoire sur quelques épisodes de mon règne*, Brussels, Racine, 2001).

Leton, Anton and Andre Miroir, *Les Conflicts communautaires en Belgique*, Paris, Presses Universitaires de France, 1999.

Liebaers, Herman, *Beyond Belgium, Royal and other Adventures of a Librarian World-wide*, Leuven, Van Halewijk, 2003.

Lijphart, Arend (ed.), *Conflict and Coexistence in Belgium: The Dynamics of a Culturally Divided Society*, Berkeley, University of California, IIS, 1981.

Littlell, Jonathan, *Le sec et l'humide*, Paris, L'arbalète Gallimard, 2008.

Loades, David, *Elizabeth I*, London and New York, Hambledon and London, 2003.

Loze, Pierre and François, *Belgium Art Nouveau—From Victor Hugo to Antoine Pompe*, Snoek-Ducaju & Zoon, 1991.

Lucas, Henry S., *The Low Countries and the Hundred Years War, 1326–1347*, Ann Arbor, MI, University of Michigan, 1929.

Luykx, Theo, *Politieke geschiedenis van Belgie*, Brussels/Amsterdam, Elsevier, 1977.

Luykx, Theo and Marc Platel, *Politieke Geschiedenis van Belgie van 1944 tot 1985*, Antwerp, Kluwer rechtsweten schappen, 1985.

Lynn, John A., *The Wars of Louis XIV*, London, Longman, 1999.

Mabille, Xavier, *Histoire Politique de la Belgique*, Brussels, Crisp, 1992.

MacCulloch, Diarmaid, *The Reformation*, London, Penguin, 2004.

MacDonnell, John de Courcy, *Leopold II: his Rule in Belgium and the Congo*, New York, Argosy-Antiquarium, 1970.

Maltby, William, *The Reign of Charles V*, New York, Palgrave, 2002.

Maltby, W. S., *Alba: A Biography of Fernando Alvarez de Toledo Third Duke of Alba, 1507–82*, Los Angeles, University of California, 1983.

Mansel, Philip, *Prince of Europe, The Life of Charles-Joseph de Ligne*, London, Weidenfeld & Nicolson, 2003.

Martens, Wilfried, *De Memoires*, Tielt, Lannoo, 2006.

Maurois, Andre, *A History of France*, New York, Farrar, Straus and Cudahy, 1956.

McKitterick, R., *The Frankish Kingdoms under the Carolingians, 751–987*, London, Longman, 1983.

———, *Charlemagne, The Formation of a European Identity*, Cambridge University Press, 2008.

McManners, John (ed.), *The Oxford Illustrated History of Christianity*, Oxford University Press, 1990.

McRae, Kenneth D., *Conflict and Compromise in Multilingual Societies* (vol. 2), Belgium), Waterloo, Ont., Wilfred Laurier University, 1986.

Meeus, Adrien de, *History of the Belgians*, New York, NY, Praeger, 1962 (published in French as *Histoire des Belges*, Paris, A. Fayard, 1928).

Meier, Christian, *Caesar*, New York, Basic Books, 1996.

Mercator, Geraldi, *Atlas Minor*, Joannes Janssens, 1621.

Mercier, Jacques, Anne Fontaine and France Debray, *Les Belges du XXe Siecle*, Bruxelles, La Renaissance du Livre, 1999.

Mole, John, *Mind Your Manners, Managing Business Cultures in the new Global Europe* (3rd ed.), London, Nicholas Brearley, 2003.

Motley, John Lothrop, *The Rise of the Dutch Republic* (3 vols.), London, Bickers & Son, 1864.

Muller, Jeffrey and Jim Murrel (eds), *Miniatura or the Art of Limning*, New Haven, CT, Yale University Press, 1997.

Murray, James M., *Bruges, Cradle of Capitalism 1280–1390*, Cambridge University Press, 2005.

Ndaywel e Nziem, Isidore, *Histoire generale du Congo: De l'heritage ancien a la Republic Democratique*, Paris, Duculot, 1998.

Neillands, Robin, *The Hundred Years War*, London, Routledge, 1990.

Neve, Franz, *Deux mille ans de l'Histoire des Belges* (four vols.), Brussels, Librairie de Lannoy/Editions 'Verbe et Lumière', 1923–26.

New Cambridge Modern History, The (Volumes I-XIV), London and New York, Cambridge University Press, 1957–71.

Nicholas, David, *The Metamorphosis of a Medieval City: Ghent in the Age of the Arteveldes, 1302–1390*, Lincoln, NE, University of Nebraska, 1987.

———, *The van Arteveldes of Ghent: the Varieties of Vendetta and the Hero in History*, Ithaca, NY and London, Cornell University Press, 1988.

———, *Medieval Flanders*, London, Longman, 1992.

Nicolson, Adam, *God's Secretaries,The Making of the King James Bible*, New York, NY, HarperCollins, 2003 (published in Great Britain in 2003 as *Power and Glory*).

Northrup, David, *Beyond the Bend of the River: African Labor in Eastern Zaire, 1865–1940*, Athens, OH, Ohio University Center for International Studies, 1988.

Nugent, Neill, *The Government and Politics of the European Community*, London, Macmillan, 1991.

Osborne, Harold (ed.), *The Oxford Companion to Art*, Oxford, Clarendon Press, 1970.

Ostler, Nicholas, *Empires of the World, A Language History of the World*, New York, HarperCollins, 2005.

Palmer, Alan, *Metternich: Councillor of Europe*, London, 1972.

———, *Northern Shores, A History of the Baltic Sea*, London, John Murray, 2005.

Paret, Peter, *Clausewitz and the State*, New York, Oxford University Press, 1976.

Parker, Geoffrey, *The Dutch Revolt*, London, Cambridge, 1977.

———, *The Grand Strategy of Philip II*, New Haven, CT, Yale University Press, 1998.

Parker, Geoffrey and Geoffrey Barraclough (eds), *The Times Atlas of World History* (Fourth Edition), Maplewood, NJ, Hammond, 1993.

Pauwels, Henri and Andre Moorman, 'Belgium' in *The Encyclopedia of World Art*, New York, McGraw-Hill, 1959.

Payne, Robert, *The Dream and the Tomb—A History of the Crusades*, New York, Stein and Day, 1984.

Pierre, Stéphanie, *Les Années vingt et trente*, Braine l'Alleud, J.-M. Collet, 1997.

Pinder, John, *European Community*, Oxford University Press, 1991.

Pirenne, Henri (ed.), *Chronique rimée des troubles en 1379–1380*, Ghent, A. Siffer, 1902.

———, *Belgian Democracy, Its Early History*, New York, AMS Press, 1970 (published in Manchester 1915).

———, *Medieval Cities, Their Origins and the Revival of Trade*, Princeton University, 1925 (published in French in Brussels in 1927).

———, *Histoire de Belgique des origines à nos jours* (5 vols.), Brussels, La Renaissance du Livre, 1972 (first published 1900).

Plisnier, Flore, *Ils ont pris les armes pour Hitler, La collaboration armée en Belgique francophone*, Brussels, Editions Luc Pire, 2008 (also published in Dutch).

Pliesnier, Flore and Maertens Fabrice, *Te Wapen voor Hitler: gewapende collaartie in Frantalig Belgie 1940–1944*, Antwerp, Meulenhoff/Manteau, 2008.

Pol, Paul von, *Flanders in Flooded Fields, Before Ypres there was Yser*, Barnesley, Pen & Sword Military, 2006.

Prevenier, W. and Wim Blockmans, *The Burgundian Netherlands*, Cambridge, Cambridge University Press, 1986 (published in French as *Les Pays-Bas Bourguignons*, Antwerp, Mercatorfonds, 1986).

Previté-Orton, C. W., *The Shorter Cambridge Medieval History* (two vols.), Cambridge, University Press, 1962.

Purtle, Carole, *The Marian Paintings of Jan van Eyck*, Princeton University Press, 1982.

Reynebeau, Marc, *Histoire Belge 1830–2005*, Brussels, Racine, 2005 (also published in Dutch: Tielt, Lannoo, 2005).

Roxburgh, Angus, *Preachers of Hate: the Rise of the Right*, London, Gibson Square Books, 2002.

Sadie, Stanley, *The New Grove Dictionary of Music and Musicians*, London, Macmillan, 1980–83.

Sanderus, Antonius, *Flandria illustrata...*, Cologne, ab Egmondt, 1644.

Sawyer, Peter (ed.), *The Oxford Illustrated History of the Vikings*, New York, Oxford University Press, 1997.

Sebag-Montefiore, Hugh, *Dunkirk, Fight to the Last Man*, Cambidge, MA, Harvard University Press, 2006.

Seward, Desmond, *A Brief History of The Hundred Years War, The English in France 1337–1453*, London, Constable & Robinson, 2003.

Shepherd, William R., *Shepherd's Historical Atlas*, New York, Harper & Row, 1976.

Shirley, Rodney W., *Mapping of the World*, London, Holland Press, 1984.

Shorto, Russell, *The Island in the Centre of the World*, New York, Doubleday, 2004.

Siedentop, Larry, *Democracy in Europe*, London, Penguin, 2000.

Sigmann, Jean, *1848: Les revolutions romantiques et Démocratique de l'Europe*, Paris, Calmann, 1970 (published in English as *1848: The Romantic and Democratic Révolutions in Europe*, New York, Harper & Row, 1973).

Simpson, Jonathan, *The Hundred Years War* (two vols.), Philadelphia, PA, University of Pennsylvania, 1990.

Skelton, R.A., *The History of Cartography*, London, C. A. Watts, 1964.

Soly, Hugo (ed.), *Charles V 1500–1558 and His Time*, Antwerp, Fonds Mercator, 1999 (published simultaneously in Dutch as *De Wereld van Keiser* and in French as *Le Monde de Charles Quint*).

Spufford, Peter, *Power and Profit: The Merchant in Medieval Europe*, London, Thames & Hudson, 2002.

Stallaerts, Robert, *Historical Dictionary of Belgium*, London, The Scarecrow Press, 1999.

Stengers, Jean, *La Place de Léopold II dans l'Histoire de la Colonisation*, Brussels, La Nouvelle Clio, 1950.

———, *Combien le Congo a-t-il couté à la Belgique?* Brussels, Academie Royale des Sciences Coloniales, 1957.

———, *Aux origines de la question royale, Léopold et le gouvernment. Les deux publiques belges de 1946*, Gembloux-Paris, Ducolet, 1980.

———, *L'action du roi en Belgique, Pouvoir et Influence*, Brussels, Racine, 1997 (published simultaneously in Dutch as *De Koningen de Belgen, van Leopold I tot Albert II*, Leuven, Davidsfond).

Strayer, Joseph R., *Western Europe in the Middle Ages*, New York, Appleton-Century-Crofts, 1955.

Strien, Kees van, *Touring of the Low Countries, Accounts of British Travellers, 1660–1720*, Amsterdam University Press, 1998.

Strikwerda, Carl, *A House Divided: Catholics, Socialists and Flemish nationalists in nineteenth century Belgium*, London, Rowman & Littlefield, 1997.

Sumption, Jonathan, *The Hundred Years War* (two vols.), Philadelphia, University of Pennsylvania Press, 1991.

Taylor, A. J. P., *The Habsburg Monarchy 1809–1918—a History of the Austrian Empire and Austria-Hungary*, Harmondsworth, Penguin Books, 1964.

Terlinden, Charles, *Charles Quint Empereur des Deux Mondes*, Bruxelles, Desclée de Brouwer, 1965.

Theuerdank (Maximilian I, Melchior Pfintzing, and Marx Treitz), Nuremberg, Johann Schonspergher, 1517.

Thomson, W. G., *A History of Tapestry*, London, Hodder and Stoughton, 1930.

Toynbee, Arnold J., *The German Terror in Belgium*, New York, George H. Doran, 1917.

Tuchman, Barbara W., *A Distant Mirror, The Calamitous 14th Century*, New York, Alfred A. Knopf, 1978.

Tyler, Royall, *The Emperor Charles V*, Fair Lawn, NJ, Essential Books, 1956.

Vandekerckhove, L. and Luc Huyse, *In de buitenbaan*, Antwerp, Standaard, 1976.

Vandeputte, Robert, *Histoire économique de la Belgique 1944–1990*, Brussels, Labor, 1993.

Vangroenweghe, Daniel, *Du Sang sur lianes*, Brussels, Hatier, 1986.

Vanthemsche, Guy, *De werkloosheid in Belgie 1929–1940*, Brussels, Labor, 1961 (published simultaneously by same publisher in French as *Le chômage en Belgique, son histoire, son actualité 1925–1940*).

Vaughan, Richard, *Philip the Bold, The Formation of the Burgundian State*, Cambridge, MA, Harvard University Press, 1962.

———, *John the Fearless, The Growth of Burgundian Power*, London, Longman, 1966.

———, *Philip the Good, The Apogee of Burgundy*, London, Longman, 1970.

———, *Charles the Bold, The Last Valois Duke of Burgundy*, London, Longman, 1973.

———, *Valois Burgundy*, London, Longman, 1975.

Velaers, Jan and Herman Van Goethem, *Leopold III, de koning, het land, de oorlog*, Tielt, Lannoo, 2001.

Vellut, Jean-Luc et al. (eds), *La mémoire du Congo: Le Temps colonial*, Ghent and Tervuren, Editions Snoeck/Musée royal de l'Afrique centrale, 2005.

Vellut, Jean-Luc, scientific director, *Memory of Congo, The Colonial Era*, Tervuren, Musée Royal De L'Afrique Centrale, 2005.

Voet, L., *Antwerp, The Golden Age*, Antwerp, Fonds Mercator, 1973 (published simultaneously in Dutch by the same publisher as *Tot Cierat deser Stadt*).

Warmbrunn, Werner, *The German Occupation of Belgium, 1940–44*, New York, P. Land, 1993.
Watelet, Marcel (ed.), *Gerard Mercator, Rupelmonanus*, Antwerp, Fonds Mercator Paribus, 1994 (published simultaneously in French as *Gerard Mercator, Cosmographe*).
Wegge, David, *Atlas of Tooneel des Oorlogs in Europa*, Amsterdam, 1753.
Weightman, Christine, *Margaret of York Duchess of York, 1446–1503*, New York, St. Martin's, 1989.
Weintraub, Stanley, *Albert, Uncrowned King*, London, John Murray, 1997.
Wheare, K. C., *Modern Constitutions*, London, Oxford University Press, 1962.
Wheatcroft, Andrew, *The Habsburgs Embodying Empire*, London, Penguin, 1995.
Whitlock, Brand, *Belgium, A Personal Narrative* (two vols.), New York, NY, D. Appleton, 1919.
Wickman, Stephen B. (ed.), *Belgium, A Country Study*, Washington, D.C., Government Printing Office, 1985.
Wijngaert, Mark van den, Michael Dumoulin and Vincent Dujardin, *Een konings drama, de biographie van Leopold III*, Antwerp, Manteau, 2001.
Wilde, Maurice de, *L'ordre Nouveau*, Gembloux, Ducolet J., 1984 (published in Dutch as *De nieuwe orde*, Leeuwarden, De Nederlandsche Boekhandel, 1982.
Willequet, Jacques. *1830, Naissance de l'état belge*, Brussels, Sablon, 1945.
———, *Albert I, koning des Belges*, Sint-Stevens-Woluwe, Elsevier, 1979 (also published in French as *Albert I, roi de Belges*, Brussels, Presses de Belgique, 1979).
Wilson, Peter H., *The Thirty Years War: Europe's Tragedy*, Cambridge, MA, Belknap Press of Harvard University Press, 2009.
———, *La Belgique sous la botte: résistance et collaboration 1940–1945*, Paris, Editions Universitaires, 1986.
Witte, Els (ed.), *Geschiedenis van Vlaanderen van de oorsprong tot heden*, Brussels, La Renaissance du Livre, 1983 (published in French by the same publisher as *Histoire de Flandre des origines à nos jours*).
Witte, Els, Jan Craeybeckx and Alan Meynen, *Politieke geschiedenis van belgie sinds 1830*, Antwerp, Standaard Uitgevering, 1985 (6th edition, 1997. Published in French as *La Belgique Politique de 1830 à nos jours*, Brussels, Editions Labor, 1987; in English as *Political History of Belgium from 1830* Antwerp, Standaard Uitgeverij/VUB Press, 2000; *Political History of Belgium from 1830 Onwards*, Brussels, Academic and Scientific Publishers, 2009).
Witte, Els and Harry Van Velthoven, *Language and Politics*, Brussels, VUB Press, 2000 (published in 2000 by the same publisher in French as *Langue and Politique* and in Dutch as *Taal en Politiek*).
Zamoyski, Adam, *Rites of Peace, The Fall of Napoleon and The Congress of Vienna*, New York, HarperCollins, 2007.
Zee, Henri and Barbara van der, *William and Mary*, Penguin, London, 1988.

Ziegler, P., *The Black Death*, Harmondsworth, Penguin, 1982.

Zuckerman, Larry, *The Rape of Belgium, The Untold Story of World War I*, New York, New York University Press, 2004.

Articles

Béland, Daniel and André Lecours, 'Nationalism, Public Policy, and Institutional Development: Social Security in Belgium,' *Journal of Public Policy* 25.2, May-Aug 2005, pp. 265–85

Billiet, Jaak, 'Church Involvement, Ethnocentricism, and Voting for the Radical right-wing party: Diverging Behavioural Outcomes of Equal Attitudinal Dispositions', *Sociology of Religion*, vol. 56, no. 3, Fall 1995, p. 303(24).

Brans, Marleen, 'The Politics of Belgium. A Unique Federalism', *Public Administration*, vol. 761, Spring 1998, p. 194.

Buruma, Ian, 'Postcard from Europe—The Divorce', *The New Yorker*, Jan 10, 2011, pp. 38–40.

Conway, Martin, 'Building the Christian City: Catholics and Politics in Interwar Francophone Belgium', *Past and Present* no. 128, Aug. 1990, p. 117 (35).

Economist, 'Charlemagne—The Real Trouble with Flanders', 29 Jan., 2011, p. 51.

Evans, R. J. W., 'The Most Dynamic Ruler', *The New York Review of Books*, 24 June 2010, pp. 55–57.

Judt, Tony, 'Is there a Belgium?', *The New York Review of Books*, 2 Dec. 1999, pp. 49–53.

Kalyvas, Stathis N., 'Democracy and Religious Politics: Evidence from Belgium' *Comparative Political Studies* 31. no. 3 (June 1988, pp. 293–29).

Keating, Michael, 'Asymmetrical Government: Multinational States in an Integrating Europe (Critical Essay)', *Publius* vol. 29, no. 1, Winter 1999, p. 71.

Kitschelt, Herbert and Staf Hellemans, 'The Left-right Semantics and the New Politics Cleavage', *Comparative Political Studies*, vol. 23, no. 2, July 1990, p. 210 (29).

Laurent, Pierre-Henri, 'Divided Belgium Walks a Tight Rope', *Current History*, vol. 83, Apr. 1984, p. 169 (5).

Swingedouw, Marc and Gilles Ivaldi, 'The Extreme Right Utopia in Belgium and France: The Ideology of the Flemish Vlaams Blok and the French Front National', *West European Politics*, vol. 24, no. 3, July 2001, p. 1.

Verougstraete, Ivan, 'Judicial Politics in Belgium', (Special Issue—Judicial Politics and Policy-Making in Western Europe), *West European Politics*, vol. 15, no. 3, July 1993, p. 93 (16).

Witte, Els, 'The Formation of a Centre in Belgium: The Role of Brussels in the Formation… (1830–1840)', *European History Quarterly*, vol. 19, no. 4, Oct. 1989, p. 434 (34).

INDEX

THE AUTHOR

Samuel Humes lived in Belgium for twenty-four years, from 1984 until 2008. He is a graduate of The Hill School, Williams College (BA), Wharton Graduate School of the University of Pennsylvania (MGA), and Leiden University (Drs and PhD). After serving as executive director of the Metropolitan Washington Council of Governments and county administrator of Baltimore County, he directed graduate programmes of administration in Africa, North America and Europe—most recently Boston University's Brussels campus.

His latest books are *Managing the Multinational: Confronting the Global-Local Dilemma; Government and Local Development in Western Nigeria* (with R. L. Ola); and *Local Governance and National Power: A Worldwide Comparison of Tradition and Change in Local Government,* which track and analyse the growth and adaptation of government and corporate organisations. Earlier publications include *The Structure of Local Government Throughout the World* and its successor, *The Structure of Local Government: A Comparative Survey of 81 Countries*, which have been described as the seminal works in its field. He now lives in Williamstown, Massachusetts with his wife Lynne De Lay.